W9-CJI-782

Praise for *Old Age*

"Detailed, easy-to-understand information . . . discusses everything from nutritional needs for the elderly to the most common financial scams used to prey on older people."
—*Cleveland Plain Dealer*

"With good sense and humor, Linkletter here addresses problems and preoccupations of the elderly." —*Publishers Weekly*

"He manages to highlight the most important items in a seemingly artless manner that makes his message accessible to most readers. A useful resource." —*Kirkus Reviews*

"We all need to ponder Art's 'Golden Rights of Senior Americans.' They are an incisive challenge to ageism and the ignoble status that it gives to the elderly."
—James A. Peterson
Professor of Gerontology, Director,
Emeriti Center
University of Southern California

PENGUIN BOOKS

OLD AGE IS NOT FOR SISSIES

A television and radio star for more than forty years, Art Linkletter has performed in two of the longest-running shows in broadcast history—*People Are Funny* and *House Party*. His books, including *Kids Say the Darndest Things* and *Wish I'd Said That*—have made him one of the all-time bestselling authors. In addition to ten honorary doctoral degrees for his humanitarian work, he has been named Speaker of the Year; Grandfather of the Year; Chairman of National Easter Seal Week, National Cancer Week, National Heart Week, the National Arthritis Foundation, Foster Parents Plan, Goodwill Industries, and the National Advisory Council of the American Family Society, among many others. He has served on the President's Advisory Council for Drug Abuse Prevention and is a past President of the National Coordinating Council on Drug Abuse Education and Information. He was recently named Ambassador by President Reagan and appointed Commissioner General for the Brisbane, Australia, Expo '88.

Art Linkletter

• • •

OLD AGE IS NOT FOR SISSIES

Choices for Senior Americans

PENGUIN BOOKS

PENGUIN BOOKS
Published by the Penguin Group
Viking Penguin Inc., 40 West 23rd Street,
New York, New York 10010, U.S.A.
Penguin Books Ltd, 27 Wrights Lane,
London W8 5TZ, England
Penguin Books Australia Ltd, Ringwood,
Victoria, Australia
Penguin Books Canada Ltd, 2801 John Street,
Markham, Ontario, Canada L3R 1B4
Penguin Books (N.Z.) Ltd, 182–190 Wairau Road,
Auckland 10, New Zealand

Penguin Books Ltd, Registered Offices:
Harmondsworth, Middlesex, England

First published in the United States of America by
Viking Penguin Inc. 1988

Published in Penguin Books 1989

1 3 5 7 9 10 8 6 4 2

Grateful acknowledgment is made for permission to reprint definitions from *Taber's Cyclopedic Medical Dictionary*, Fifteenth Edition,
© 1985 F. A. Davis Company. Reprinted by permission of
F. A. Davis Company, Philadelphia, Pennsylvania.

LIBRARY OF CONGRESS CATALOGING IN PUBLICATION DATA
Linkletter, Art, 1912–
Old age is not for sissies : choices for senior Americans / Art
Linkletter.
p. cm.
Includes index.
ISBN 0-451-82204-8 (pbk.)
1. Aged—United States—Life skills guides. I. Title.
[HQ1064.U5L56 1989]
305.2'6'0973—dc19   88-22805

Printed in the United States of America by
Krueger-Ringier, Inc., Dresden, Tennessee
Set in Times Roman

Special Acknowledgment

This book would never have been written without the research and writing abilities of Judith Patterson. Her long experience in the health field, along with her compassion and understanding, inspired by her many years of leadership in the fight against drug abuse, made her an invaluable associate in the writing and organization of the material.

As important, she has been a firm friend and enthusiastic companion throughout the long months of work required to cover this complex subject.

Writing this book was not for sissies. Judy is a champion.

Art Linkletter

Acknowledgments

Without the help of many people, this book wouldn't have been possible. I've talked to more Senior Americans throughout the United States than can be listed. Each one, in his or her own way, has contributed to *Old Age Is Not for Sissies*. The people who are listed have made exceptional contributions, given freely of their time, assisted with the research that was needed, taken time to review copy, and have provided encouragement every step of the way. I extend my deep and sincere thanks to each of them.

Tracy Brown, my editor at Viking Penguin
James J. Breuss
Mrs. Betty Thom Foster
Dr. James A. Peterson, Director, Emeriti Center, University of Southern California
John Pleas, Ph.D., Middle Tennessee State University, Murfreesboro, Tennessee
Jamie Pope, M.S., Registered Dietitian, Director of Nutrition, Vanderbilt University Weight Management Program

Lee Ray
Sally Vaci, Research

APPLE COMPUTER, INC.
Many thanks to Apple Computer, Inc., a company
with dynamite equipment, the Macintosh Plus, and
dynamite people, Keri Walker, Doedy Hunter,
and the local Apple representative, Dave Barwick. Also, thanks to Microsoft and their word-
processing program. Without these, I might still
be typing.

SENIOR AMERICAN FOCUS GROUP—
SPRING LAKE VILLAGE, SANTA ROSA,
  CALIFORNIA
Mr. and Mrs. Clifford L. Anderson
Mrs. Dorothy Bell Becker
Dr. D. W. Betts
Mr. and Mrs. Robert Deasy
Dr. Naomi D. Green
Mr. and Mrs. Frank Hamilton
Mrs. Betty McEachron
Mr. and Mrs. Hubbard Parker
Mr. Al Piette, Assistant Administrator
Mr. L. T. Saalwaechter
Mrs. Helen Vidak
Mr. and Mrs. Robert H. Wesson
Mrs. Rosalind H. Westgate
Mr. and Mrs. James Williams
Mr. and Mrs. Woody Woodward

SENIOR AMERICAN FOCUS GROUP— WAUSAU, WISCONSIN

Mrs. Winnie Gooding
Mr. and Mrs. Carl Gotz
Mr. Larry Hoyt
Mrs. Jane Morse
Mr. and Mrs. Robert Plisch
Mr. Willi Preu
Mrs. Helen Pugh
Mrs. Vera Schmieden
Mrs. Beth Scott
Mrs. Helen Staples

SPECIAL CONTRIBUTORS

Mrs. Phyllis Ashton, Assistant Vice President, Citizens Bank & Trust
Mrs. Cheryl Bahr
Lucille Ball
Sibylle and David Barwick, Team Electronics, Apple Computer, Inc.
Kathy P. Belgea, M.D.
Carole Bibeau, Hospice Coordinator, Mt. Diablo Hospital Medical Center, Concord, California
Loretto B. Breuss
Richard Buechel, M.D.
George Burns
John Caffry
Mr. Harold Chopin
Mr. and Mrs. John W. Chopin
Mrs. Janet Crowe, Realtor
Richard Delap, Director, Social Services, Marathon County, Wisconsin

Darwin Dennison, Ed.D., President, Dine Systems, Inc.

Drs. Susan and Andrew Dibner, Founders LIFELINE®

Phyllis Diller

Justine and Daniel Dorchester

Elderhostel

Mrs. Julie Gebhardt

Anthony Gillette, Ph.D., Clinical Psychologist

Senator Barry Goldwater

Jack and Lynda Gunion

John Hattenhauer, M.D.

James Hoops, Moving Consultant, Graebel Moving & Storage, Inc.

Bob Hope

Jack Jackson, Registered Pharmacist

Elizabeth Jacobs

Robert D. Junion, CFP, IDS Financial Services, Inc.

Mili Katz

Michael Knauf

Carol Kriemelmeyer, Wisconsin Governor's Ombudsman

Kay and Bill Lainhart

Mike Murphy

Michele Panucci, Social Services Specialist, Bureau of Quality Compliance, Wisconsin Division of Health

David W. Patterson

Jack Potter, Attorney

Charlie Redman

Thomas Rengel, M.D.

J. Allen Reynolds III, Attorney, Evans, Jones & Reynolds, Nashville, Tennessee

Richard Riley, Vice President Marketing, International SOS Assistance, Inc.

Barbara Schneider, Travel Counselor

George C. Schnitzer

Michael P. Scott

Mrs. Maggie Sherard

Peggy Stoeger, Coordinator Transportation and Information Referrals, Commission on Aging

John Vaci, A.I.A., Project Architect

Betty White

Iris Winogrond, Ph.D., Clinical Psychologist, Director Adult Resource Center

Norma Woodcock, Supervisor, Social Security Administration

Howard Woodside, Attorney

Judith Zitske, Program Director, Bureau of Long-Term Support, Madison, Wisconsin

Contents

OLD AGE
IS NOT FOR
SISSIES

Introduction

> *"Since I intend to spend the rest of my life there,*
> *my interest is in tomorrow—and the best thing about*
> *tomorrow is that it comes one day at a time."*
>
> —Art Linkletter

Straighten up, shoulders back, sharpen your senses of humor, keep control of your lives, and remember what Thomas Jefferson recommended: "A little rebellion now and then is a good thing."

Old age definitely is not for sissies.

It is for people who can laugh as hard as the seventy-eight-year-old lady who told me what made her realize she wasn't twenty-one anymore. She described standing near a curb waiting for a friend to pick her up so they could drive to a restaurant for lunch. A man observing her waiting assumed something was wrong. He came up to her and asked if there was anything he could do to help. She told him there wasn't and said, "I'm just waiting to get picked up." She said he looked at her like he couldn't believe what she'd told him before replying, "Well, lady, as old as *you* look, you could be in for quite a wait."

And, it's for people like George Burns who, at

the age of ninety-one, when he'd finished testifying in the court dispute over Groucho Marx's estate, was asked if an eighty-year-old man could find happiness with a thirty-year-old woman. His answer? "No, not often. Only once or twice a night."

What about feisty eighty-one-year-old Charlie who lives alone with his dog, cats, and bird, wears blue and red flannel shirts, spends most of his time tying fishing flies, and claims Campbell's Scotch Broth soup is superior to anything made with loving hands at home? He described being not too subtly questioned about his lifestyle one day and the accompanying suggestions that maybe he'd slipped into senility. "Senility? I'm no different now than I was thirty years ago," he said. "My entire family combined isn't as much fun as one of my dogs and not one of 'em—including my wife—ever made decent soup."

Until recently, Betty lived on the front lines leading the charges behind all the interests that were part of her life in a small community in the Midwest. Because of her desire to maintain her independence while being freed from the fear of ever being forced into a nursing home, she decided to move across the country and live in a retirement center that provides lifetime health care. Although beautifully situated and complete with every amenity, the most important element for a woman like her is missing. There are no risks left or mountains that need climbing—everything that needs doing gets done. I visited her four weeks after she'd moved in and asked her how she liked it.

Her reply? "There are two things wrong with it. It's filled with old people and has all the excitement of a 300-bed morgue."

I'll never forget interviewing the oldest new father in the United States on *House Party*. After I'd announced a national search to find this man, we were flooded with letters and phone calls. I wouldn't have been astonished at an eighty, maybe even ninety-year-old winner but was incredulous when he turned out to be 104 years old. We flew him and his thirty-eight-year-old wife to Hollywood to appear on the show and he was completely at ease as he walked into the studio to face the lights, cameras, and the live audience. He said he'd never considered retirement and still worked as an undertaker during the week and as a minister on Sundays. I remember commenting that he had the perfect setup—he could take his customers from here to eternity in one operation.

Then he recounted how he'd married his present wife shortly after he'd turned ninety-eight. Finally, I asked what everyone really wanted to know—to what did he attribute his extraordinary virility at such an advanced age?

He looked at me and said, "Well, Art, you're just born with these things in your blood and bones. I got a hint how true this was when I became the father of twins at a hundred."

Twins at a hundred . . . a hint? I felt as though I had received a shot of the Fountain of Youth just by sitting next to him. I walked with a spring in my step for the next six months.

One afternoon a friend of mine was in the middle of telling me something and forgot the details essential to making his point. He sat there a moment and then almost remorsefully said, "I hate getting old, Art . . . can't remember a thing anymore." I leaned forward and said, "Who are you kidding, Jack? You never could remember details like those you're searching for right now." We both laughed as he admitted how well his advancing age was working to excuse his lifelong poor memory. Even though I never heard the end of his story, it reminded me of one of my favorites.

Martha and her husband, Fred, were sitting in their small living room watching TV one evening. Out of the blue, Fred said to Martha, "Say, I'll bet you'd like some ice cream, wouldn't you?" "Oh yes, that would taste good—I'd just love some—but we don't have any in the house," she said. "That's okay," her husband of fifty-two years replied. "I'll walk over to the store and buy some. While I'm there, I'll also get some chocolate and whipping cream so we can make sundaes." "That would be just wonderful," Martha said. As he was getting ready to leave she said, "You know your memory isn't what it used to be, dear. With three things to remember don't you think you should make a list?" "No, I don't. The store is only two blocks away. I won't forget," he said.

With that, he left.

About forty-five minutes later he returned carrying a brown grocery bag. Martha walked into the kitchen and watched as he took out three pounds of bacon. "Oh, Fred," she said, "I told you to make a list . . . you forgot the eggs."

I learned a long time ago that the most interesting interviews are with children or people older than eighty. Both are refreshingly and surprisingly frank, as well as completely unaffected by what other people think. Children are too young to know any better. People over eighty are opinionated, unguarded, have no time for hypocrisy, and, instead of saying what their friends think they should say, they just say what they think without worrying if it's right or wrong. What's conveyed is: "Who cares? I'm not trying to impress anyone . . . at my age, I've seen it all."

A classic example was Dr. Richter, a professor emeritus from Cal Tech who had devised the world-renowned Richter Scale used to measure the magnitude of earthquakes. About twenty-five years ago we had a good-sized earthquake in California. That same day researchers from our show rushed over to Cal Tech to see if Dr. Richter would agree to be interviewed on our show the next day. He said he would. He arrived at the show and at first the interview went well. I asked him all the predictable questions leading up to, "Dr. Richter, the big question I must ask you that everyone wants to know is when the next earthquake will occur?" He was a small man about eighty years old with a high voice. Furious, he leaped to his feet, looked down at me, shook his finger at me and yelled, "Dammit, don't you ever—not ever—ask me that question again! If you do I'll walk out of this studio right now!"

Astonished at his reaction I said, "Dr. Richter, believe me, I'll never ask the question again."

He didn't care whether or not he was on national television and that millions of people were listening. After a lifetime of work, research, and accomplishment, I'd asked him the one question he couldn't answer and he let me have it.

Growing older is startling the first time one confronts it. It happened to me when I accepted an invitation to entertain in a senior citizen retirement community some years ago. I had looked forward to it because I thought it would be nice to make those old people happy—to cheer them up and make them feel good. What a revelation to discover that I was older than most of the people living there. I'll admit it gave me cause for thought—but not for long.

I've never had any particular feelings about my age. I've never felt I ever missed anything; I never experienced a "middle-age crisis"; and I've never regretted the beginning of a new decade. Age has never had an impact on something I enjoy. For me, the future holds only anticipation.

Although I can be included in the category commonly referred to as old, I'd rather think that when someone describes me that's the last thing that comes to mind. It has nothing to do with who I am, what I am, or how I live my life. My age now, like my age twenty years ago, marks the year in which I was born. That's all. It makes me eligible for Medicare and, as I discovered one evening when my wife and I decided to go to a movie, it qualifies me for a senior citizen discount at a movie theater whether I request it or not. As I stood at the window purchasing tickets, the woman selling them informed me in a matter-of-fact voice that the senior citizen discount had been subtracted. No questions asked, no request for proof of age. Obviously there was some reason she allowed the discount but, for the life of me, I still can't figure out what it was.

Not a Sissy Among Them

One of the greatest rewards I've enjoyed as a broadcaster, world traveler, celebrity, and businessman has been the opportunity to meet some of the most successful and fascinating Senior Americans of the twentieth century. They've been colleagues, advisers, role models, and good friends—each has made an unforgettable impression in my life.

Of course, the first person who comes to mind—even though there isn't a day in my life that I've ever thought of using the words "Senior American" to describe her—is my wife of over fifty years. Lois is a beautiful, small, sparkling, creative, and energetic person. We share many interests, in-

cluding skiing. She's never faltered as my staunch-
est supporter.

I met her at an Alpha Tau Omega fraternity
dance. In fact, she was with a fraternity brother
who often was an unwitting pigeon for me in scout-
ing beautiful girls. When he showed up with Lois
as his date, he knew I'd be interested and refused
to introduce her or let me talk with her. I took
one look at this beautiful brunette and decided I
had to meet her. When I finally found out her
name, I made a cold call without ever having met
her. She said her mother would never let her go
out with a boy she didn't know and had never met.
So I said, "Put your mother on the phone." When
she picked up, I gave her mother "the Art Linkletter commercial"; I had only one product to sell—
me.

We went together for two years before getting
married in 1935, on Thanksgiving Day. While we
dated, we'd spend three or four hours at a time
dancing—in fact, we wore out one of her mother's
rugs. And did I like her mother's cooking! I ate
more dinners there than anywhere else.

Not only did I fall hopelessly in love with Lois,
she came with a bonus I wanted and didn't have—
a close, loving family. Our love for each other is
bonded even more tightly by the love we have for
our children, grandchildren, and great-grandchildren. And we still love to dance.

I've known every President of the United States
since Herbert Hoover even though I didn't meet

him until after he'd completed his term as our thirty-first President. I was a young broadcaster in my twenties and met him just before I introduced him at the San Diego World's Fair in 1935. Although he was portrayed as an austere, forbidding man, I found him to be anything but the cold, serious "engineer" statesman presented in newsreels during his years as President.

There's little doubt in my mind that most people don't associate this President with television. But when Herbert Hoover was nominated for the Presidency in 1928, it marked the first time ceremonies were televised at the Assembly Chamber in Albany, New York. The "telecast" notified Democratic candidate Alfred Smith of Hoover's nomination. The pictures were transmitted by television to Schenectady, New York, and sent out by short wave by the General Electric Company. Perhaps it was his pioneering contribution to show business that led to his warm and sly humor.

As the former President and I discussed the length of the material he intended to use during the CBS radio broadcast from the World's Fair, I timidly mentioned that I thought his "copy" might be too long and cause timing problems on the network. He looked at me with twinkling eyes and said, "What kind of timing problems?" I replied, "The governor of New York might have to cut some of his remarks." To this, a smiling former President Hoover responded, "In that case, obviously, he'll have less to say."

After that brief encounter with him backstage

at Balboa Park, I didn't visit with him again until years later at the Bohemian Club's famous "Grove Encampment" among the redwood trees along the Russian River near San Francisco. He was now an elder statesman in his eighties but still managing a busy, involved life writing and giving speeches. I remember him as a warm, delightful man surrounded by adoring friends and family.

A United States President must be able to withstand harassment and the turbulence that is part of the job. In my opinion, of all our Presidents, Ronald Reagan stands out in his ability to handle it. He hasn't visibly aged as have so many others serving under the twenty-four-hour-a-day, seven-day-a-week burden of responsibilities. And I know that's because of his attitude and mental outlook. He's resilient and has a wonderful sense of humor— a sense of humor that has been used against him at times. When he makes an off-the-cuff comment in a radio studio, he does what every broadcaster or former broadcaster does. The studio is where everyone has a little fun before air time. I couldn't believe it when the press let a throwaway remark lead them to conclude that he's a careless cowboy. In fact, his patriotism, upbeat approach to life and sense of humor have helped make him one of our best-loved Presidents. In that sense, we're very much alike. Every time I see him, he'll ask if I have any good stories. He knows as well as I do that there are times when you have to laugh because, if you can't, you'll probably be tempted to scream.

Although this remarkable President has many qualities I admire, perhaps the one that most stands out in my mind is his ability to take a risk. A circumstance comes to mind where he could again have had the press all over him because of his age. I'm a member of the President's Physical Fitness Committee that's headed by one of the greatest-ever football coaches, George Allen. During a meeting that was being held at the White House, two things happened: The President dropped in, followed by the two dozen photographers that record everything he does, and congratulated the committee for its efforts in helping him make the public aware of the importance of physical fitness. Following his remarks, the committee presented him with a gold-plated handgrip exerciser. The next thing that happened was that the President accepted it and, without giving it a second thought, said, "Let me see if I can bend this thing." With one deft move, he squeezed it flat as everybody cheered. But, supposing he hadn't? The press probably would have used it as an example to illustrate that he's weak and old. You know something? Even that wouldn't have stopped this President. He would have been the first to laugh and suggest he needed another bowl of Wheaties in the morning. He's genuine and has the courage to take a risk. I admire him.

Later, I had a few moments alone with President Reagan and commented on his great physical condition. He said, "Art, I've probably never been in better shape in my life. Every night when I'm finished reviewing papers and documents, I work out for at least half an hour. As a matter of fact, my chest muscles have built up to where my suits are beginning to be uncomfortable when I flex them." Then, in a boyish way, he said, "Reach inside my suit and check them out for yourself." I said, "You've got to be kidding. Before I got my hand within an inch of your jacket, I'd have my arms pinned behind me by the Secret Service."

I admire Nancy Reagan in the same way I do the President. She also is capable of taking a risk and proved it when she launched her efforts in the fight against drug and alcohol abuse. When she first became involved, she had no idea of the range and extent of the problem or where it would lead her—any more than I did nearly two decades ago. She started out by being concerned and that led to studying, doing research and learning. She sought knowledgeable advice, studied the complexities, and talked to kids. She went to halfway houses and into the streets to confront the problem. Then she asked her friends in politics and show business to help. What began with a simple "Just Say No" campaign has swept the nation. She talks to heads of state, and works unceasingly in a cause to which she is deeply committed. That's not just an achievement for a First Lady; it's the kind of contribution that will leave a lifetime legacy.

When I talk to audiences, I love to tell them that Nancy was once my wife—even though the marriage only lasted thirty minutes on CBS' *General Electric Theater* on a Sunday night. We were matched as husband and wife in a picture called *The Oddball.*

Nancy is a warm, obliging and delightful person with whom to spend time. And I find it baffling that so much attention has been paid to her clothes. Anyone who knows her would be the first to say that she's always been beautifully dressed. As long as I can remember—years before she became First Lady—she was considered by everyone to be one of the best-looking, best-dressed, best-coiffed women around. Her role as wife of the President didn't present a new challenge for her regarding her appearance or choice of clothes, her reputation was well established—why would she be expected to change?

I've known and liked this lady and have been her friend for a long time. And one of her strongest and most admirable traits is her overriding loyalty to her husband. She's his best friend as well as his wife, and it's to her everlasting credit that she protects, defends, and cares for him the way that she does.

President Reagan epitomizes the kind of positive thinking that is universally accepted as a key to success and a principal element in an attitude that cloaks someone with whom we like to spend time. The modern "father" of positive thinking, however, is Dr. Norman Vincent Peale. His most recent book, *The True Joy of Positive Thinking,* was published in 1984. When it came out I was asked to comment on its content and said, "I have often thought: Wouldn't it be wonderful if we could catch, preserve, and bottle the magic essence of Dr. Peale, then produce and market this elixir to humankind. Well, this is it, between the covers of this modest, warmly written book by the great man himself." Dr. Peale has inspired millions of people to be better than they ever planned to be, to worship God, and to think positively. In his own words, he cites the influences that conspired to make a minister out of an unlikely prospect for that profession:

One was Father's preaching. The way he described Jesus Christ gave me, early in life, a profound admiration and enthusiasm for the Master. He had an incomparable way of making Christianity real and very exciting. He was a fascinating public speaker. I had enormous respect and affection for Father and always liked to hear him preach. So I was a regular churchgoer.

One summer Sunday in my boyhood, my mother was teaching a Sunday School class in the little Methodist church in Lynchburg, Ohio. Mother started out by commenting on the current status of the Cincinnati Reds, our baseball heroes. Then she launched into a description of Jesus, how He set his face to go to Jerusalem knowing very well what would happen to Him. What a man. What courage. Mother called it guts. But He resolutely walked straight into the camp of His enemies because He loved me and was willing to die for me. That belief gripped me for life. It made me love Him forever. To me there has never been anyone like Him.

Although I tucked up this love and admiration for Jesus against my heart, had an accompanying love for the old hymns, liked to hear a good preacher, and was a believer, still I was what they called "not in the Kingdom." I was a vital, virile boy and attracted by the fleshpots, though I never did quite find out what they were all about.

What a debt I owe this man. Following the tragedy of our daughter's death, he called to console us for our staggering loss and to suggest that God works in mysterious ways. He went on to suggest that perhaps God could use me in the crusade to save other children from the epidemic of drug abuse that was threatening an entire generation. His advice and guidance helped change my life and open new avenues for helping others. Never had I dreamed of my present life that includes lecturing and writing about inspirational subjects. After the session with Dr. Peale, there were no doubts left regarding my mission in a new life far from the bright lights of Hollywood.

Dr. Norman Vincent Peale is over ninety years old. With his beloved wife, Ruth, he travels hundreds of thousands of miles every year lecturing, preaching, and counseling. As a man who once described himself as an unlikely prospect to become a preacher, he hasn't done too badly. He's been at it for almost half a century at the Marble

Collegiate Church in New York City. It was my privilege and high honor to share a platform once again with him as master of ceremonies for his ninetieth birthday party. He's been one of the most important spiritual advisers in my life.

I met President Dwight D. Eisenhower during my first appearance at a formal White House dinner. Having declined to run in 1948, he'd been elected President in 1952. I wasn't certain what to expect. Here was a man bigger than life—the Supreme Commander of the Allied Expeditionary Force who'd led the D-Day invasion of Normandy on June 6, 1944. He looked straight into my eyes and shut out all the other conversation around us as we discussed the details of the program. He was reserved and taciturn in his manner but impressed me with his immense strength of concentration.

Mamie, on the other hand, was "down home" friendly. She smiled warmly and said, "I'm one of your biggest *House Party* fans . . . surely you're not going to look through my purse!" Then she turned to Lois and apologized for not having us come up to their private quarters, saying in a true, housewifely way, "We're doing some redecorating and I wouldn't want you to see our house in such a mess."

One of my later memories of Mamie and her beloved "Ike" comes from a time when he was quite ill. The news media had gathered below his window on the hospital lawn. The President came to the window in a wheelchair and gave his famous wave and broke into a grin. As he was exchanging comments with the media, a sudden breeze began to blow, catching strands of his hair and randomly rearranging them. With a loving gentleness that touched me, Mamie unobtrusively brushed them back into place. He turned and looked at her in a way that told their lifetime story.

When he died in 1969, he left a legacy few Americans will ever match. During his two successive administrations, the armistice was signed ending the Korean War in 1953, the U.S. occupation of Germany ended in 1955, he signed acts admitting Alaska and Hawaii as our forty-ninth and fiftieth states in 1959, and appointed five U.S. Supreme Court Justices. When he retired to his Gettysburg farm in 1961, he became an author and published three books before he died at the age of seventy-eight.

Ike was buried in Abilene, Kansas, and I joined a nation mourning one of our greatest contributors to the freedom we enjoy today. The minister who spoke at his graveside ceremony chose Timothy II 4:6–7 from the Bible: "For I am now ready to be offered, and the time of my departure is at hand. I have fought a good fight, I have finished my course, I have kept the faith." As his casket was slowly lowered into the ground, the last remaining five-star general, Omar Bradley, brought his hand to a salute. As General of the Army and President of the United States Dwight David Eisenhower was buried, I remembered the firm and purposeful hand he had extended to me in 1952.

We have County Down in Northern Ireland to

thank for providing a place of birth for a cum laude university graduate named Greer Garson who went on to become one of the best-loved actresses of this century. Who will ever forget the performance in *Mrs. Miniver* that caused her peers to vote her an Oscar for the best performance by an actress? This fascinating woman and dear friend is a mixture of two people—the gorgeous movie star and a mischievous prankster ready for any adventure that will enliven a party.

My favorite story about Greer is one that took place "under the sheets" with the lovely redhead. Lois and I were guests at her ranch near Santa Fe, New Mexico, and we'd all been invited to watch a traditional Indian ceremony. The highlight of the ceremony was setting fire to a fifty-foot-tall, papier-mâché figure of Gloom as young boys and girls danced around the blazing symbol beneath white bed sheets. There we were, watching intently, when Greer leaned over and whispered to me, "Art, let's sneak out and get under the sheets with the kids!" I never hesitated to leap at this chance to "co-star" with the fabulous actress. No one saw us as we crept away from our group, and you should have seen the looks on the kids' faces when they discovered we'd joined them in a wild dance "under the sheets." And believe me, we *weren't* kids.

Someone else who never lost a child's enthusiasm and spirit was a giant figure among inspirational Senior Americans. One of my closest and dearest friends, Walt Disney, was imaginative, daring, and a perfectionist in everything he did.

He was a key player in my career. At his invitation, I helped plan the entertainment for the world-class athletes at the Winter Olympics in Squaw Valley. Lois and I lived with the Disneys during part of the planning for this triumphant effort. It resulted in the most spectacular display of Hollywood All-Stars ever presented exclusively for the participating athletes and officials of an Olympic Games. Every night a group of entertainers like Danny Kaye, Red Skelton, Roy Rogers, and Jack Benny was flown into Lake Tahoe to participate in the production at the Olympic Village.

But perhaps the highlight of all my years of friendship with Walt came when he asked me to emcee the opening of Disneyland as his dream was about to come true. For years I'd watched him plan and create a place he'd dreamed of for every American family's enjoyment. As the grand opening drew nearer, Walt was overspent, overworked, and worried about whether he'd made the correct "bet" when he created Disneyland. He called me and told me he couldn't afford to pay the usual fee and felt badly about asking me to do the job for "scale" (the standard union fee of $250). I told him I'd be happy to do it if he'd agree to two conditions: First, I asked for the concession at Disneyland for the sale of all film and cameras; second, I said I'd like two of my good friends in show business to be co-emcees with Walt and me. He agreed. It turned out to be the highest paid broadcast in history. A two-hour job paid with a film concession turned out to be worth several million dollars in the next ten years. Best of all, when Bob Cummings and Ronald Reagan agreed to be co-hosts for the world premiere of Disneyland, it solidified friendships that have continued for nearly four decades.

Lois and I have Lowell Thomas to thank for our passion for skiing. He was seventy years old and we were in our fifties when he encouraged us to start skiing. We quickly grew to love it and often met to ski together in Colorado. He insisted on renting a helicopter so we could go up to the highest peaks and ski the slopes where no one had been. Standing at 11,000 feet looking down on a tiny village 4,000 feet directly below us was a breathtaking experience. I thought he was the gutsiest man I'd ever known. It wasn't until much later that I found out he had double cataracts and could only see about thirty or forty feet ahead. If he was worried, he never showed it. But then again, *I* was the one who could see all the way down!

Without question, Lowell Thomas was my personal and number-one role model. He was a world-famed adventurer, traveler, author, news commentator, and athlete. He was the first nationally known newscaster and voice of the Movietone News shown on movie screens across America. He also was a friend and confidant of Lawrence of Arabia, he climbed the Himalayas, he was the pioneer in a new film process known as Cinemascope, and he was married to the same lady for more than sixty years. When she died, he remarried in a few years. He was in his eighties.

Following the wedding, he set off for a honeymoon around the world. I wired him in Hong Kong at the Mandarin Hotel: "LOWELL: I HAVE GREAT FAITH IN YOUR STRENGTH AND VIRILITY, BUT A HONEYMOON LIKE THIS COULD BE FATAL." He wired back: "IF SHE'S GOT TO GO, SHE'S GOT TO GO!"

Lowell Thomas was approaching his ninetieth birthday when he died. He was in the process of completing a new book, editing his old TV films into a new series of adventures, and looking forward to yet another winter of skiing. There'll never be another like him—when he died they broke the mold.

When I think of adventurers and heroes another friend comes to mind—General Jimmy Doolittle. I met him while I was sitting at a river's edge, casting for trout. Suddenly, flying through the air in a front flip from the riverbank above me, came the agile body of a sixty-five-year-old man who turned out to be the General himself. He said that he recognized me as he was taking his daily five-mile walk and decided to stop and say hello. Can you imagine that? There he was, a genuine four-star American hero who'd literally "dropped in" to say hello.

This great, courageous man was born in 1896, and holds the air record for the first flight across the United States in less than twenty-four hours. He was the first man to fly faster than 300 m.p.h. in a land plane, and in 1930 retired from the Army with a reserve commission to become manager of aviation for the Shell Oil Company. He set a new transcontinental flight record in 1931 and a new world speed record for land planes in 1932. Then his country needed him and he was recalled to active duty with the U.S. Army in 1940. Who can forget the Lieutenant Colonel who led the famous Tokyo Raiders in 1942? Later, he commanded the 12th and 15th Air Forces and, in 1944, he commanded the 8th Air Force. He retired as General Doolittle in 1959.

Throughout the years, we've maintained a friendship that I cherish. Even though Jimmy is like an "old shoe," there are some differences. He has an effervescent sense of humor, a body to be admired by athletes in their thirties, and no pretensions, and there are one or two honors that set him apart. He's been awarded the Congressional Medal of Honor, the Distinguished Flying Cross, the Distinguished Service Medal with Oak-Leaf Clusters, the Air Medal wth three Oak-Leaf Clusters, the Silver Star, the Bronze Star, and foreign awards too numerous to list. Now in his early nineties, he lives every minute of every day and is never too busy to talk to a youngster like me.

My role model in the *writing game* is Irving Stone. He is my dear and close friend and undeniably one of the ablest practitioners of the biographical novel. To mention just a few, his books include *Lust for Life, The Agony and the Ecstasy, The Passions of the Mind, The President's Lady, The Story of Michelangelo's Pietà,* and *False Witness.* It would take a page and a half to list all his books, his honors, and other recognitions.

Irving, now in his eighties, is still turning out a best-seller every three or four years. He and Jean, his wife of more than fifty years, spent much of their lives researching the backgrounds of subjects like van Gogh, Freud, and Michelangelo before sitting down to the task of writing. They've traveled in remote and wild places, as well as actually living in the houses of the French, Italian, or German subjects of their books.

Irving writes and Jean edits. I can't think of anyone *but* a wife who would dare to throw out two or three hundred pages of *his* work and live to tell about it. Lois and I enjoy spending time with them. It's a special experience to watch Jean glaring at Irving while complaining, "You write the same thing too many times!" One of the things we look forward to is being invited to their lovely home high in the hills above Los Angeles so we can share the reading of the Seder during Passover—the beautiful service that commemorates the exodus of the Jews from Egypt.

Another Senior American whose mind can be in the stars while his feet are on the ground—*running*—is Si Ramo of the world-renowned Thompson, Ramo, and Wollridge. On the New York Stock Exchange this blue-chip company is known by its initials: TRW.

It's tempting to categorize a scientist who deals with intercontinental ballistics and advises Presidents about aerospace as an "ivory tower" professor, far removed from the sweaty crowd of we "commoners" . . . a man engrossed only in deep, intellectual thought. My friend Si Ramo is all of the above. Yet, in addition to being at ease in the company of the highest of the high-tech scientists, he's equally at ease on a tennis court or at the head table during a dinner party. More than that, he's an accomplished humorist who can write and deliver lines well enough to be a professional wit. His classic and amusing book, *Tennis by Machiavelli,* explains how duffers should play tennis. Rounding out this unbelievable man is his ability to sit in with a classical string quartet and play a violin well enough to qualify him to be a symphony artist. Si is an inspiration to watch as he continues to lead an active, productive, fun-filled life—long past retirement.

Former President Herbert Hoover wasn't the only inspirational person I met in San Diego. Sally Rand was the original Fan Dancer who'd "knocked 'em dead" at the Chicago World's Fair. She also was an actress on both stage and screen, but it's her dancing people remember. It was in San Diego that we became good friends. In 1936, we went on to appear at the Dallas Centennial and then the New York World's Fair in 1939. Although we performed very differently—to say the least—our friendship sprang out of an entirely surprising mutual interest in history and social problems.

This glamorous, voluptuous dancer had the reputation of being a high-class "stripper" who never fully revealed anything of importance while giving an audience the alluring impression of "now you see it . . . now you don't" behind her constantly moving feather fans. She ran a tight ship with her company of showgirls billed as Sally Rand's Nude Ranch at the World's Fair.

Sally loved to lecture at ladies' clubs and delighted in surprising the giggling, tittering, expectant crowds of gussied-up society ladies by dressing very conservatively. When they recovered from that surprise, she'd give them an intellectual speech that touched on everything but show business. Generous, kind and warm-hearted, Sally kept dancing behind frills and feathers until she was almost seventy years old. When I think of Sally, two words come to mind: Whatta Girl!

Who hasn't heard of the Manassa Mauler, the ferocious tiger of the ring, the knockout world champion Jack Dempsey? Jack was born in Manassa, Colorado, in 1895 and his real name was William Harrison Dempsey. He won the heavyweight title from Jess Willard in 1919, in a fight where he knocked Willard down seven times in the first round, then battered him in the second and third. Willard's seconds tossed the towel in before the fourth round ever began.

The picture of him standing under the hot lights with a prostrate body beneath him is an unforgettable memory. Jack was finally beaten by Gene Tunney two times and, after the second fight, he retired. Later he changed his mind and made a "comeback" tour which ended in Chicago. He was still appearing in exhibitions in 1940 at the age of forty-five.

I knew Jack as a sly, practical joker who loved

to palm off an exploding cigar or pinch someone's bottom in a crowded elevator while innocently staring skyward. He was a Senior American with a child's sense of play and he grew old with grace. He appeared on *People Are Funny,* after being beaten by Tunney, to face his conqueror in a gag replay of the "long count." The audience loved this 6′ 1½″ hulk of a man—and so did I.

During World War II, I became Henry Kaiser's employee as a public relations and morale executive at the Richmond Shipyards. I'll never forget his enthusiasm and drive. In his late sixties, he could galvanize a crowd of 5,000 welders and engineers with shouted exhortations of "I love you . . . I love all of you for what you are doing to build a pipeline of liberty ships to the South Pacific islands where our boys are fighting the Japanese!" His vitality and determination were the driving force behind the miracle of his "ship-a-day" schedule.

This famed industrialist built great dams, revolutionized the building of ships during World War I, pioneered a new automobile company, steel mills, and aluminum manufacturing, and forever changed the face of Hawaii with his hotels and residential developments. The fact that he did most of this after he was sixty-nine years old is nothing less than inspirational.

The last time I had dinner with him, we were at his gorgeous home overlooking the Pacific at Hawaii Kaii on Oahu. He was ill and had only a few months left to live. His wife, Allie, had just scolded him for reaching for dessert. He pretended to cry while complaining, "Here I am in my eighties. I sit as head of a worldwide empire and I can't even have a piece of apple pie! Art . . . can't *you* have some influence on my heartless bride?" What an incredible leader; what an incredible man.

Eleanor Roosevelt was the niece of Theodore Roosevelt and lost both her parents by the time she was ten years old. Her early bent for helping others began when she was seventeen years old when she worked as a volunteer in settlement schools and joined the National Consumers' Council.

She married her cousin, Franklin, in 1905 and they had six children. Her third son died in infancy. By 1917 she'd become an energetic organizer for the war effort. In 1920 she began working for the League of Labor voters. In 1921, her husband was struck down by polio and became paralyzed. She lobbied first for her husband when he ran for governor of New York and was one of the driving forces behind his successful bid for the Presidency in 1932. Because of Franklin's disability, it was Eleanor who undertook nationwide tours on behalf of his New Deal policy in 1933.

In 1945, after Franklin's death, President Truman appointed Eleanor as delegate to the United Nations. Her part in the drafting and pressing through of the Declaration of Human Rights in 1948 was recognized with a standing ovation. There are no adequate words to describe this remarkable woman whom I was privileged to consider a friend.

I knew Eleanor best when she was an elderly ex-President's widow who worked untiringly to help the hungry, the homeless, and the racially demeaned. With every year she grew older, she gained speed. Her newspaper column "My Day" was read by millions and she told stories about herself better than anyone. Here's one she whispered to me while I awaited my introduction at a dinner: "You know, Art, I used to send a wire ahead to the local politicians asking them to be brief in their remarks about me so they wouldn't run on and on and take up my time. One old farmer in Kansas took me at my word. He got up and said, 'Here's Mrs. Roosevelt—the less said about her, the better!' "

When she died in 1962, I was one of millions throughout the world who mourned her loss. No matter which century she'd appeared in, or by what standard she'd been judged, Eleanor Roosevelt would have been the same—one of the great women of her time.

It Comes Down to One Word: Attitude

"Attitude" may very well be the most important word in the English language. It explains what makes us think and act like we're forty on our seventy-fifth birthday or what makes others act and

behave as though they're seventy-five on their for-
tieth birthday. There are so many myths surrounding old age and, in my opinion, the vast majority
just don't hold water. Although I have many, many
friends who meet the age requirements to have
earned the adjective "old," that's the last word
that would ever occur to me to use when describing
any one of them.

I've talked with a lot of people I call Senior
Americans in this book, but I'll confess that I don't
really know what the definition for that term is any
more than I know what old age means. Betty White
says, "It's one of those invisible barriers that other
people see you go through—but you never go
through it. If you're a vital person, inside your
head that same person is still going on. If you were
a dull young person, you probably entered old age
at thirty."

Trite as it may sound, age—any age—is defined
by an individual attitude. Betty's right. I know
people in their thirties and forties who give every
appearance of having entered the final phases of
their lives. It's as though some kind of stereotype
must be assigned with a change in decade. People
younger than twenty are "kids"—nothing more
needs to be said. People in their twenties can be
forgiven for not having "dried out behind the ears"
because they're "still too young." Although people in their thirties improve, they still have "a way
to go." It's turning forty that's a shock. You see,
most people believe what's said about the twenties
and thirties and think they're still young at thirty-

nine. Then, they blow out the birthday candles on one lousy cake and turn forty. Young one day, middle-aged the next. Fifty? Well, let's face it, even though the media provide shining examples of fifty-year-old people who are exceptions to the rule, the truth is "you're getting there." After sixty there isn't much to say. Retirement is at hand and the end is in sight. There you have it.

Regardless of the timetable in the preceding paragraph, there's a growing problem: People have stopped cooperating. No longer do people start cleaning out their desks a week ahead so they can retire promptly at 5:00 P.M. on the day they turn sixty-five. And other people have the audacity to begin new careers in spite of the fact that they've entered "old age." Still others kick the stereotypes out the window and do things old people shouldn't even consider doing—like run for President of the United States.

But, never at a loss for a solution, we've coined new terminology. We now describe people as being *young* old, *old,* and *old* old. Based on this alone, I've decided what *I'm* going to do—I'm going to live long enough to make *them* figure out how to describe me five years from now. I can't wait—in fact I'm watching carefully—to see who will be first to describe somone as *old* old old (I'm still not sure which "old" will get the emphasis).

The problems, rights, and choices I discuss in this book are as individual in their solution as are the people dealing with them. There are people who, when you know them, aren't a heck of a lot different than anyone else except where financial wherewithal is concerned. They may have been admired, honored, looked up to, and enjoyed for years, but it isn't just their abilities to entertain us that shine through and make us love them. We somehow know that they share a lot in common with us and that they're as real as we are. In fact, it's that suspicion that makes us want to find out more about them because we discover things that inspire *us*.

In order to set the stage for the Senior Americans I talked to throughout this country—people with whom you'll also find a lot in common—I'd like you to know how five of my famous friends feel about their families and the attitudes that guide their lives.

Betty White is one of the most genuine people I know—real to the core. And what she and the other Golden Girls—Rue McClanahan, Bea Arthur, and Estelle Getty—have done for Senior America deserves a standing ovation.

She shines because she's the authentic article. When she answered my telephone call she began by explaining the sounds in the background: "I just happened to be going through some mail and I sat down on the bed. I've got a black cat on the bed, a black poodle on the bed, a little shelter puppy on the bed, and a golden retriever—so there! Do you know Tom Sullivan, the blind singer and writer? Well, he had to retire his guide dog because of cataracts. I've known Tom forever and so I took

Dinah—she's the golden retriever—and she's just a joy—you can actually discuss things with her."

You can discuss things with Betty, too. Her love for animals and tireless work to help in their behalf is well known. She doesn't just talk about it; she carried that interest over into working to get the legislation passed that now mandates any federally operated aging facility to allow pets. She says pets give people a reason to get up in the morning, to eat on time, a reason to do all the things that people tend to let slip when they're alone. But she's not fanatical on the subject and gets angry when she describes people who ruin it for others: "Unfortunately, it's not always the wicked old landlord who is at fault. A lot of individual pet owners ruin it for everybody else when they refuse to take responsibility for their pets. And when that happens, everybody has to suffer."

As we talked, we covered a lot of subjects and she told me a number of things I'd never realized. It was no secret that she adored Allen Ludden and that they were very happily married for almost eighteen years. However, I didn't realize how ill he'd really been before he died. In fact, Allen was very sick for two and a half years during the four years that his cancer ran its inevitable course. No one really knew that or that it was Betty who cared for him. She described his ordeal, and her own, as a book in itself. "You just put one foot in front of the other and live moment to moment."

An only child, Betty describes her parents as "my best buddies . . . they were the greatest parents in the world." Betty's incredible attitude allows her to make this statement: "I was fortunate because I lost Allen before I lost my mom. By that time, I was able to give my full attention to her." That she did. After her father's death, her mother lived in Century Towers about five miles from Betty's home. She laughed as she told me how much time they spent on the phone talking and being together. Her mother told her flat out that she wouldn't move in with her daughter because she refused to disrupt her life. "I'm just *not* going to do it!" Betty acknowledges that it took some doing to pry her mother out of her apartment, but she finally won the battle. She said, "I was so privileged to have her here. It gave me so much to look forward to when I came home from work at night. I had somebody to yak with and someone with whom I could talk anything through. You know, Art, that relationship just doesn't exist between a lot of parents and children because the kids have just turned the parents off—they get rid of them."

Betty learned to give diabetic injections and to do a lot of other things she never thought she'd have to do. Her mother died at the age of eighty-seven. Betty's assessment after she'd lost the two people she loved most in the world: "I don't know the meaning of the word guilt . . . I'm so lucky. We didn't have to try to make everything up at the end or anything like that—and that goes for Allen and my mom. And that left *me* with the strength and comfort they'd wish for me."

As we discussed catastrophic illness, I shared an

opinion Betty supports. No one would argue the devastation that catastrophic illness imposes, particularly when it involves an extended length of time in a skilled care or other nursing facility. However, as we hear this subject discussed by the media, without fail someone laments the tragedy that will occur if a nest egg is used up paying for care—leaving nothing to pass on as an inheritance. I'm not certain when it happened, but we've come to view health care and all its costs as something that must be paid by insurance and/or the government. It's human to want to leave a legacy, including financial assets. That notwithstanding, there *are* circumstances that direct us back to the original purpose behind building a nest egg. I don't think there is any reason on earth why anyone should feel guilty about having to spend whatever was earned and saved to pay for care. In fact, we consider ourselves fortunate that our years of hard work have made it possible for Lois and me to pay for whatever care we may someday require. The important word is "care"—not who will be denied an inheritance after our death if the money is used up.

Betty responded by saying, "I cared for two people with catastrophic illnesses—Allen and Mother—and I put in plenty of time at the hospital. I saw how a lot of people behave in the hospital—not in a nursing home situation—but in a regular hospital situation. They'd stand in the hall and you'd hear these conversations and what they were *really* worried about: 'I wonder how long this is going to take . . . can you believe how much this is going to cost—there won't be a thing left.' It made me sick."

We also talked about how times had changed. She applauded the increased attention being given Senior Americans. "I think one thing that's positive is that at least it lets the world know that we exist. For such a long time—once you passed thirty—you might as well have dropped off the edge of the planet. Now, with all the talk about the 'Graying of America' and the available demographics . . . well, at least we have a voice in what's going on. Frankly, I think we live in a good time to be this age. Fifteen years ago, there were a lot of differences in public consciousness about Senior Americans. I don't think the attention hurts anyone as long as the people behind them are as front and center as they ought to be."

George Burns is in his early nineties. I'll openly confess that my "interview" with George didn't follow the pattern expected in a typical interview . . . in fact, throughout our conversation, I found myself being questioned by him. George is a very funny man and, as I learned, he's also a very wise man. I began our conversation by asking everyone's favorite question first:

"What's the secret to long life, George?"

In typical George Burns fashion he answered *with* a question to set up his answer:

"Tell me, Art, do you love what you're doing for a living?"

"Of course I do."

"See . . . that's what's important. It's the secret to long life . . . to be able to get up in the morning and do something you love to do. And I love what I'm doing. I don't care what you do for a living. Let's say you're making felt hats. The only thing that's important is that you make sure you *love* to make felt hats.

"For instance—I started in show business when I was seven years old. I was singing with three other kids in the Pee-Wee Quartet. From seven to twenty-seven I did all kinds of acts. They were all failures and flops but I didn't think so because I loved what I was doing—that's why I didn't think I was a failure.

"I'd rather be a failure at something I loved than be a success at something I hated. You know, I love show business as much today as I did when I was with the Pee-Wee Quartet. There were three other kids, all about seven or eight years old. Two of 'em ended up in the taxicab business."

"George, what do you think about the way the media portrays Senior Americans?"

"Well, I'll tell you something. Sometimes it's good, sometimes it's bad. I don't know what all this talk is about getting old. I was old when I was eighteen."

"Eighteen? Why?"

"I couldn't get a job. When you're not working, you're old. And when you're ninety-one and you're working, you're eighteen."

Before I could pause to ask the next question,

he continued by telling me he had some important advice to pass along:

"I'll tell you something, Art. I smoke, I drink martinis. I don't believe that everything gives you cancer. And there's no such thing as bad food for me. I'm not a connoisseur of food. It's got to be hot, that's all—stove hot, I mean. I came from a very poor family and in a poor family the food is always very hot so you never knew if it was good or bad. I like my food hot and I like the girls hot . . . and if I don't like the food, I send for catsup. And if I don't like the girl I send for catsup. Anytime I don't like something . . . I send for catsup."

George was on a roll and he knew he'd won over his audience when he heard me laughing out loud. He went on without missing a beat.

"Let me tell you something important to tell old people. I don't do anything that isn't right for my age and I think that should go for everyone. I think if you're a fifty-year-old woman and you dress beautifully for your age you look like you're forty. But if you're a fifty-year-old woman and you dress like you're twenty-five, you look like you're seventy. That also goes for jokes—the jokes have to be right for your age and they have to fit your mouth. Everything I do is my age. I dance my age, I sing my age. And at my age I do a lot of talking . . . at least let me *talk* about it."

"What about Gracie, George?"

"I had a wonderful marriage. You know, Gracie and I were married for a long time—until she left

this world. I'd still be married to her if she hadn't.
And the reason our marriage was a big success was
that it was a byproduct of what we did for a living.
Don't forget, Art, when I was married to Gracie,
I not only worked with Gracie, I dressed with Gracie, I slept with Gracie—I was with Gracie twenty-
four hours a day. It wasn't like somebody going
to work in the morning and coming back twelve
hours later. I was with Gracie thirty-eight years—
no, more than that, forty—I was with Gracie two
years before I married her."

"Could anyone ever have replaced her?"

"No—no. I'd never get married again. I've *been*
married. But let me tell you something, Art. I bet
very few comedians get divorces. For instance, Jack
Benny, Alan King, Red Buttons . . . you know,
any comedian. They don't get married because
they're great lovers; they get married because they
make their wives laugh. Let me tell you something:
When you get to be married for twenty-five years
or so, it's much easier just to make your wife laugh.

"I'll tell you something else. The subject of dying
seems to come up a lot around old people. If you
ask me about dying, you're asking the wrong fella.
I've already done it. I 'died' in Altoona. My trunk
is still there . . . I was so bad the people who booked
me wouldn't even give me back my trunk!"

"Any last thought you want me to pass along,
George?"

"Well, I don't think you should retire. All you
do is sit around and play with your cuticles . . . did
you ever play with your cuticles?"

"No . . ."

"It's nothing. Trust me."

"Thanks, George."

And that was that.

Phyllis Diller and I share the same birthday—July 17. That's one of many things we have in common. She still travels nearly fifty percent of the time, has never felt better in her life, and doesn't hold a drop of resentment toward the recent birthday that made her seventy years old.

Phyllis was thirty-seven when she picked up a book entitled *Life Begins at Forty*. She told me the book proved to be inspirational. When the motivation she received from the book was combined with the insistence of the husband we all came to know and love as "Fang," she found the impetus to launch her career as a comedienne.

Phyllis has five children and four grandchildren and they all live within thirty minutes of one another. She was born in Lima, Ohio, and studied music in Chicago. In fact, she played with 100 symphonies between 1971 and 1981. "Then," she said, "I just gave it up and walked away from it because I couldn't find the time to practice anymore. Besides, my attitude had changed. I had that wonderful experience but, in my life, I concentrate on the priorities and I insist on enjoyment. When practice became work, that was the end."

One of the most delightful aspects of sharing a friendship with Phyllis is her ability to speak in a straightforward fashion about everything. She de-

livers lines in conversation with the same deftness
she uses doing standup comedy. When we talked
about retirement, her response was predictable.
"That's the most awful thing I could ever think
about doing. However, I can understand it when
people have worked all their lives in jobs they've
hated—that *is* a reason to retire. But . . . gee whiz
. . . me retire? I'd find something else to do . . .
immediately . . . in fact, I never would have stayed
in a job I didn't like." Those aren't hollow
words . . . they come from a mother of five who
began a career at thirty-seven.

Her advice for people who I suggested may not
have any options? "Everyone has options,
Art . . . c'mon, you know that. If people really
want to do something, they can. The real word is
'fear.' There's a big difference between deliberately choosing to do something and not doing it
because you're afraid. I think just about everyone
can find something to do that will put some fun in
their lives. I don't really understand loneliness that
comes as a result of being alone. In fact, my 'prime
time' is when I'm alone. What I really enjoy is the
total sense of freedom it allows me. The other kind
of loneliness comes from deep inside and the saddest people are those who suffer that kind of loneliness."

As we talked, we shifted into one of the concerns
I've heard expressed by so many Senior Americans
concerned about the growing role of government
in their lives. Phyllis's response was swift and to
the point: "I don't like government's involvement.

It already has too much. People are getting weaker and weaker . . . look, why did all those people kill themselves in Guyana? They wanted to be taken care of. Why do people send eight million dollars to Oral Roberts? They want to be taken care of. They'll go for anything that will assure them health, happiness, and a long life. I just abhor that. I go back to the old days when people worked their tails off for what they wanted. Look at the situation with the government now—we're bankrupt and it's no wonder. Three generations of people have grown up with relief and they don't know how to work—their children don't know how to work. They're taken care of and it's no surprise everyone wants to come to our country. They swim rivers and drop out of the sky because we have the greatest system in the world. No one wants to take care of everybody . . . but we are!

"In fact that makes me think of my own parents. I remember their brightness. They were always working and always looking forward to the next move. They were vital . . . and fun. My parents were very old when they died and for them it was the easiest thing in the world—they just died. I think that's the way to go . . . it's how *I* want to go. Pow! Just pop off."

Phyllis Diller is perhaps the only woman in the world who got more attention than Betty Ford because she *chose* to have a face lift. And, I'm here to tell you she looks wonderful! I asked her if she was happy with her decision. "You bet I am. It's done wonders for me . . . absolute wonders and I'm all for it! That's why I talk about it. There's only one problem: It does cost money. But you feel young inside and you get a boost from it every day. The best thing about it is that when I look in the mirror, my face matches what I feel inside—young!"

Phyllis said that the biggest change she's seen in her lifetime has been transportation. She described the contrast this way: "Today I travel on jets—including the supersonic Concorde. When I was a child, my family traveled by horse and buggy to the town where Neil Armstrong was born. Imagine that—the first man who stepped on the moon!"

Bob Hope, born in England, one of seven boys, had as "happy a childhood as you can have with six brothers." He has four kids of his own and I met him years ago on *People Are Funny*. We've been friends ever since.

According to Bob, what's changed most in his lifetime is his appearance. "As you get older and somebody sends you a picture of yourself to autograph you think, 'Did I really look that good?' " Bob is in his mid-eighties and, by any standard that can be applied, he is a national institution.

As we started to talk about Senior America, he reminded me that it was President Eisenhower who originally said, "There are three stages of life: youth, maturity, and 'God you look good!' "

Bob credits his mother, who was a concert singer, with his start in show business. It was from her that he inherited his singing voice. He inherited the bent for comedy from his dad, an amateur comedian who worked full time as a stonemason. It was in 1922, after the Hopes had moved from London to Cleveland, that he began his career as a singer. He "hit the road in '24" and has been in show business ever since. Ever since means more than sixty years.

Bob's known every U.S. President since Hoover and has been extended literally every honor this country can bestow. Among all that he's done, he still considers his extraordinary efforts for the USO the high point of his life and has no intention of slacking off. He also has an interesting attitude about his age. He doesn't consider himself old— he says he's a combination of all ages.

I asked him what was the best time he could remember in which to be alive. He said, "I don't think there's any better time than right now. There's more chance for people—youngsters—everybody—to get going. This country keeps building and building and building. As I look out I see progress everywhere, see businesses and the way they are building . . . this country is fantastic. If I could speak at one time to all Senior Americans, I'd tell them to forget their age and do exactly what they feel like doing. It all comes down to attitude. Excitement is what really keeps you going. We had a party Saturday night and this gal—eighty-nine years old—had just come back from Alaska. She brought me a cocktail napkin that had a 'naughty' poem on it—all the way from Alaska. What a great sense of humor. Eighty-nine years old and she has it all together—still loves to laugh. And let me tell you, she looks just as sharp as she acts. That's what it's all about."

When I asked Bob if religion was important to him, he answered seriously when he told me it was. But Bob will be Bob. He continued by reminding me that he's a Presbyterian and his wife is Catholic. He said he once had to go to Vietnam to get meat on Friday . . . "that's how religious *she* is. In fact, when she saw my first act, she knew somebody had to start praying, and she's been praying for me ever since."

I asked Bob who he thinks inspires Senior Americans today. It wasn't surprising that he cited the President and Nancy Reagan first or that he followed by acknowledging all that Senator Claude Pepper has done. "He has Senior Americans getting up and trying to *do* things. It's wonderful and he's earned his reputation as one of the real champions of the elderly. He's inspiring . . . almost as inspiring as George Burns. Did you know he was on *Dance Fever* the other night—as a contestant?"

Lucille Ball, in a recent article, described herself this way: "I wasn't beautiful or even all that talented. I was just in show business. I was never the wrong age because I could play different ages. Nobody ever pounded on my door for my beauty or youth."

How wrong can any one person be? Lucy is one of the most talented women who ever lived and, in this man's opinion, one of the most beautiful inside and out. And that isn't a casually held opinion. Not too long ago an hour-long tribute to Lucy was aired on network TV that was attended by an impressive list of her peers. During the show, her children surprised her with a tribute of their own. You only had to watch her face—and theirs— to know who Lucille Ball really is and what kind of an example she provides for Senior America. When I say old age is not for sissies, there isn't a better example than Lucille Ball.

Lucy has the distinction of having garnered more newsprint and higher television ratings than even the Eisenhower inauguration when Desi Jr. was born in 1952. In fact, even though it seems as though *I Love Lucy* has always been on television, Lucy was thirty-nine years old when the first episode was filmed.

Now in her mid-seventies, she stands firmly against retirement. "I'm so-called retired because I don't do the *Lucy Show* anymore. But I'm still traveling, I have a show coming up with Bob Hope, I'm going to New York for a couple of things, I have dinners and award things scheduled, I'm working with Dr. Norman Vincent Peale and Armand Hammer. It's a full schedule. The best advice I could ever give to another Senior American would be: Make sure you have something to do— have a reason to get up in the morning."

Lucy's deep love for her son and daughter is easy to understand when you hear her describe her own childhood. She and her brother were raised by their grandparents when their father died at the age of twenty-three.

"My mother was very young, so we went back to her parents' home in Jamestown, New York, and were brought up by our maternal grandparents. We were very close. My grandfather died at seventy-eight and I knew him all my life as Daddy. My mother's name was Desirée but everyone called her Dede. She was a very strong factor in my children's lives as they were growing up. I'm only sorry that she's not here to see my daughter Lucie's children grow up. She was a mentor for all of us . . . our Dede. She never lived with us except in New York when I was doing the show *Wildcats* for a year. Even though she always had her own place, she was always a part of us. For years she lived very close, but always had her own independence. She helped me in so many ways. I was working and Dede was always there watching over everything. Whenever we traveled, she always went with us. And on our weekends, vacations, and holidays, it was always with Dede. I needed her advice and her know-how. Just as I appreciated my mother, my daughter appreciates me and welcomes a little help now and then."

I asked Lucy if families are different today than when she was growing up: "By necessity, families are getting back together today because of economics. I think it's going to happen even more and it's wonderful, although, at the moment, it's also a little scary for everybody. So many families have been separated for the last twenty years because of airplanes. It's easy to get somewhere that's 3,000 miles away. However, it's also easy to move somewhere miles and miles and miles away. So, by necessity, we haven't had the wonderful family togetherness that the older generation had. Now, because of the economy, people are finding they have to get back together again and I think that's all to the good—it's wonderful when children have their grandparents around. It's not happening overnight, but I'm all for it."

Lucy has been married to Gary Morton for twenty-five years and she acknowledges that what's most important in her life are her husband and the knowledge that her children are well, taking care of themselves, and living happy lives. When I asked what makes *her* happy, she said, "I'm happiest when I'm able to hold up my end of things; when I can make people around me happy; and when I can keep my hands off what's not my business."

I've given you a brief inside look at five of my friends who are admired, loved, and respected. What shines through everything they had to say is an exciting attitude toward life. And they also know, as I do, that people who are the happiest face the future with anticipation and a willingness to make choices. I now know what wisdom really is—it's a product of experience that comes from years and years of trying and failing; trying and succeeding; getting involved and discovering you *were* the best person for the job; raising kids; suffering pain; knowing what really causes happiness; knowing when to keep your hands off something that's none of your business; considering yourself lucky to care for your mother in a catastrophic illness after burying your husband; considering time alone "prime time"; and knowing you don't have to die because you already did it in Altoona.

Rights are those things we are entitled to as human beings. The seven Golden Rights of Senior Americans were specifically developed for this book to encompass those areas of living that I believe are most significant for Senior Americans. Choices, on the other hand, grant us the freedom and power to choose how we exercise those rights. It is my sincerest hope and intention that the rights and choices described on the following pages will bring a better quality of life to all Senior Americans in this great country.

ART LINKLETTER'S

Golden Rights of Senior Americans

1. Irrespective of individual status or achievement, Senior Americans have the right to expect to be held in esteem and treated with consideration and dignity because of age alone.

2. Senior Americans have the right to independence, privacy, and choice of persons with whom they live and associate; they also have the right not to fear abridgement of those rights because of advancing age.

3. In all instances where decisions governing personal health are concerned, Senior Americans have the right to complete and accurate information necessary to ensure freedom of choice in selection of health care services. They have the further right to expect medical treatment from persons whose knowledge is strengthened with compassion and whose judgment is governed by moral restraint.

4. Senior Americans have the right to manage their financial affairs, as well as the right to complete information and full disclosure of possible consequences from those through whom they seek assistance with the management of those affairs.

5. Senior Americans have the right to freedom from fear of mental and physical abuse, as well as from chemical or physical restraint except in medical emergencies.

6. Senior Americans have the right to the information and assistance needed to ensure a continuing healthy lifestyle.

7. Senior Americans have the right to choose how and with whom they spend leisure time, as well as the right to expect considerate assistance when they travel.

1
The Right to Consideration and Dignity

Irrespective of individual status or achievement, Senior Americans have the right to expect to be held in esteem and treated with consideration and dignity because of age alone.

"Old is old, people are people . . . be kind to everyone, age doesn't matter." —Art Linkletter

Senior Americans are not a separate race of people who speak a foreign language. They aren't typified by senility, frailty, or their boring, repetitive stories. They're just an older version of younger Americans. And by all that's holy, advancing age *should* be accompanied by a certain respect if only for what it took just to live long enough to be considered "old."

People are people. They live in warm climates and cold climates, vote for Republicans and Democrats, are happy and sad, ambitious and lazy, good and bad parents and grandparents, recognized and unrecognized, rich and poor, and their dreams may or may not have been fulfilled. They run the gamut of everything applied to anyone in this country no matter who they are and regardless of their age.

What *is* different is that, by virtue of age, their remaining life-spans are shorter. Maybe that's what gives so many Senior Americans the fortitude to answer questions directly and cut through to the core of issues being discussed in superfluous language. What we view with delight as Senior America's refreshing candor may just be annoyance at having time wasted—which makes sense. After all time *is* running out, isn't it?

When we stand back and look at Senior America, we see a composite of people, many of whom are just two or three generations removed from being immigrants to the United States. They remember parents who began working the day they finished school and, for many of them, that was the day after they finished the sixth or eighth grade. Role models were parents, grandparents, and friends within a very close area because travel and communication—as we know it now—just didn't exist.

All the news was printed in extraordinary detail in the newspaper. When a couple married, the bride's wedding dress down to the fabrics and laces that were used to make it were described with a thousand words of detail. The journalistic style of the day allowed complete descriptions of wedding gifts and who gave them. What the guests wore and how they socialized, what they ate and drank, and who did or didn't have a good time went on— paragraph after paragraph. And when guests were from out of town, the reporter described how they traveled, what their relationships were to the bride, groom, and their families—everything was included. Anyone reading an account of the event knew, in detail, what had happened, what the weather had been and whether or not people conducted themselves in a manner that was morally in tune with the times.

Local political figures became folk heroes whose exploits and daring deeds were reported in serial fashion as they unfolded. There were no "gray areas" that clouded a subject and writers freely included broad editorial comments. Right was right. Wrong was wrong. And when someone was described as "morally upstanding," no further explanation was required.

Men and women married and raised children. The hub of family life was the church or synagogue. If someone stepped out of line, it wasn't considered meddling when the minister, priest, or rabbi arrived to deliver the dressing down. It was expected.

Housewives were measured by the manner in which they did their housework and cared for their families. Justine, one of the ladies in a group I talked with, described her mother's assessment of a "good" or "bad" woman. Her mother said a "good" woman's first responsibility was to be a wife and mother. And if she couldn't be that, she was expected to be a respectable maiden lady—with the key word being *lady*. A "bad" woman needed no description.

Her mother vied with her neighbors to be the first one with her laundry on the line on Monday mornings. Justine described how her mother clucked in dismay at one neighbor who had the habit of letting Mondays slip into the afternoon before the first bed sheet or towel appeared on her wash lines. Justine's mother expressed her sympathy for the woman's husband and the burden he had to bear as a result of having married "that kind of woman."

As Justine unfolded her story, embellishing it with wonderful detail, she was encouraged by nodding heads as people remembered similar events in their own lives. The subject of her story, and the others that follow, illustrates people who subscribed to a common value system and the standards of the times. They were people with a sense of purpose who passed along what they believed were the important lessons they'd learned from their parents. One of those lessons was to be considerate and respect the dignity of everyone who reached "old age." Being old was reason enough.

Jack was next to launch into a story about his father and the role he'd played in the lives of his children and grandchildren. Jack grew up in an Italian neighborhood in Chicago. Houses weren't built side by side with their own yards; they were attached row houses. Their neighborhood spanned three city blocks connected by back alleys. Each summer neighbors competed to see who would produce the first ripe tomato.

Families who chose to live there—or move there—

had a reason. If neighbors weren't related Italians, they had other common roots. The neighborhood ended at the parish boundaries of the Catholic church and, in Jack's neighborhood in Chicago, that was Sixty-ninth Street. Everyone knew everything about everyone.

Jack's father was called "Poppy" by children and grandchildren and was the head of his family. His trademark was the cigar he always had pinched in his teeth. When World War I began, he enlisted in the Army. After the war, he started his own construction business. Then, because he possessed badly needed skills, he enlisted again during World War II as a construction battalion "seabee." He was sent to the Pacific to help to clear land and build airstrips so the Army could follow. After the war, Poppy returned to his construction business in Chicago.

When Jack and his brother grew up and married, they settled in the same neighborhood in which they'd grown up. Jack had distinguished himself by graduating from West Point and had also served his country at the end of World War II during the occupation of Japan. Poppy was immensely proud of his "West Point graduate" but was always concerned lest his son forget his origins or seek some form of recognition based on West Point status alone.

After the war, Jack joined his dad in the construction business starting at the bottom as a bricklayer. Poppy found the perfect way to keep his son humble. He delighted in waiting until Jack was knee-deep in mortar and bricks, and sweating as he worked in the heat of the day. These were the times Poppy deliberately selected to bring someone over to meet his son. After the introduction, his father and the visitor would stand and "shoot the breeze" as Jack labored on his hands and knees. Jack said Poppy had the patience of Job as he waited for the perfect moment to casually mention, "By the way . . . did I tell you Jack graduated from West Point?"

Humility wasn't the only lesson that Poppy taught with a wry sense of humor. According to Jack, his father had a unique way of teaching every lesson he considered to be significant. "Poppy was the one with the straight answers, a man who could pare anyone who needed it down to size." He was a man venerated by his family and remembered by a son in his late sixties with warmth and affection.

The lack of veneration for age was further described by a woman named Helen. When Helen's husband died nearly thirty years ago, she was astonished to discover she'd been left with almost no financial resources to support herself. Fortunately, her children were already on their own and she had only herself to worry about as she took control of her life. Although she never thought she'd use the degree she'd earned thirty years earlier, it enabled her to begin a teaching career in her late fifties and buy a small house just two blocks from school. After retirement, she continued substitute teaching for another ten years and paid off her house and bought a car. At eighty-one, she no longer teaches and is living on a very limited income.

Helen's friend told us about the next-door neighbors who share a common driveway with Helen. They're people in their late forties who have two large vans that they deliberately park in a way that blocks Helen's access to her half of the driveway. Shortly after they rented the house next door, Helen baked cookies, walked over to introduce herself, and unsuccessfully tried to make friends. She walked next door a few weeks later to ask if they could leave a little more room when they parked. The neighbors—and their adult children—responded by taunting and yelling epithets about the way "the stupid old lady" parks. After several months of increasingly abusive treatment, Helen finally decided to call their landlord, who issued a stern warning the same day. The neighbors responded by escalating their abuse. Her friend says Helen refuses to complain again because she fears what they'll do next to "get even." This frail eighty-one-year-old woman has been terrified into silence by neighbors who are taking advantage of her age and vulnerability.

Times *have* changed. The good old days weren't all good by any means. They weren't times without crime, everyone didn't live in an idyllic American town with a bandstand in the park, all children weren't happy-go-lucky, and there were plenty of problems. There were as many hard times as good times and Senior Americans didn't get discounts. What they did get, however, was a greater level of respect and more consideration. Old age was venerated.

Many Senior Americans don't like our new ways or the inhuman contribution of machines and technology. And this isn't exclusive to the United States. It's also true in Japan—the nation that has always been viewed as the leader in caring for and venerating its elders. In a *Chicago Tribune* article published August 7, 1986, Ronald E. Yates quotes Tsuneo Iida, a professor at Nagoya University: "While much of the world still thinks Japan is a society where the children look after their elderly parents, that simply is no longer the case." He states that according to a survey conducted by the Japan Institute of Life Insurance, only one in four Japanese between the ages of fifty-five and sixty-four feels children should be financially responsible for aging parents—an attitude credited with having its origin among Japan's young adults. He also quotes a seventy-six-year-old former gardener he interviewed in a tiny Tokyo apartment that he shares with another elderly man: "I don't like this new Japan—it is a lonely, cold place. Everything is electronic, nothing is human. Even my two daughters are more concerned with their kitchen appliances than with their father."

As I talked with Senior Americans around the country, it often took considerable time to bring their memories and outspoken comments to the surface. It was almost as though the people speaking feared they would bore someone or appear to be suffering from terminal cases of nostalgia. The stories exchanged were nostalgic, humorous, and sentimental. For the most part, they recalled people who were loved, respected, and deeply missed. The agreement my Senior American friends and I reached was that consideration and dignity are rights that belong to every human being—respect and love, on the other hand, are earned. And, in my opinion, the manner in which we venerate advanced age is a significant measure of the strength of the society in which we live.

Grief

It's terribly difficult to know how to comfort a friend or family member who is grieving. Perhaps more than any other time this is when we must do our utmost to show consideration and bestow dignity on the grieving individual. It's public knowledge that Lois and I have lost two of our five children. There is no way to describe the depth of our pain and level of our grief. Children are not supposed to die before their parents—period. Because our daughter Diane's death was the result of experimenting in the drug culture, her death threw me into the fight against the problem and I've spent nearly twenty years committed to helping others prevent what happened to our beautiful daughter. Lois, however, was asked one day why she refused to listen to me speak when I talked about drugs. She said, "It's like having a deep, terrible cut that finally begins to heal. I know Art has to talk about what happened in order to reach his audience. But when I listen to him speak it's like ripping the Band-Aid off the wound—it begins bleeding and I have to start healing all over again."

Our son Robert died in an automobile accident. For a family that shares so much love, and to whom family is so important, things like this just shouldn't happen. But they do. As Diane's death brought me into the fight against drugs and alcohol, Robert's death caused me to continue the work he'd begun through his invention of a safety top for drug containers that is now being widely used in the pharmaceutical industry. Our memories of our children are happy. Life isn't the same without them, but it's still a good life. The sun still comes up and the grass is still green and tomorrow still holds hope and expectation. We're happy for the years we had them with us and can do nothing about the years we lost.

A few years ago a friend of mine lost her mother after an eighteen-month battle against cancer. I watched her anguish as she watched her mother's and did what I could to help—mostly listen as she unfolded the terrible progress of her mother's cancer. A few months after her mother died, I urged her to put what she'd told me into writing. I decided to include her "Tribute to My Mother" because it carries an underlying message that says more about grief than all the studies I've read. Perhaps the most important point it makes is that she dealt with many of her concerns while her mother was still alive.

She died just a year and a half ago—the day before Thanksgiving—having suffered terribly from a virulent form of cancer that had ravaged her from the moment it struck.

Never—during the time she fought, went through three major surgeries, became despondent, fought again, and finally resigned herself to the inevitable— did she lose the qualities I miss so terribly. Her death, like her life, she did with class, style, and a sense of humor.

One day she made her wishes about her funeral known to my sister and me with an almost belly-laugh sense of humor. "Remember, you two, this will be my final appearance. I know they don't put shoes and a girdle on you in a coffin but they better do it for me . . . you see to it," she said. "And make sure you wash that blouse of mine—I think the last time I wore it I spilled lobster butter on it. I refuse to lie there and have everyone see the spots." My sister and I laughed and cried at the same time. Even as she made her wishes known, she eased our pain by doing it with humor.

Oh yes, she was some woman. She was my mother and I miss her more than any words will ever express.

Because I lived many miles away, I drove on the weekends to where she lived. As I drove the 100 miles each way I thought about seeing her weaker, in greater pain, and slowly slipping away. I would think to myself that this time I must tell her—somehow—what she meant to me before it was too late. Each time I drove home it was with tears streaming down my face because I'd been unable to find the words.

The third weekend in May was magnificent. It was sunshiny and warm. Everything looked like life—lacy, beautiful, and green. How my mother loved the spring. It was the time she began to work in her wonderful gardens where she grew roses and every other supporting flower. I can see her with her cat purring and flitting in and out while she worked on her hands and knees. He purred just because he could be near the person he loved best in the world—the person who said she never spoiled him but who drove across town in the snow to buy him smelt in the middle of winter.

One more weekend had passed and I hadn't told my mother what I felt and it worried me. This particular weekend she'd looked so much weaker.

I got up at six o'clock the next morning. In our short summers it is a time I love—peaceful and quiet—and I enjoy sitting outside on the patio. I made a pot of coffee, took a sheaf of paper with me, and went outside to write what I'd been unable to say.

I did write the letter and I'm so happy I did. My mother didn't get on the telephone to comment when she'd received it. I neither wanted that nor expected she would. All she said the next time I saw her was,

"I love you so much and I'm proud that you're my daughter." As I write this the tears run down my face again for the lovely woman with the quiet strength and wonderful laughter.

The last time I saw her was three days before she died. I'd received a call telling me she was no longer able to hear or be aware of anyone's presence. But a dear friend of mine who is a doctor told me this wasn't true. She said my mother would be able to hear—it's the last of the senses to disappear.

The moment I went into her room I knew it would be the last time. I bent and kissed her and took her now fragile hand in mine. Because her bones were so brittle they could break at the slightest movement, I cradled her carefully and finally said—out loud— what I'd put in writing.

I don't know how long I held her like that but as I was talking to her, she somehow managed to put her hand on my shoulder. She had heard and was telling me good-bye and that she loved me, too.

I know that three days later when she finally was at peace and free from suffering God must have said, "It's good to see you, Sally, you're one of My best."

We buried her in a blouse free of lobster butter wearing a girdle and shoes. The roses that surrounded her were peach to match her suit. The minister talked of her with tears and with laughter and the hymn we sang was "How Great Thou Art."

I can never again buy her a card or send flowers on Mother's Day. But in my heart I can thank her every day of my life and remember her with love, warmth, laughter, and tears. The world is better for her having been here. She leaves a legacy of wisdom and love that were hers alone. Every time I see a rose and look at its beauty I see my mother. And I miss her terribly.

Conventional thinking says that grieving people come to terms with their loss and recover normal functioning in one to two years. Yet that may not always be true. University of Michigan psychology professor Camille Wortman reported findings of recent studies about grief to the American Association for the Advancement of Science. These studies suggest that some people come through bereavement relatively unscathed while others take years to recover. Those who manage well often feel guilty because they aren't plunged into overwhelming distress following the death of a loved one, though they think it's expected of them. The studies suggest that we should learn and understand what resources protect these lucky individuals.

On the other hand, the same studies found that fifty-seven percent of surviving spouses and seventy-four percent of parents who'd lost a child said memories still were painful four to seven years later. The studies also uncovered new findings that clash with other conventional beliefs about grief, such as assuming that a display of grief will help a person come to terms with a loved one's death more quickly.

There isn't a right or wrong way to grieve. Chaplain Philip W. Williams, author of *When Death Draws Near*, says, "Death is the ultimate loss and accepting it is a struggle. We all struggle in our own way. Acceptance comes with more or less difficulty or not at all, depending on who we are and what we believe."

The complete course of grief takes us through shock, emotion, depression and loneliness, physical distress, panic, guilt, resistance, hope, and finally the confrontation with reality. This course progresses at different speeds and with differing visible clues.

And grief doesn't occur only because of the death of someone we love. Regardless of age, as human beings, our senses of personal dignity and self-respect are closely related to our levels of independence and freedom. Consequently, when Senior Americans are forced to surrender their independence in order to survive, the grief that accompanies this loss is profound and can be permanently devastating. It's one thing to be physically, mentally, and financially able to make choices and decisions; it's quite another to have these abilities compromised, or removed, because one becomes dependent on others for survival.

Grief can also be a symptom of our mobile culture that uproots people and relocates them, cutting off relationships with community, friends, family, and a lifetime of feeling comfortable just because they knew their way around. Or it can be caused by divorce, which has been described as a living death; by retirement, which isn't always welcomed by people who leave their jobs feeling as though they've lost their reason for living; by losing one's employment; by losing a child through marriage; by losing one's sight or hearing; by becoming disabled as a result of injury or disease—and many other reasons too long to identify in a single book.

The most important thing to remember is that there isn't a right or wrong way to survive grief or bereavement. There are a lot of people who can help—clergy in particular. In the past few years most clergy have had special training that allows them to effectively help people get through it and eventually recover. Interestingly, funeral home directors are more often than not receiving training that allows them to better understand grief. And many hospitals are offering support groups for grief and bereavement.

Accomplishing a recovery doesn't mean we have once again become our old selves. Grief is a result of unwanted or unavoidable change and people come through it permanently strengthened or permanently weakened. Life after grief will never be the same as what preceded it, but there can be much remaining that's good and worthwhile. We *can* learn to love life again even though we thought that day would never come.

The conclusion of my friend's tribute to her mother clearly says that she knows full well what's been lost and that it can never be the same. It also recognizes the memories she'll hold in her heart forever. It expresses the hope of a tomorrow that, although changed, will allow her to continue her life saddened but strengthened by someone she loved. The day I knew she'd finally healed was when she said, "You know, Art, the saddest thing about my mother's death is that I realize I no longer need her. Just the other day I wanted to telephone her and realized I couldn't. When I thought about it I realized what I really wanted was to hear her voice. But I didn't need her advice and direction— I knew what she would have said . . . she taught me well."

Loneliness

Loneliness is pervasive in this pell-mell world we live in today and it takes all forms up to and including suicide. Even though being alone is often considered synonymous with loneliness, they aren't the same. There's a big difference between being alone and being lonely. People alone can do well, especially if they are people who preferred being by themselves throughout their lives. Others, however, who find themselves suddenly alone can slip into a loneliness that becomes devastating. After the death of someone with whom they've shared their lives, the comfortable pattern of familiarity is shattered. Then a breeding ground opens for anger, fear, resentment, depression, and lethargy.

It's all well and good to say that someone can deal with loneliness *if* he or she chooses—which is true—but it isn't always that simple. For the person who has maintained an active, involved life it's a lot easier to remain involved. For the person who has shared activities with someone else, the loss of that person can be total.

Jake is a man who comes to mind. He was married to a woman he adored. They had shared everything from the first day they met, including the responsibilities related to children and grandchildren. Jake always told everyone that his wife earned half his salary just by the manner in which she handled the household and all the daily responsibilities which freed him to work. And he meant it. Vacations were with family until all the kids married and left home. Then they were with his wife—just the two of them.

When she was struck down with a terminal illness, the tenderness with which Jake cared for her was a testimony to the word "love." Until the day she died with him at her side, Jake never really believed it would happen. It was as though, without warning, she'd vanished. Jake didn't turn against anyone or reject his children; he just couldn't stand the loneliness in a house that reminded him everywhere he turned of the woman he'd loved. He refused to consider selling it and lived, for the most part, in the kitchen and bedroom. Even though he'd loved playing golf, it wasn't the same when he came home to an empty house at the end of the day. He began staying up late at night and sleeping later in the morning. Although he was cordial to his friends, he turned down most invitations and eventually his friends stopped asking. Jake was happiest when someone stopped in and he could talk about his wife—it was as though she was there again.

Another man—Harold—had a similar experience, although his wife died suddenly and there was no extended illness. They'd never had children and had spent literally every moment of their fifty-one-year marriage together. She'd been an excellent cook and housekeeper, and had completely taken care of Harold. He's doing splendidly. Harold's description of his early forays into the cooking arena are sidesplitting and were inspired when he decided he wanted food like she used to cook. His greatest triumph came when he felt he had a simple chicken dish mastered well enough to invite his friends over for dinner. They gave Harold's culinary skills a 10 and he now hosts a Monday night ritual dinner during football season that has all the appearances of continuing year round. The friends are two other widowers and a woman who never married. Harold laughs when he describes how guilty he felt allowing the dishes to sit until Tuesday, knowing what his wife would have said. He quickly pushes that aside with the acknowledgment that he has all day Tuesday to clean up. He's also discovered that the dirty dishes have no impact on how much he and his friends enjoy the game. The last time I talked to Harold, he spent fifteen minutes telling me why he thought he was ready to try Peking duck. If you'd asked me twenty years ago what this man would have done without his wife, I would have predicted he wouldn't have lasted a year. Harold decided he liked living and, since the woman he loved couldn't do it, he'd have to do it himself.

Women usually are the glue in a household that holds everything together. Consequently, they tend to manage better after the death of a spouse than men do. They also have an additional advantage where friends are concerned. They share their feelings more openly than men who maintain casual friendships with "buddies."

Although the loss of a husband is profound, women manage day-to-day activities better. They're accustomed to doing the cooking when the kids and grandkids come over and they already know how to load an automatic washer. Lifetime roles related to mothering and grandmothering help a lot. My advisers tell me that most men really don't put a household back together in the sense that most women do—they manage it just fine but the touches that make it "home," or the way it used to be, often aren't there.

When illness or a handicap is part of a Senior American's life, loneliness is intensified. This is where the right to privacy has to be carefully considered in terms of what I'll call an invasion inspired by genuine caring. When people who can't manage on their own summarily turn down an invitation, it may be because they fear being "too much trouble" or that their special needs create too burdensome an imposition. This is when it's worth a little forceful insistence to break the pattern. People have different ways of reaching out, and although the first response to an invitation may be, "No, thank you . . . I don't think so," don't be too sure it isn't just a test to see if you really mean it. Go ahead, insist. It's worth a try.

My expert advisers tell me that following the death of a loved one, family members and others will rally round the surviving parent or relative, showering him or her with attention. That continues for a while and then gradually tapers off. Visits become further apart and the person grieving can easily conclude no one cares. During this period of discovering that one really *is* alone, many people don't know how to reach out and find it easier to withdraw.

Pets help. There is overwhelming evidence to support the contribution a pet makes in someone's life. First of all, you *have* to get up in the morning because a pet needs to be fed and cared for. Animals are like people—they respond to love. The best thing about pets is their unqualified love. Rain or shine, happy or sad, their love is constant and their trust is total.

A woman named Neva had always had an Irish setter when she and her husband lived in their own home. After his death, her children insisted she move into an apartment where she could more easily manage. Although she finally agreed, she missed everything that had been familiar in their house. She missed her children and their families who lived far away just a little more than she missed her dog.

It was a neighbor named Amy—a woman young enough to be her granddaughter—who helped her carry groceries in one day and stayed for coffee. That became the beginning of a fast friendship. In time, Neva would call and tell Amy that she'd baked cookies for the kids or invite them over for lunch. As the coffee visits became regular events, Neva and Amy covered every subject worthy of discussion. They also shared a love for animals. Even though Neva had never had a cat, Amy knew she could manage one. Anyone who had the capacity for love that Neva did wouldn't reject a kitten.

On Neva's birthday, Amy and her kids arrived with a cake, a litter box, cans of food, a pint of milk, dishes, and a tabby kitten with white paws that weighed less than a pound and a half. It was love at first sight for real. When Amy told Neva the dire straits from which she'd "saved the kitten" in a farmer's barn, he was home free—he'd found his champion. I'm here to tell you that there isn't a smarter, more beautiful, entertaining, wonderful cat on earth. And if you doubt me, call Neva— she delights in reporting his every activity. He's a full-grown neutered cat that now weighs seventeen pounds, and his favorite place to sleep is on her lap. He eats only 9-Lives sliced veal and behaves like a king, as well he should—he's in complete control. He destroyed Neva's plants but she didn't really mind. In fact, she thought it was the funniest thing she'd ever seen when he climbed her ficus tree and broke the trunk. She said he jumped three feet in the air when it snapped in two. Mittens and his mistress were made for each other. He eats regularly at 7:00 A.M. and 5:00 P.M. Their favorite days are the sunny ones when they can enjoy a nap in the chair in front of the window—together.

Senior Americans who are healthy and able to make choices have to deal consciously with being alone—there *are* options out there. I've talked with lots of Senior Americans who have come up with some real solutions: Some form restaurant groups and go out for lunch once a week; others travel together; others extol the marvelous experiences they've had as participants in the Elderhostel program. (See p. 422.) Two men living side by side in a condominium complex discovered they shared a love for woodworking. They spend hours going between workshops and have a number of projects under mutual construction. Others are active in volunteer work and their churches, and some serve as foster grandparents. In some communities, there are babysitting services staffed entirely by Senior Americans, who receive a nominal fee for their services. Their experience and care free young women who need help with children at an affordable price. Many communities—through Commissions on Aging—sponsor a retail store that's stocked entirely with handmade items furnished by Senior Americans. And with the nation's renewed interest in nostalgia, there's another market at craft fairs and flea markets. If a person who can get out of the house chooses to do so, the options are limitless.

Senior Americans confined to nursing homes and those who live in rural or isolated areas have the toughest time. Here is where friends and family need to understand the importance of a phone call just to say "Hello . . . I'm thinking about you," and cards that are sent just to say you care. Reasonable people understand that visits aren't always possible—it's the regular, tangible reminders that you *haven't* forgotten that brighten a lonely person's day.

Children and younger friends can help a great deal by encouraging independence and getting out of the house. I know one group of kids who banded together and decided they were going to get their dad involved in something if it was the last thing they ever did. It took a lot of work and they hit a lot of dead ends before they found it. Their dad was a retired executive in his middle sixties and he'd always been keenly interested in politics. With his kids' active participation in his campaign, he's now a county supervisor. Now they have a new complaint—he's so busy they have to call him a week ahead of time to schedule dinner or other events. And when he is at one of their houses, all he talks about is politics.

Loneliness is real and painful. If you are a Senior American confined or unable to get out, let people know what they can do to help. And if someone wants to be part of your life, don't turn him or her aside because you think you are an unnecessary burden. People who care want to help, and when those who need the help deny them the opportunity, they also suffer. If you are a lonely, healthy Senior American, I urge you to make a conscious choice to get involved in something right now. Let the barriers down, take a chance—there are a lot of people who need you and what you have to contribute.

Kids Who Parent Parents

A healthy family isn't one where members are enmeshed in one another's lives to the point that no one can stand on his or her feet without the continuing support and approval of everyone else. It's essential that family members treat each other with consideration and dignity, especially as parents grow older and children are tempted to begin making decisions for them. As wonderful as it is to hold people we love close to us, mature and healthy love lets go. Good parents do the best they can raising kids and, when the time comes, they let go knowing they've done all they can. Even though they may not agree with the timing, they let their kids leave the nest. And that isn't always easy. But family life becomes even more complicated when parents and children start reversing their traditional roles.

Elizabeth and George raised three children. The first to marry was their oldest daughter. When she announced her intentions, they couldn't have been more disappointed. She was leaving college just a year before graduation to marry a man who didn't fit the picture of the man they'd imagined marrying their headstrong daughter. Compounding the disappointment, she and her husband-to-be planned to locate more than a thousand miles away from "home." Finally out of arguments trying to convince her to finish college, they decided to get on with the wedding and keep their feelings and concerns to themselves.

Elizabeth described her daughter Marty's call just a week later when she and her husband arrived at their first apartment. She could hear the homesick quavering in Marty's voice as she asked how everyone was. Elizabeth said it took all the strength she had not to cry, to comfort her, and to tell her everything would be okay. Then and there, she made the decision to "play it casually." She described talking to her daughter about unimportant family happenings while never asking what had occurred in her life as they drove across the country. She described the noises Marty could hear in the background as the family enjoyed a summer picnic. Marty asked who was there and what was going on. Her mother's answers were bright and cheery. Finally, she asked if she could say hello to her dad. Although he was standing two feet away her mother said, "I'm afraid not—he's up to his ears grilling hamburgers and you know how he gets when he's interrupted." Elizabeth said it nearly killed her to make her point that way, but she felt she had to let her daughter know that her life had changed.

When I spoke to Marty, she described herself as incredulous. "Here it was," she said, "just a week later and they were having a picnic without me . . . and enjoying it! Then, to be told that my own father was too busy grilling hamburgers to talk to me—well, I couldn't believe it. I was so mad when I hung up all I could think of was that I'd show *them*—and I did. I grew up and, somewhere along the way, realized what kind of nifty parents they really were."

Nearly ten years later, Marty and her family moved back into the area. Then, without warning, the tables turned. Marty's phone rang in the early morning and her mother tersely told her George had collapsed at work and was in an ambulance en route to the hospital. As soon as she'd blurted out the message, she began to cry and fall apart. Without hesitation, Marty stepped in and took control. She told her mother to be at the front door in five minutes—that she'd drive her to the hospital. On the way there, her strong, in-control mother was disintegrating as she watched, and by the time they arrived at the hospital Elizabeth was allowing herself to be led like a small, terrified child. They were ushered into the cardiac intensive care unit to see George positioned upright in a bed with tourniquets on his arms and legs as he choked, trying to breathe. His color was blue-gray and he was in congestive heart failure. The doctor told them his chances were no better than fifty-fifty and that the next twenty-four hours would tell the story. Marty said her mother didn't cry and said very little—she "tuned out." Marty called their minister and asked him to come over; she notified the rest of the family and made her mother's decisions.

Late that night, George's doctor suggested they go home after assuring mother and daughter they could call the hospital at any time and get a report on his condition. It was on the way home that Marty began to really worry about her mother. She described Elizabeth's exhaustion and terror regarding what she was facing. "All of a sudden Mother broke down and began to cry uncontrollably. I had to help her out of the car and lead her into the house, where she threw herself in a chair, crying. Then she told me that there was no way she could handle this . . . that I'd have to continue to make decisions . . . that she'd do what she could but she didn't think that would be much. It was when she told me she was no good to anyone that I got mad, really mad. I stood yelling down at her, using something my dad had once said to snap me around when my own daughter was very ill. 'Mother,' I said, 'knock it off. Here you sit blubbering and feeling sorry for yourself while Dad fights for his life. I'll tell you what I think—I think it stinks and I also think your selfishness stinks. If you really want people to feel sorry for poor Elizabeth, why don't you carry a sign on your back, march up and down the street, and tell the neighbors it's you they should worry about instead of him. I don't feel sorry for you, I feel sorry for Dad and I'm going home—now. If you keep this up, don't worry—I will be there for Dad and *will* stand in for you so you can cry. I hurt, too, and right now I don't need your problems. I'm going to have all I can do to manage my own family while I attempt to replace you. I'll just tell Dad you're crumpled in a corner feeling sorry for yourself.' "

With that soliloquy behind her, Marty slammed out the door and went home. She described her own anguish as she told her husband what she'd said to her mother and the hurt look on Elizabeth's face as she heard her daughter's brutal, angry words. She'd just about decided to go back to her mother's house to apologize when the phone rang. It was Elizabeth, sounding exhausted but in quiet control. She thanked her daughter for the courage it had taken to say what had to be said and made her promise she'd repeat it if she slipped.

In the conversation that followed, Marty explained that the hardest thing she'd experienced as her role reversed with her mother's was the anger she felt when her mother didn't comfort her—after all, it was her *father* and everyone knows parents should comfort children first.

Herein lies the dilemma between parents and children. Role reversal is scary for adult children. Everything in them says, "What's happened? Our parents used to take care of *us.*" Like it or not, nearly eighty percent of all Senior Americans—sooner or later—will be involved with their adult children or other relatives—an involvement that can be healthy in spite of growing dependencies.

Experts report that the majority of kids think they *should* accept responsibility for their parents, including moving them in with their own families. They also tell us that the majority of Senior Americans, however, want to remain entirely independent. As parents do become unable to keep up in some areas, it isn't helping children they resent, it's the diminishing of capabilities they'd always taken for granted.

Because people really don't change all that much, most difficulties experienced as Senior Americans relate to old, unresolved conflicts. People who have always been demanding, abrasive, or thoughtless aren't likely to change; in fact, those qualities may intensify. And people who are easygoing, happy, and upbeat are more than likely to stay that way.

Unfortunately, when illnesses like Alzheimer's, a debilitating stroke, or anything causing human devastation occurs, the brunt of pain—particularly for the children—is terrible. Elizabeth's husband recovered and with minimal help from their children, he and his wife have remained independent. They're lucky. All the dynamics work and the family almost sounds too good to be true.

However, if George had been discharged from the hospital as a man consigned to a wheelchair, never again able to manage without help, he could be spending his remaining years as a man embittered by his loss of independence. And Elizabeth might not have sat beside her middle-aged daughter remembering the crisis as a time when their love had grown deeper than ever. She might very well have remembered it only as the time their lives drastically changed—the crisis that added a permanent burden of responsibility, costly medical bills, and a lot of unhappiness.

For the most part, children who help *want* to help. If anything, they want to do too much and, inadvertently, cause parents to lose self-respect. That doesn't mean, however, that there aren't times when a son or daughter must step in and say, "Dad can't be allowed to drive anymore," and regardless of a loss of self-respect, take action. It's maintaining an even balance that's the trick.

When children are needed to help manage a parent's affairs, by necessity they share power and often gain knowledge in areas that once were closed in their parents' lives. This subtle erosion and shift in control can cause deep resentment—regardless of the needs that bring children in to help. It's also natural for children to resent parents who ask and then put up barriers, hurl insults, or treat them like hated interlopers.

We often hear that the most common problem for children who are the only siblings is living close by their parents. They bear the brunt of the care-giving and responsibility—often at considerable interruption in their own lives—while often being reminded what saints and heroes the kids are who live a thousand miles away. This is further compounded when out-of-town brothers and sisters literally "dust off" the complaints a sibling shares related to Mom and/or Dad. It's easy and convenient to ignore what really *is* involved when you don't deal with it on a day-to-day basis.

Many children honestly and devotedly care for parents and share their lives. They often spend a lot of time and money doing it in spite of being unappreciated or having to deal with unreasonable demands and anger.

One of the complaints associated with caring for parents comes when in-laws are involved—and it's a legitimate complaint. Many Senior American women are crystal clear in their descriptions of resentment toward husbands who didn't carry their fair share as *they* cared for parents and in-laws. This resentment continues in today's middle-aged children bearing the same burden. What they describe is having been caregivers all their lives—first for their own kids and families, now for parents and in-laws. One woman described a treadmill of work and more work performed while listening to continual criticism. To make it even worse, her husband often supports his parents' criticisms even though he does little, if anything, to help. One feisty woman said, "What does it mean to be a woman, Art? Does it mean any job that doesn't absolutely require a man automatically becomes *my* responsibility?"

Unfortunately, some children do want to control a parent or parents to get their hands on an inheritance or available dollars while parents are still living. Fortunately, they don't represent a majority. The good news is that younger generations haven't "gone to the dogs" in spite of the incredible changes experienced in their lifetimes. And they aren't as negative toward Senior Americans as they're often portrayed. In fact, most of them have the same stereotypical images of parents and grandparents held by generations who preceded them.

There are no easy answers where "parenting" parents is concerned—except this one: Children *shouldn't* parent parents. There's a considerable difference between helping, caring and doing something for a parent and "parenting."

2
The Right to Live Independently

Senior Americans have the right to independence, privacy, and choice of persons with whom they live and associate; they also have the right not to fear abridgement of those rights because of advancing age.

"Senior Americans who prefer their pets and friends to the company of relatives are no different than younger Americans who do the same."
—Art Linkletter

Individual habits and preferences are the by-products of good and bad experiences, families and friends, jobs, interests, and our mental and physical health. In fact, one of the things that make life interesting is the differences among people. Nevertheless, while most people would agree that we are a nation of individuals, the temptation is always present to conclude that someone who marches to a different drummer has a problem—particularly if that person happens to be a Senior American.

It makes no difference how well-intentioned we may be, becoming involved in another's life is unfair when involvement isn't wanted by the other party. Senior Americans resent invasions of privacy and meddling in their affairs as much as any younger person would.

However, ignoring a problem under the pretense of "being respectful" of someone's privacy isn't right either. There are circumstances where someone is needed to make a judgment call, step in, and help. There's a powerful difference between being thoughtfully concerned and intruding on another's privacy.

Many Senior Americans have a preference for friends over family members and, in some cases, the friends are pets. Does preferring pets to people constitute strange enough behavior to allow someone to let himself in with a key to "check up," if that's the only reason for concern?

Consider this example. Should a license be provided to enter a Senior American's house because he feeds four dogs from one dish that he puts on the coffee table in the living room? As much as I love my dog, Max, I can't envision myself feeding him on the living room coffee table or Lois permitting it more than once. But when I met a man I'll call Elmer, I didn't think it was so strange. His arthritis makes it tough to bend and it's easier to put the dish on the coffee table than on the floor. Besides, he can watch to see that each dog gets a fair share. A different approach maybe, but a workable solution to a problem. His son doesn't agree with that any more than he does with the fact that his dad and his buddies play cards, drink beer, and tell war stories into the small hours of the night. They fight constantly and Elmer has asked his son to stay out of his house and mind his own business. He's had the house rekeyed a number of times but his son always manages to get a duplicate. Elmer said, "He comes and goes at will checking up, threatening, and making a fool out of me." Elmer's opinion of his son's meddling is unprintable.

A woman I'll call Emily has only one child, a daughter whose husband is trying to get a failing business off the ground. The couple has four children ages ten and younger. When Emily's husband died, her daughter and son-in-law urged her to sell her small home and turn the profits over to them. They promised to combine monies and build one large house with a mother-in-law apartment exactly as Emily specified. She'd be near her only child, her grandchildren—everything would be splendid. In the midst of her grief, she was all too anxious to have someone else step in and help.

Emily's house sold quickly and she moved into her daughter's small house while the new one was being completed. It took longer than they thought because her son-in-law insisted they build in the country, where land was less expensive and there'd be room enough to add the machine shop he needed for his business. By the time the merged family moved into the new house, everyone's nerves were jangled to the point of no return.

For a while things were almost tolerable in the new, big house. Then the grandchildren began to come and go as they pleased, using their grandmother's things, and interrupting her when she was on the phone. Instead of having access to the city bus system, Emily had to take cabs if she went anywhere. She didn't feel she could impose on a daughter who chauffeured kids all day.

Emily had always been a movie buff. She enjoyed going to an afternoon double feature and then to a restaurant for dinner by herself or with a friend. The first time she called a cab and went to a movie without telling her daughter, the evening ended as she was picked up by the police—who'd been called by her daughter—in a department store restaurant. From then on, she promised she wouldn't go anywhere without letting someone know. Unfortunately, her daughter usually didn't agree with her plans and more often than not, she ended up staying home. She did a lot of babysitting.

There were other problems. Emily loved cats but two of her grandchildren were allergic to them. As sad as it was, her son-in-law informed her that her cat had to stay outside or be put to sleep. Even though she'd raised him from a kitten, fed him, and kept his box in her room, she decided to put him to sleep rather than force him to try to survive outside. Her daughter promised they'd consider a dog instead, but that never worked out—her husband didn't like dogs any better than cats.

A friend of Emily's urged her to accept an invitation to move in. It seemed like the perfect answer—they'd been lifelong friends and got along well. And her friend welcomed the idea of sharing

expenses and lifting the burden of her own loneliness. When Emily's family found out, they
wouldn't hear of it. Rather than hurt anyone's feelings, she decided she'd better stay put. She's still
alive but her health has rapidly gone downhill and
she doesn't have a lot of energy anymore. Her son-
in-law manages all the money now, including hers,
but he always reminds her that if she wants anything, all she has to do is ask.

What about Senior Americans who, through no
fault of their own, end up in nursing homes? When
people cannot help themselves is it okay to put
them on display, diapered, wearing bibs, and tied
in wheelchairs in the hallways? Does helplessness
provide sufficient reason to leave people unclothed
or partially clothed in rooms with doors open, even
when bedpans are being used? When Senior
Americans can no longer care for themselves, aren't
they still entitled to personal privacy?

I often wonder why more younger Americans
don't watch how Senior Americans treat friends
their own age—they could learn a lot. When Senior Americans are physically encumbered or handicapped, their friends will provide the needed
assistance cheerfully. Every consideration is extended to protect a friend's dignity. When friends
are visited in hospitals or nursing homes, Senior
Americans work at keeping their visits centered
on what's going on in the community and other
things that have always been of interest. Their visits relate to life.

The bottom line? If a dog, cat, canary, or talking parrot makes someone happy, why not? If people like sitting in the park with friends talking about the good old days, what's wrong with that? If a man thinks the widow up the street is a pretty cute package, does he need his kids' approval before he can ask her out for pizza? If someone wants to drop in to make certain a person is okay, is it too much to expect that he or she knocks first?

Thomas Jefferson considered it a human right for Americans to be free to direct their own lives when he drafted our Declaration of Independence in 1776. The Continental Congress agreed when its representatives put their signatures to the document that contained these words: "We hold these Truths to be self-evident, that all Men are created equal, that they are endowed by their Creator with certain unalienable Rights, that among these are Life, Liberty, and the Pursuit of Happiness." Unless I'm mistaken, no changes have ever been made that terminate these rights at a certain age.

"My Home Is My Castle"

"My home is my castle" is a cliché, but it is indicative of where the right to privacy begins and ends. It serves notice that no matter what we may have to put up with on the outside, our homes are our own turf. While some people enjoy unan-

nounced visitors who "drop in" at any hour of the
day or night, others prefer to extend an invitation
or be telephoned before someone visits. Regardless, I can't think of anyone who would argue against
each person's right to set the rules in his or her
own home. Our sense of a private space is further
defined by the personal possessions that make every
house, apartment or single room feel like "home."
They remind us of people we love, significant events,
and other things that are important to us. No matter where we move or how different our new housing may be from what we've been used to, we feel
like we're "home" when our possessions have been
unpacked.

Lois and I live very differently than we did when
our kids were growing up in Holmby Hills, California. We're surrounded by reminders of a lifetime and everything we enjoy—not the least of
which is her cat, Mai Tai, and my dog, Max. I'd
like to have you believe this big German shepherd
is a fierce, macho prototype of the breed. But that's
hard to sell when you see him with an orange ball
he'd gladly let me throw all day for him to chase
or when he lies next to the patio door with his
paws in the air and one ear cocked looking like an
overgrown stuffed toy. Mai Tai? What can you say
about a cat that fetches and looks at your wife as
though she were the only person in the world who
ever *could* matter to a cat with his superior intelligence? The only reason he bothers to saunter past
me at all is because it fulfills his need to ignore
me.

We have seven grandchildren and two great-grandchildren and I'm here to tell you that Lois hasn't taken the birth of our second great-grandchild any less seriously than she took the birth of *our* first child. Our lives are full, active, and involved, and the house we live in is a home.

Everywhere I look I see the evidence of fifty-one years of marriage in what we keep prominently displayed: our son Jack's magnificent sculpture on a pedestal near a doorway; Lois's beautiful needlepoint rugs that, to this day, I've never set foot on except accidentally; pictures everywhere of our children, grandchildren, and great-grandchildren; a collection of individual pieces of crystal given as gifts to commemorate special occasions; an African violet on the table where we eat breakfast each morning that has bloomed without stopping for more years than I can remember; a comfortable easy chair and ottoman that has my outline worn into its fabric; a grand piano that provides me with enjoyment (and a ready reminder that I probably won't get a call in the near future to appear with the New York Philharmonic); paintings and other artifacts we've collected from the Orient; and all those other touches Lois has added, offering proof throughout that this home is filled with love.

Our panoramic view spans everything from Dodger Stadium to Los Angeles International Airport. In daylight it's remarkable. Outlined with a million lights at night, it's breathtaking and we never tire of it. Like dogs in many other houses in California, Max uses the pool as his favorite water dish, standing knee deep to take a drink and cool off at the same time. I just use it for swimming.

We don't have full-time help because we no longer need it. And we prefer our privacy. No matter how much we've liked people who've lived in and worked for us, we never enjoyed the sense of complete privacy that we do now. We aren't involved in the hectic Hollywood mainstream and, measured by visible standards, maintain an unpretentious and unassuming lifestyle. Lois and I enjoy each other's company and that of our family and friends.

Our home is a place where I can be stretched out on the bed watching a football game while my grandson tells me about his latest business venture, at the same time Lois is in the kitchen talking to his mother. It's a home where holidays are celebrated and happiness or sadness is shared by everyone. It's a home that smells good and is surrounded by flowers and Lois's rose garden. It's a home that provides a base for her charity and volunteer work and the place I'm anxious to return to whenever I travel. And it's a home that had to have a pair of Arnold Palmer's golf shoes removed from where they'd been welded to hide a floor safe after he'd sold it to us seventeen years ago.

Lois and I are comfortable where we are, the surroundings are warm and familiar, our roots in the community are deep, our circle of friends is well-established, we're familiar with a pharmacy, our doctors, a hospital, veterinarian, bank, and people we need to repair things. It suits our style of living. We like it and intend to remain where we are. Best of all, we're among the many fortunate Senior Americans who can afford the privilege of this decision.

House, mobile home, condominium, apartment, retirement community, life care center . . . a mother/father-in-law apartment with the kids? Live in your hometown, in Florida, in California, on the East Coast, in the Midwest or Pacific Northwest? Start over again making new friends, go for the climate, go for security, go for the promise of lifetime health care? Stay where you are and let the chips fall where they may? Among the many alternatives, the real question is what makes it home? The answer lies in the intangibles I've described. Size, location, and climate aren't important when the dwelling contains those elements that tell its character, provide its memories, and give it substance enough to make it a home.

According to available statistics, adults between the ages of fifty-five and sixty-five have the highest per-capita income in the country and those between sixty-five and seventy-five score highest in average total assets. Most adults over sixty-five own their homes outright and eight out of ten Senior Americans say their financial health is good.

Although this is good news for the majority of Senior Americans, it in no way diminishes the problems of those who are unable to work, unable to make ends meet, who don't qualify for assistance and spend the last years of their lives uncared for, in fear of tomorrow, unloved and alone. There is no question that this problem is one that won't go away and must be faced head-on in the years ahead.

Not everyone who decides to give up his, her, or their home does so because it's financially necessary. There are other reasons, including climate. Hard winters or excessive heat can be reason enough to relocate after retirement. There may be reasons like having four bedrooms and only needing one, half an acre of grass to cut and snow to shovel, an aging house imminently in need of major repairs, a neighborhood that has become dangerous over the years, the death of a spouse filling a home with sad memories, or children, grandchildren, and friends living in other parts of the country. When any of these are the circumstances, what's wrong with moving?

Then again, if things add up—the mortgage is paid off, or nearly paid off—there's some kind of discount on property taxes because of age—or the neighborhood is familiar and secure—or kids, grandchildren, and friends are nearby—or you're a member of a church or synagogue and have been for many years—or you're a member of clubs and enjoy doing volunteer work—or you like yard work or have found a boy up the block to help out—or monthly expenses are manageable and fit your income—why would you want to move to Sun City when you've never even visited Arizona?

Without a doubt, decisions governing where and how to live are as complicated and emotional as anything Senior Americans face. I illustrate my point with a series of decisions and choices made by two lifelong friends who have been widows for many years. Each of them is financially secure and they're loved and respected by many friends. Their children love them and will do anything to see that their happiness is assured. They often travel together and have, by any standard that can be applied, what appears to be the best of all worlds. Until the day they moved, each of them had a private world in a home she loved and both were actively involved in their community.

In spite of all this, like many other Senior Americans, they have no desire to be a burden if something happens to their health—and they fear someday ending up in a "typical" nursing home stripped of everything that is important to them. With these concerns in mind, they began to search for a life-retirement center.

By no means did they make their decision capriciously. They had traveled to several life-retirement centers in California when they concluded this was the climate they wanted after lifetimes of punishing Midwest winters. They read all the books, did research like candidates for Ph.D.s, and finally found *the place* situated in one of Rand McNally's top-ten climate choices. They even had a financial review of the facility conducted to make certain they weren't buying into something that was likely to go bankrupt in the years ahead.

They paid well in excess of $100,000 each for units that include two bedrooms, two full baths, a gracious living room, lovely entrance, and a small kitchen. The grounds are connected by covered, lighted walkways and the landscaping is no more than a tenth of a degree from perfect. The dining room is centrally located, beautifully appointed, and includes every luxury. Meals are served by waiters and waitresses, and there are no assigned tables or seating. The look is elegant and although no one is required to eat meals in the dining room, they are served three times a day between certain hours. The only effort involved is walking to and from the dining room.

Indeed, there is a nursing home on the premises but, as one of my friends said, "A nursing home is a nursing home is a nursing home regardless of how well it's decorated or where it's located." Acute care—if and when needed—is provided by a local hospital and the doctors available for residents to select from are organized in a PPO. (See p. 250.)

Then the anguish of moving began. One friend sold her home and gave away furniture to children and grandchildren and severed her ties with her hometown and state. The other decided to keep her condominium "just in case." As they sorted and packed they were hit with memory after memory, to say nothing of the daily reminders of how much they would be missed by their friends.

When the moving van had been loaded, my friends boarded a plane certain their decision was well-researched, sound, and would secure them against the worst that could happen.

What's interesting is what took place when they got there. One threw herself into getting along, making friends, and working to convince herself she "absolutely loved" the place. The other was unhappy from day one. She made a genuine effort but not with the zealousness of her friend. The first chink in the armor came when she admitted— out loud—that she found it depressing to be "surrounded by so many handicapped and sick old people." Her description? "Another day of sunshine with nothing to do except watch 300 gray heads bob in unison."

Three months after they moved, they decided to return, believing that full refunds would be forthcoming as the contract promised. That wasn't the case. They'd missed the deadline by a couple of days and would be held to another ninety days paying $1,500 a month maintenance fees unless their units sold before then. Over the Christmas holidays, they were angered by an impassioned plea from the administration asking for a $25 monthly commitment from each resident for "tips" to enhance minimum wages paid dining room staff. Shortly after the holidays, they heard that plans were under way to raise the residents' monthly fees ten percent and that the contract's fine print allowed additional arbitrary raises at any time management decided it was necessary. Compounding everything else was the growing annoyance at having to walk three city blocks to parking spaces that were theirs for life.

The plug that let the water out of the dike was pulled the day the friend who "gave it her all" finally admitted, "I'm so damn sick and tired of walking to the dining room I could scream—it's like eating three meals a day with the same people in the same restaurant." With that admission, they talked it through and decided to chuck it then and there. As much as anything, they missed the sense of privacy they felt they'd lost when they became part of a retirement community. They wanted to go home to punishing winters, kitchens that were big enough to allow them to really cook, friends, familiar surroundings, and a lifestyle they discovered was more important than knowing that if and when nursing home care was needed, it would be provided in a nice climate.

Neither friend is bitter, angry, or regrets having made the move. They realize the decision to move was a good one and so was the decision to return. No doubts remain that—for them—friends, activity, familiarity, and the privacy of their own homes provide the essence of life and put purpose into their days. These friends would be the first to agree that the majority of people who chose the same life-retirement facility are well pleased with their decisions. Many residents candidly acknowledge their pleasure at being relieved from cooking and other daily chores. Others who are alone look forward to companionship available everywhere. For the people who are natives of the community where the facility was built, it's the best of all worlds. The only thing that changed for these residents was a street address—community, friends, and everything "hometown" remained the same.

Most Senior Americans—if surveys and statistics can be believed—will stay right where they are. Most enjoy having friends of many differing ages and a sense of familiarity everywhere. Those who will eventually become residents of retirement communities—which still is a relatively new concept—will think hard before they make the move.

It's safe to say that with the entry of large corporations into the development of life-care and life-retirement communities, the years ahead hold promise of some changes that are bound to meet Senior America's needs even better than ever before. It's exciting.

In my opinion, the choice of permanent housing isn't something that has to be decided by the time a person reaches sixty-five. There are so many things that affect why people live where they do that no one book could address them. I think the most important goal is to end up where the greatest numbers of people and things you best like are located—if that's possible.

Each person, couple, or group of friends has his, her, or their own criteria for making decisions and there are no rights or wrongs. What makes me happy may not make the next ten people I meet happy. Lois and I love California, its weather, our lifestyle, and having family and friends nearby. This is our home. We have other friends who couldn't exist without four distinct seasonal changes and those who would move to the middle of nowhere if that's where their children were located. Lois's mother, Peg, lives in a life-retirement community and enjoys every second of it, including all the activities and the secure surroundings. Whenever she visits, she starts talking about going home three hours after she arrives.

Some people thrive on adventure and change, others don't. Some people love working in a yard no matter how they complain at the end of the day about their backs hurting. For others, the yearly maintenance tasks are familiarities that provide continuing stability. Many Senior Americans would choose a lesser kind of housing rather than be forced to give up their pets. Although I have no desire to live in a remote area, other people consider it an invasion of their privacy to have a neighbor living closer than two miles away. What's home to you, and home to someone else, cannot be defined by anyone. No one should be allowed to "sell" you on an idea that is inherently opposed to the way you've lived all your life.

Consider, for example, the alternative of "living with the kids." It's interesting that greater numbers of children think parents should live with them than vice-versa. What parents are most afraid of is encumbering their own independence and forfeiting their privacy. Living with children can work, but it's difficult—blending families spanning many ages is not easily achieved. Here again, if you agree that old age is not for sissies, with or without a spouse, you'll make a careful assessment of all the implications before you make any changes. *Then, whatever you decide, allow room for having made a mistake that can be undone.*

Old age certainly doesn't mean that even if a move occurs it is the last one allowed to happen. There's nothing wrong with saying, "I made a mistake." Let's face it, even *Senior* Americans aren't perfect.

HOUSING CHOICES

Life-Care Retirement Centers

Life-retirement or life-care communities are for people who want to remain independent as age robs them of the ability to maintain a house. In addition to the unit in which they live, housekeeping, property maintenance, meals, and a lifetime guarantee for whatever nursing care they may need is included in the cost. A large front-end fee is charged, ranging from $50,000 to more than $200,000, in addition to monthly payments. Depending on where they are located, these communities may include golf courses, swimming pools, craft workshops, educational courses, and health fitness centers. Retirement communities usually are made up of people who have compatible tastes and often are sponsored by corporations or religious groups.

The number of life-care retirement communities is growing. There are about 700 retirement communities already providing some form of continuing care for an estimated 200,000 people in the United States. In the next ten years, that number is expected to double.

Not all life-retirement centers or communities are alike. Perhaps the most serious concern of anyone considering a life-care community is its financial soundness. Prospective residents should read the fine print carefully and seek some expert counsel before signing anything. At the present time, only seventeen states license life-care retirement facilities. Even though authorities often require providers to maintain a trust fund to cover longterm expenses, bankruptcy or sale of the business could cause untenable difficulties for residents.

Like any other investment, a life-care retirement facility may or may not pay off. When residents die without receiving a significant amount of nursing care, they don't get full value from their entry fees. Some communities offer partial refunds to families of deceased residents. Other liferetirement centers hold down payments in escrow as a "security deposit" that is fully refunded when a resident moves or is paid heirs after death. Others offer a full refund only when the decision is reversed in the first ninety days and a resident leaves. From then on, the investment depreciates at a rate of $1\frac{2}{3}$ percent each succeeding month. Regardless of when death intervenes, the deceased's heirs get nothing. Then there are facilities that refund ninety percent of the entry fee and no longer charge residents monthly payments if they are permanently transferred to the nursing home.

However, residents then are charged $65 a day for nursing care, which exceeds the average $1,800 traditional monthly nursing home fee.

Condominiums

In 1960 the word "condominium" was just beginning to be heard in the United States. Since then more than two and a half million units have been built and more are being constructed every day. The two biggest purchasers are young couples buying their first homes and Senior Americans wanting more easily maintained homes, security, and neighbors their own age.

By definition, condominiums are apartments or townhouses owned by residents who share ownership of common areas like hallways, elevators, parking lots, land, and recreation facilities. Owners—or residents—become members of an association that oversees the property and makes joint decisions, as well as sharing costs of maintenance, insurance, and taxes on jointly owned property.

Regardless of how affordable they're advertised to be, the average condominium costs in the neighborhood of $90,000. According to *Rand McNally's Places Rated Retirement Guide,* the greatest numbers of them are found in Hawaii, Florida, Maryland, South Carolina, Nevada, and California. In fact, in Maui, Hawaii, condominiums represent thirty-two percent of the total available housing.

"Condos" have advantages and disadvantages. The advantages are obvious: no worries about outside painting, lawn mowing, gardening, landscaping, external plumbing, electrical items, or just about anything that is common to the entire building. The lifestyle is virtually maintenance-free. Many units also include recreational facilities and common rooms that can be used for larger scale entertaining. Since condominiums are purchased, you own your own home and realize whatever it gains in property value.

Condominiums have become very attractive to the many Senior Americans who travel frequently or for extended periods of time. Residents can pack and leave at the drop of a hat with the peace of mind that results from having good overall security which generally is part of a condominium project.

On the other hand, "condos" can be noisy if they are poorly constructed or built too close together. And some residents resent the lack of personal control in the sense that outside painting, landscaping, and other common improvements and costs are decided by an association. Only the inside of your home is your castle. The outside belongs to everyone and, where decisions are concerned, the majority rules.

Although townhouses often are referred to as condominiums, there are differences. Townhouse complexes sometimes are called planned unit developments (PUDs). Generally, there is less density in numbers of units and, although the buildings are close together and side by side, they usually are built singularly—not one on top of the other. Townhouse owners also have title to the land their units occupy and control the air space above.

Regardless of the development, however, you'd be well advised to have an attorney or an accountant review the books of the corporation or the association, which often is called a homeowners' association (HOA), to see that adequate reserves have been set aside for emergencies and repairs. The review should also include a close scrutiny of monthly association fees. Homeowner association fees can change if something of major consequence occurs. And in new developments, monthly fees often are advertised at a low price to attract buyers; then, when the complex is fully occupied, owners discover that the actual fees are far too low to cover maintenance, utilities, and other costs. Although some states have passed laws requiring realistic estimates of HOA dues, this remains an area of concern requiring close review.

Mobile Homes or Manufactured Homes

When you consider that many mobile homes are fourteen feet wide and seventy feet long, the word "mobile" hardly seems appropriate. They are manufactured homes that are transported from the factory to an intended site and, once in place, only two percent are ever moved again. Mobile homes come from the factory in one or more sections to a concrete foundation on the owner's property or to the one of the 24,000 mobile home parks located throughout the United States. The majority of these parks are located in Arizona, California, Texas, Missouri, New Mexico, Delaware, and Oklahoma. One-third of the purchasers of mobile or manufactured homes are older than fifty-five years of age.

Today's manufactured homes may have as many as three bedrooms, two baths, a living room, dining room, and kitchen complete with its own appliances. Everything, including furniture and window coverings, is included, and any number of additional amenities can be added—including sunken bathtubs and fireplaces. It's clear that the image of a shoddy metal "trailer" is no longer accurate.

There are small mobile homes under 400 square feet and others combining more than one unit that are as large—or larger—than 2,000 square feet. Smaller units are called "single wides" and the larger units "double wides," meaning that one or more units are attached. When you consider that a 1,500-square-foot traditional home can cost in the neighborhood of $100,000 and a 1,500-square-foot mobile home $50,000, there is no question as to the economic value. A very nice manufactured home can be obtained for about $30,000.

Finding a location for your mobile home in an area of the country you really want, however, can be difficult. Because of the high cost of residential land in certain areas, mobile home parks and park developments aren't found in Hawaii or Cape Cod and very few are found in Virginia, New Jersey, Colorado, Texas, or in the large metropolitan areas. However, mobile homes have become a major housing choice in the rapidly growing rural retirement areas.

The advantages of a manufactured or mobile home are its lower purchase price, the great variety of interior designs, and good construction. Many Senior Americans also like the social atmosphere of mobile home parks and the recreational facilities that often are included. The newer "trailer parks" are attractively landscaped and many mobile homes include porches, patios, and carports.

A mobile home has several disadvantages, however. It is not as good an investment as a traditional home unless you own the land on which it's located. Another problem can be that the mobile home park owner might levy large rent increases. In some parks tenants have formed organizations or associations to control these increases, as well as to have a say in the overall atmosphere of the park. If a manufactured home is something you are considering, you'd be well advised to find out if these kinds of associations exist in the parks you're considering. And it's important to do a full financial review *before* choosing a park because, for example, the costs of building a permanent foundation of concrete blocks or poured concrete can vary from $2,000 to $5,000. And if you want to add a walkway, garden, carport, or other improvements, your final setup cost could rise to as much as $10,000.

On a national average, prices are lower for mobile or manufactured homes than for single houses, or the even higher-priced condominiums and townhouses.

What About Buying a Smaller House?

If this is what you're considering, be sure you understand that smaller houses are no different than larger houses in the sense that they remain single-family detached homes in neighborhoods selected by owners. They continue to appreciate in the same manner that all residential real estate does. Depending on the home purchased, "smaller" may or may not mean less maintenance. However, obtaining financing for its purchase will be less complicated than for newer types of housing such as condos or life-care communities, because lenders understand traditional home purchases.

Maintenance—regardless of how much or how little—will continue to be your responsibility and so will taxes, and you'll be living in a neighborhood just as you were before, without any expanded opportunities to socialize. And finding the right neighborhood could put you beyond easy access to shopping areas and other necessities.

However, the 57 million single houses in the United States still offer the greatest variety of housing choices simply because there are so many of them for sale.

Retirement Communities

Retirement communities were in existence as long ago as the 1940s. Although nonprofit organizations—including church groups and health agencies—remain in the forefront when it comes to developing retirement communities, there are also other developers on the scene. Real estate professionals have discovered that a profit-oriented market exists because of the growth in the Senior American population. Consequently, the retirement community industry has grown dramatically in the last few years, and increasing rates of growth continue to be projected as large corporations enter the market.

What defines a retirement community today is no longer a simple answer. There are many differing configurations—including a "clustered" community with attached homes, single-family homes, condominiums, and mid- or high-rise apartments. Some developments have been converted from hotels and old nursing homes.

Sun City, Arizona, with its population of 40,000, is large enough to have its own shopping centers, medical centers, and golf courses. It's a planned retirement community tailored for the needs of Senior Americans.

Sun City inspired other planned retirement communities throughout the country that offer recreational facilities and self-containment in the sense that residents never have to go very far to find anything. However, ninety percent of them have less than 500 residents.

Many Senior Americans enjoy the wide variety of social activities that are continually taking place in retirement communities, as well as the fact that the smaller houses have been designed to require minimal inside maintenance. For the most part, security is part of the community service and medical attention is readily available. In most cases, once the initial large purchase is over, monthly payments are not likely to escalate.

The negative aspects of this lifestyle relate to the almost mandatory high level of personal activity required to fit into the accompanying lifestyle. Some people resent the "clubby" atmosphere and constant socialization. Others miss the traditional mix of families and ages found in neighborhoods. Regardless, retirement communities have been highly successful, and although they aren't for everyone, they seem to satisfy a larger number of people every year.

If You Plan to Move . . .

According to the moving consultant who advised me, the greatest problem for Senior Americans who decide to move is the expense itself. As he said, "There's no getting around it, Art, moving is expensive. Just the packing of an average household can cost $500." He went on to explain that large national moving companies make their money from corporate contracts, not individual residential contracts. Therefore, they're usually unwilling to offer special discounts to individuals. He said that there really are only two ways Senior Americans can contain costs during a move: (1) Get help from family and friends with packing and the disconnecting and reconnecting of appliances. (2) Obtain competitive bids—*not estimates*—from several moving companies.

It's important to understand the difference between an estimate and a competitive bid. An estimate is just what it says—an *approximation* of the total expense. It doesn't guarantee a certain price. Reliable moving companies not only can—but should—be willing to submit bids that aren't subject to change (a guaranteed price) and which outline in detail all services that are to be provided.

My consultant feels it's a good idea to get two or three bids—"to shop around." And be sure to read the fine print carefully so that the complete bid is fully understood.

Most moving companies offer a number of services, including:

Insurance—Although most moving companies offer some insurance with every move, it is likely to be minimal coverage, usually in the neighborhood of sixty cents a pound for each individual article. What that means is that a damaged or lost twenty-pound chair would result in insurance coverage of $12. The best buy for your money is what's called depreciated value coverage and costs about $5 for each 1,000 pounds of household contents. The average move would cost about $50 to insure at this level, compared to $200 for the "Cadillac" insurance policy offering full-replacement coverage. It is extremely rare that an entire load of household contents is lost or destroyed, so unless you have extremely valuable possessions, there is no real reason to purchase full-replacement insurance.

Guaranteed Pickup and Delivery—This usually is an automatic feature if the weight of your move meets the company's minimum requirements (usually 8,000–12,000 pounds, depending on the time of year). A guarantee means that you and your mover will agree on the date that you'd like to have your contents picked up and you'll also agree on one or two days that are acceptable delivery dates. Then, if for some reason your shipment is delayed, the moving company will pay you a fixed rate plus hotel and meal charges for each day you are inconvenienced.

Retired Employee Benefit Clause—When a corporation signs a contract with a moving company (usually on a one-year basis), a feature that sometimes is included that may not be widely known to employees is the retired employee benefit clause. This means that if you happen to retire and then move during the time your company's contract is valid, you may be entitled to extra moving benefits under the corporate contract. You will still have to pay for the move, but your cost may be reduced and you may be entitled to insurance, guaranteed pickup and delivery, and other "extras." Make certain you check your company's policy when you retire.

If you do move and intend to do your own packing, here are some tips my moving consultant suggested I pass along:

- Limit the weight of each container to about fifty pounds.
- Use small cartons for heavy items like books, tools, and canned goods.
- Use large cartons for light, bulky items like blankets and pots and pans.
- Pack flat, fragile items like mirrors, marble, and plates on edge, not flat.
- Seal and label each carton, describing contents and the room where it belongs.
- Don't ever pack cartons beyond the top edge.

- Don't pack flammable or explosive items. The Department of Transportation forbids transporting these items in a moving van.
- Appliances: Disconnecting appliances is important and can pose a hazard if it isn't done correctly. Most moving companies will do this for you for a small charge.
- Lampshades should be packed individually and separate from their bases.

Do You Need a Licensed Real Estate Agent?

Yes, in my opinion you do, unless you are willing to take the time to put some real effort into learning enough to handle the job yourself. The reason people want to sell their own homes is to save the real estate commission. But you should know that the odds on that happening aren't on your side. Most people who do sell their own homes don't realize a higher net profit.

For example: Let's assume you list your house at $100,000 and that a real estate broker's commission would be five percent, or $5,000. First of all, it's impossible for the seller *and* the buyer to save the same commission. Most prospective buyers realize that they, too, have the chance to save the commission when a house is listed by an owner and therefore are likely to reduce any offers by $5,000 (the real estate commission). If you should accept such an offer, you won't have saved the commission, and if you don't accept the offer, you run the risk of losing the sale and indefinitely extending the time before the house sells.

It's possible that you and the prospective buyer can agree to split the difference where the commission is concerned, which would result in your saving $2,500. But before you think this is good news, consider other potential costs, such as advertising. The average length of time your home will be on the market from the time you first decide to sell it to the time you receive an offer to purchase is ninety days. Assuming that you advertise in the weekend editions of one newspaper and one other day during each week, you could easily spend $750 to $1,000, depending on where you live. At this point your "savings" have been reduced to $1,500—assuming the prospective buyer agrees to "split the difference." Then, ask yourself another question. Are you really knowledgeable enough to write and execute a contract that is certain to be valid and legally binding, or is it possible you'll have to spend more money to hire an attorney or other expert to help you? These are only the most obvious problems you might encounter. I'm not suggesting that anyone who decides to sell his or her own home should throw the idea out; I am suggesting that if you do, it should be with sound preparation and your eyes wide open.

Perhaps the best way to make my point is to explain what a realtor does and doesn't do. Then you can compare your own skills with those that a good real estate broker provides for his or her clients.

First of all, licensed real estate agents or brokers are professionals. Their full-time job is selling property and their sales efforts are guaranteed because they work without pay until houses are sold for the prices, terms, and conditions agreed upon. No commission checks are written until the sellers have been paid.

Brokers know what comparable properties are selling for in a given area. They advise clients on ways to enhance the features of their homes to make them more attractive to prospective buyers. Brokers are in continual contact with people looking for homes, and they work to generate additional prospects through advertising and open houses. And through the multiple listing service (MLS), homes are shown by real estate agents throughout the area in which clients live. In addition, many real estate people have contacts with other brokers in different offices, in different cities and states. Real estate agencies often maintain contacts with corporations that move transferred employees into an area, and most agencies have answering services to take calls that might be missed by clients operating on their own.

Many buyers dislike dealing face-to-face with sellers but won't hesitate to have agents make lower offers or enter into other negotiations. Realtors are familiar with all aspects of real estate and have the necessary experience to act as negotiators between buyers and sellers—they're qualified to negotiate contracts through to conclusion. In fact, brokers, more often than not, are the catalysts needed to conclude transactions.

When it comes to financing, most people have no qualms about revealing their financial status to professionals, but resist disclosing personal information to private parties. It's the real estate broker's personal knowledge and experience in real estate financing that can be responsible for significantly speeding up a transaction which could, for example, save a client from making payments on two houses at the same time. An agent also can work with an interested party who is considered a "marginal buyer." There are times when an agent can use his or her financial resources to help such a buyer qualify for a loan. In addition, many agencies have an attorney, an accountant—or both—on retainer to assist if complications arise during a transaction.

Another important consideration during the time a house is being shown to prospective buyers is keeping unwanted people from going through your property. Getting ready to show a house is a lot of work and you don't want unqualified buyers or those who just want to snoop looking through your house. Real estate agents screen the buyers they bring through and are no more interested than you are in wasting time.

Assisted Independence

If we acknowledge that in all of our lives a time may come when doing what once were routine tasks is no longer possible, that we may fear being alone in an emergency because of a health problem, or that we may fear for our lives because the area we live in isn't safe, then we must ask: Will life continue as it has in the past or will it be necessary to forfeit our independence just to survive?

Senior Americans want to remain independent throughout their lives. They don't necessarily want to live with their kids, they resent having decisions imposed upon them, they know what makes them happy and what doesn't—they like to do it their way as much as they ever did.

As one man in his eighties said, "Hell, Art . . . I always was a loner. I'd rather watch a good football game and eat popcorn than spend every Sunday with relatives . . . and if any of 'em would bother to remember, I was just the same at forty. You know something? I'm not slipping . . . I might be the only one with enough sense to recognize that a football game is more fun than they are." I haven't a shred of doubt that if this crusty, independent man ever needs help to make certain he can continue to watch football games in his own living room, he'll ask for it.

Granted, there are people who vehemently deny any need for help and do everything possible to avoid it, as though acknowledging the need is proof of having failed—for them no amount of pleading or rational argument will make any difference. Seizing control and finding available assistance that can assure independence can't be forced on anyone.

The good news is that independence—even in the face of a serious health condition or illness—often *can* be achieved if we remember that old age is not for sissies.

Every Senior American should remember that the most important word in his or her vocabulary may someday be "assistance." It's the word that can mean the difference between living as you *want* to and living as you *have* to just because you don't know what options are available out there. There isn't a book big enough to cover each of the fifty states and every county within a state, so I've chosen one exemplary assistance program located in the Midwest to use as an example. (It's up to you to find out what services are available in *your* county.)

In addition to maintaining twenty separate phone lines that include a Medicare hotline, and separate information lines for Homebound Meals, the Visiting Nurse Association and Volunteer Exchange, this particular county offers the following standing programs:

- **Meals**—A hot, nutritious meal is served at noon in twelve different senior centers for persons who are sixty years of age and older. Meals also can be delivered to a Senior American with the referral of an outreach worker. The program is called Homebound Meals and the food will be prepared to meet certain dietary restrictions. Meals are delivered by volunteers in specially designed containers to keep them hot. The price of a homebound meal is whatever donation (if any is possible) can be afforded—there is no fixed fee. No charge exists for meals served in senior centers either; as with homebound meals, all donations are gratefully received. The obvious question I asked was how long can a person receive this kind of help. The answer was, "As long as necessary." One man in his nineties has been receiving a hot, homebound meal for several years.

- **Information and Referral**—Information is available that directs Senior Americans to where they can get assistance that will be tailored to meet specific needs. When required, referrals are made to appropriate agencies for assistance. This service is available to everyone.

- **Transportation**—Transportation can be provided on a regular basis by bus, through volunteers, or in a van equipped with a wheelchair lift.

- **Telephone Reassurance**—Arrangements can be made for people living alone to be contacted by telephone every day. The person calling will take time to talk about whatever is of interest and make certain the person is all right.

- **Home Help • Household Chores • Personal Care**—

Often, help with personal needs or household chores like cleaning, laundry, changing bed linen, or keeping appointments is all that is needed to keep someone independent. This county provides that assistance to whatever degree it is needed. Any costs for services are based on financial status and need.

- **Legal • Insurance • Banking • Money Management**—If a Senior American needs help in a specific area, a counseling appointment is scheduled with a lawyer or other trained specialist.

- **Elder Abuse**—Senior Americans don't have to tolerate any form of abuse—physical, mental, material, or other. The Commission on Aging handles all reports confidentially and follows up on any complaints that are received, going to court when necessary.

- **Senior Aide Program**—Part-time jobs can be provided for persons fifty-five years and older who meet income eligibility requirements. A typical job involves working twenty hours a week in a government or not-for-profit agency.

- **Senior Job Service Program**—This program is offered to persons who are forty years of age or older. People are placed part-time, full-time, or on a temporary or permanent basis. There are no income requirements and salaries vary according to the jobs.

- **Adult Day Care Center**—This center povides daytime care and supervision for people who cannot participate in regular senior activities but who do not need the intensive care offered in a nursing home. For people caring for elderly friends or relatives, the day care center offers needed respite and can free them to maintain their own employment. In addition, if a ride to and from the center is needed, the Commission sees that it is provided. In fact, one man confined to a wheelchair has been picked up and returned to his daughter's home each working day for three and a half years. His daughter said, "Without the Commission's help, I would have had no choice but to put my dad in a nursing home . . . all I need is someone to help him during the day so I can go to work."

- **Skill Center**—Furniture refinishing and upholstery classes are taught by qualified instructors in a shop fully equipped with modern woodworking machines.
- **Identification Cards**—Cards are issued on request to Senior Americans sixty years of age and older. These cards are used in businesses, restaurants, etc. to obtain senior discounts. The Commission also provides recreational passes and other special opportunity passes for certain events, as well as Golden Passports, which can be used to receive discounts in national parks and camping areas.
- **Meeting Rooms**—Rooms and facilities are available for Senior Americans for organized activities and other meetings.
- **Craft Classes and Consumer Awareness Programs**—These special programs are conducted periodically and are announced in a bulletin that

is printed and mailed out monthly. An extensive variety of classes and programs covering literally everything that could be of interest is offered.

• **Talent Shop**—Senior Americans can sell crafts and homemade articles to the public in a location that's really a store. And what's for sale has to be seen to be believed—everything from the amateur variety of products made with loving hands at home to the most intricate needlework and beautifully crafted, stained, and polished cabinets.

Bear in mind, this is only a summary listing and doesn't include the many classes on nutrition, basic microwave cooking, and health and fitness programs. It doesn't include the used clothing program that provides clothes free of charge for seniors who need them, or the special counseling program on how to spot a con artist. Senior Americans using Commission programs get a booklet every month that outlines what's ahead, what's new, expanded information and referral services, the schedule for the bus that takes people grocery shopping, and articles of interest on subjects that particularly relate to Senior Americans.

The Commission on Aging emphasizes that as a nation we're on our way to the realization that it is far less costly to *assist* independence than to place people in institutions or make them otherwise dependent. Even more important, it seems we're catching on to the fact that because people are no longer able to leap tall buildings in a single bound doesn't mean they should be written off as people who no longer count.

Commissions on Aging

Although Congress passed the Older Americans Act in 1965, which provides monies for Senior American programs, many people resist seeking assistance because of long-held beliefs that asking for help will cause them to give up property, savings accounts, and other monies—to say nothing of dignity. Even though that's no longer true, a pseudo sense of pride remains that causes people to be hesitant about approaching the Commission on Aging because of an assumed welfare stigma. Dignity doesn't have to be affected if we take the time to remember that it is some of *our* tax money that pays the bill.

Experts told me that learning what is or isn't available for each Senior American should begin with a phone call to the local Commission on Aging. If no separate listing appears for the Commission, telephone the Department of Social Services and ask for the number. It's this department that can put you in touch with programs that assist Senior Americans.

For the record, I didn't just sit down and write this chapter. I did exactly as I recommend and called several county Commissions on Aging in different areas of the country. The only word that comes close to expressing how I feel about what I've learned is "amazement." I'll confess to having had no idea what is available for the asking.

Unfortunately, I'm not the only Senior American who didn't know. I'm told it's a conservative estimate when I report that no more than fifty percent of the country's Senior Americans have any idea of what is available, even though monthly booklets and other print materials are widely distributed.

The programs I discovered include the services of people who will help with grocery shopping, cleaning, paying bills, money management, and transportation to and from medical appointments. Depending on a Commission on Aging's location and the number of people being served, the list of available services can run to several pages.

Community Option Program

For the majority of our national population a Community Option Program (COP) remains a distant hope. But, for the lucky people in Wisconsin, it's already an existing choice. I feel strongly about COP, and I hope a program like it will be demanded by an outpouring of mail and phone calls to legislators in every state.

In 1982, a number of people in various agencies

that work with the elderly, handicapped, mentally ill, and developmentally disabled got together and concluded that they'd seen enough. Each of them was working within a system that, with its abuses and complex problems, would take three lifetimes to correct. Since that wasn't a choice, they decided that creating a new system was a better way to go. What finally emerged began as an experiment in eight of Wisconsin's seventy-two counties. As a direct and provable result of what was achieved, the Community Option Program became law in the entire state in 1985.

In a nutshell, the COP program provides a network of support that offers options and programs that often can replace nursing home care. Judith Zitske was one of the people instrumental in the development of Wisconsin's Community Options Program. She now serves as a program specialist with the Bureau of Long-Term Support. She told me, "For every person currently in a nursing home, I can show you his or her counterpart living at home because of COP. The program has provided the first real option in thirty years that allows people to choose what *they* want—their own homes complete with all the familiar sounds and smells. When people decide they want to remain at home or leave a nursing home, we build a plan determined by the kind of help and people needed to make it work. Costs are based upon needs and an ability to pay."

Two things aided the program's emergence. One was the furor that began in the 1970s regarding nursing home abuse reported with shocking detail. This helped to create a climate that fueled legislators with enough ammunition to come down hard on defenders of the status quo. The second factor was that, on a comparative basis, Wisconsin had more available nursing home beds than any other state in the country.

It's interesting that the initial objective of the Community Option Program wasn't to save money. The objective was to develop a program that would allow Senior Americans to choose between a nursing home and assisted independence in their own homes. It not only accomplished that; it also resulted in a savings of public monies that amount to about $300 per month for each person utilizing what's offered. As one man said, "It's Wisconsin's answer to cost containment."

Although the program is open to anyone in need, irrespective of age or ability to pay, sixty-five percent of the participants are Senior Americans. The program allows people who are ill or disabled the chance to decide for themselves whether they wish to stay at home or go to a nursing home. This is accomplished by an assessment of each person's needs and capabilities, which are compared or matched with available county services. The individual then has the choice of remaining in the community or going to a long-term-care facility. No one is prohibited from nursing-home care, should that be his or her choice.

The program isn't just for the indigent and it doesn't require that only trained, licensed medical personnel provide the care that's needed. When appropriate, COP will pay a spouse, family member, or friend to do the things that can keep someone independent. Most important, the person needing help doesn't have to manage the services or people being provided. The program screens, hires, and oversees people, scheduling, payments—everything. The kind of help needed to remain independent can range from simple household chores to help with personal tasks like bathing and dressing. Some people may only need modifications made within their homes to permit a wheelchair to be used. The program will buy what's needed, pay family members to provide services, modify a household, and utilize a lot of creative energy to produce a solution. Senior Americans I've talked to who have utilized COP strongly praise what they believe has been achieved.

"Even in the very best nursing homes," Judy Zitske said, "people lose rights that can make the difference in whether or not they want to live. When we're young, we don't give a second thought to when is the right time for meals, or whether or not Rice Krispies tastes good for dinner, when to get up, when to go to bed, how loudly to play a TV or radio, where plants will be placed, or on what walls pictures will hang. These are simple decisions we make all our lives without thinking twice. Consequently, when these decisions are made by the administration and staff, the last vestiges of human dignity disappear. Try to imagine needing someone's permission to decide where a plant should be placed or whether or not someone will grant approval so you can watch a late movie on TV because you have trouble sleeping. The result is so dehumanizing, it strips people of the will to live.

"Nursing homes aren't the only solution just because someone is old, ill, handicapped, disabled, or frail." And with justifiable pride, Judy concluded, "We've proven that there *are* other options—have we *ever!*"

LIFELINE®

Assisted independence is available in another exciting program that's offered—and growing— through a third of our nation's hospitals.

It's being used by more than 100,000 people in all fifty of the United States and in Canada. That number is growing by 30,000 new subscribers each year. The patented system is called LIFELINE®, and it offers security and help at the touch of a waterproof button that can be worn even in the shower. It's the kind of assistance that can mean the difference between dependence and independence.

Dr. Andrew Dibner, a psychologist, and his wife, Dr. Susan Dibner, a sociologist, developed the device in 1972 while they were research fellows at the Duke University Center for the Study of Aging and Human Development. They began with the hope they could help postpone nursing home entry, shorten acute hospital stays, lessen fear, and instill a sense of security in the lives of Senior Americans. How well they succeeded. The result of their effort produced what's now known as LIFELINE®.

Senior Americans who are alone, disabled, frail, or recovering from surgery or illness can subscribe to the LIFELINE® program and maintain their independence and security at home, backed up by twenty-four-hour-a-day emergency help. The program links people (subscribers) to a hospital's emergency room or directly to LIFELINE® CENTRAL in Massachusetts.

The program uses a communicator that's attached to a subscriber's home telephone. A small wireless button is worn on a slender chain around the neck. When the button is pushed, a radio signal is sent which automatically dials an emergency response center at a hospital. The system works even if a telephone is off the hook—or if there's a power failure. If a subscriber loses consciousness during a medical emergency, a timer automatically continues to signal for help.

When a signal for help is received, an emergency coordinator returns the call at once. If a subscriber is in distress or fails to respond, help is dispatched immediately. This help can come from neighbors, relatives, police and fire departments, or medical rescue units. All LIFELINE® programs include file card systems that list brief medical histories for each subscriber. With this information, the hospital can respond quickly and accurately when medical help is needed.

Every subscriber's file includes names and phone numbers of people willing to respond and they have keys to the subscriber's home. LIFELINE®'s creators say half the signals for help that come in aren't serious and involve a minor fall or accident that can be managed by the person sent to respond. The emergency coordinator knows help has arrived because a signal is received when the person responding pushes a flashing yellow button near the phone.

Nationally, the average cost to subscribe is $18 a month. And in many communities money is available to help defray the cost for those who need it. If you need information abou LIFELINE®, telephone the nearest hospital or call LIFELINE® CENTRAL toll-free at 1-800-451-0525. In Massachusetts the toll-free number is 1-800-441-4014. You can write to LIFELINE® CENTRAL at 1 Arsenal Marketplace, Watertown, Massachusetts 02172.

Shared Housing

Another form of assisted independence that's already been chosen by 700,000 people sixty-five years of age or older in the United States is shared housing. Some people find their own "housemates," while others use the 400 or so house-sharing organizations throughout the country that help locate and screen people for compatibility.

An indication of the success that can be achieved was reported in a recent article written by Bill Richards in the *Wall Street Journal*. Three women who described themselves as "two widows and an old maid" share a one-bedroom house with two dogs and a pale blue parakeet named Pretty Boy. All three women are in their seventies and say that they chose to share one house because "Living alone is spooky. You eat alone and there's just you all day. We're never lonesome now."

Two of the three women found each other through Project Match in San Jose, California. Previously, they were both living alone, surviving on Social Security checks, and didn't know each other. They combined resources and later invited a third woman to live with them when they learned she'd been hurt in a fall and had lost her job. According to the article, they get along fine, comfortably trading verbal jousts like teenagers on a street corner. They shop together, use the same doctor, and have a joint predilection for soap operas. All three women emphatically agree on one thing: However cramped their cottage, they prefer it to a nursing home. "We're our own boss here . . . we do as we please."

Housemates aren't always the same age or sex. Richards describes a seventy-five-year-old widow who eventually found her match—a young automobile salesman who pays $175 a month to share her six-room apartment. For that he gets his room straightened and occasional mothering. "When will he get married?" Mrs. Nievod says over tea. "He's not telling me; I'm not asking."

Several states are giving financial help to developers willing to build or renovate housing that can be shared by elderly occupants. The intent is to keep Senior Americans not in need of specialized health care independent—as long as possible—in a family environment.

If shared or group housing is an alternative you want to look into, call the Commission on Aging. They'll point you in the right direction.

Other resources in the community to explore include churches. Many maintain and offer extensive assistance for members. The United Way provides Meals on Wheels or Mobile Meals, among many other programs, and helps to fund the Salvation Army.

Hospice

"The way people care for the dying, honor the dead and bear one another's grief reflects the value any society places on human life."
"Living with Dying," *Newsweek*, May 1978.

Most of us never think of a hospice as a form of assisted independence, but it is.

The first hospice program in the United States

started in 1971 in New Haven, Connecticut, and was the spark that touched off a national movement. The movement has grown into 1,400 hospice programs located throughout the country. Hospice is more than a program. When someone chooses a hospice he or she accepts its philosophy, which views death as part of life.

By sheer circumstance, I was serving as a member of a foundation board at a hospital that was among the first to introduce a hospice unit. I well recall the controversy surrounding the 1977 decision to appoint a committee to study the hospice issue. There was no overwhelming support at that time. The hospital had no particular commitment to leadership in a movement few people understood. It simply was responding to something everyone was talking about and wanted to be ready—just in case.

What became a catalyst turned out to be WGBH's remarkable ninety-minute film entitled *Dying*. The well-known Boston PBS broadcast station had filmed real people and their families dealing with terminal illnesses and deaths of one of their members. It wasn't scripted, it simply portrayed the actual illnesses and deaths of different people with gentle humor, touching levels of sadness, remarkable courage, grief, and—most of all—reality. Although a committee of fifty had gathered to watch the film, when the lights came on, less than twenty remained. Those who did spent the next two years developing a program the hospital adopted and opened in 1979.

The people who chose not to remain actively involved were as remarkable as those who slugged it through to the end. They were honest and open in flatly stating they would do supportive things like raise money or write letters. However, they wanted no face-to-face confrontation with the details and emotion that would be involved in getting there. They acknowledged out loud that dying was not a subject they could handle.

The hospice program that eventually was adopted didn't threaten those in the medical community doing the skilled jobs that include investigation, diagnosis, cure of illness, and prolongation of life. It recognized and reinforced the fact that they must continue to concentrate their efforts there. What it offered was another dimension of care.

Carole Bibeau, who directs a hospice program in Concord, California, says: "Hospice is not about hurrying death through mercy killing or postponing it with artificial support systems. And I chose the words 'mercy killing' instead of 'euthanasia' deliberately. Euthanasia actually means painless, happy death which, in fact, is the objective of hospice care. Terminally ill people who choose a hospice program consciously decide they want to be at home as much as possible. Obviously this means they have a family who will support that choice. It means they want to make decisions regarding their remaining lives and their deaths. It also means they are opting to prepare for eventual death in practical ways that may involve their wills, decisions regarding organ donations, and burial. They are choosing to be pain-free to whatever degree that is possible and want help from medical people and others trained in the management of their symptoms rather than in the treatment of their disease. They believe it is important to prolong living, not dying—at the same time they openly acknowledge the need for help in getting there. They are choosing to maintain as much quality in their remaining lives as they can."

Interestingly, hospice actually is based on the right to refuse treatment, as well as on the constitutional right to privacy that includes determining what happens to our bodies. More and more people are choosing to die without heroics or artificial treatment. Death—more often than not—is becoming a deliberate choice. As we continue to see technological changes that give health-care providers the capacity to extend almost any life-threatening situation, people are exercising that choice more often. Hospital chaplain Philip Williams expressed it well when he said, "Machines and things are here to serve us, not for us to serve them. We can take control if we want to."

Senior Americans fear terminal illness more than their younger friends simply because of their advancing age. Let's face it. Where in the country can anyone pick up a newspaper or turn on a TV program without being reminded of the real concerns: Where will the money come from? What will Medicare pay? Will I be alone? Would I be able to bear the pain? What about my family?

There's good news and bad. The bad first. Not

all families *can* handle terminal illness any better than some of the original committee members I described. And they shouldn't be faulted for any inability to cope as they watch someone they love in the process of dying. Hospice can help ease that pain and provide strong support; it cannot take it away.

The good news is that Medicare now supports hospice as a choice with a hospice Medicare benefit that covers home care, routine home care, and continuous home-care coverage on a short-term basis. If terminally ill Senior Americans choose hospice, they are choosing the care hospice offers and which Medicare reimburses: home care, palliative care (management of symptoms, pain control), and supportive care. There's only one problem. The hospice program chosen must be Medicare-certified. At the present time only about a third of the nation's programs have that certification. What this certification requirement has forced is a major reorganization of existing programs, and many are diligently working to meet the stringent requirements. Without the Medicare hospice benefit, only standard Medicare benefits apply. Many existing programs have serious concerns about financial risks that might be attached to certification. However, those fears have proven not to be a problem for programs already certified.

When Senior Americans have access to Medicare-certified hospice programs, they're required to waive traditional Medicare benefits and opt for the Medicare hospice benefit. All bills are then submitted directly to hospice and it's the program's responsibility to see that services are provided. The Medicare patient gets only one bill. Services covered include: all medications used at home for control of pain and other symptoms; at-home services; inpatient respite care to provide rest for those giving care at home; continuous care at home during periods of crisis; counseling services at home for patient and family; bereavement counseling; and inpatient specialized hospice care.

Not all hospice programs are based in hospitals. Some are based in home health agencies, some are freestanding, and some are community based. The growing trend—because of Medicare—is toward standardization of all programs because Medicare requires that *all* components reimbursed be included.

The best way to obtain hospice information is to contact a hospital and ask for the Department of Social Services. Even if the hospital doesn't have its own program, information you need will be available.

Nursing Homes

The nursing-home image that I carry in my mind is the one movie director Carl Reiner gave us in the 1970 MGM-United Artists film *Where's Poppa?* I laughed as hard as everyone else when George

Segal arrived at a falling-down, ramshackle nursing home trying to find out if there was an empty bed for his mother, played by Ruth Gordon. The burly manager, wearing a T-shirt with the sleeves rolled up, told him that it depended on whether anyone had died the night before—and he didn't know that answer because it was only noon and he hadn't yet had time to go upstairs and take a head count.

Nursing homes are a subject most of us would prefer not to think about. But in discussions with many Senior Americans, their children, friends, and other relatives, the subject keeps surfacing. I've heard about nursing-home residents being treated to everything from sarcasm to the most severe forms of physical and mental abuse. Hearing these actual experiences made me face the subject head-on. The commonly held derogatory opinions of nursing homes, group homes, and those who care for the elderly are not always figments of overly active imaginations. The worst imagery that we can come up with *does* happen. It makes no difference how low a percentage of people may be affected—whatever the number, it's too high.

Abuse of Senior Americans comes in many forms and occurs in and out of nursing homes. The people who do the abusing are all ages and come in all sizes and shapes, with varied backgrounds. They can be professionals or nonprofessionals. They are sometimes employees in nursing homes or group homes and they can be husbands, wives, sons, daughters, and other relatives.

Consider the following: being called grandma, grandpa, dear, or other patronizing names; continual sarcastic or insulting verbal attacks; being told what a burden you are; someone changing soiled sheets or clothing and then holding the evidence of the act under your nose; having your nose pinched shut to force your mouth open so food can be shoved in; being allowed to lie cold and shivering for hours—or days—in a wet bed unable to help yourself; being blind and having food placed in front of you, just out of reach, then having it removed because "time was up" and the trays are being collected; having someone slap your face because you said something wrong or refused to answer; being held underwater until you stopped struggling against the aide bathing you; being medicated to the point where you can do nothing but sleep or become too groggy to object or resist whatever happens; being roughed up or beaten, deliberately dropped, or raped; having personal possessions stolen; being forced to hand over money. Now picture the victims. They are old, frail, ill, suffering, blind, deaf, or mentally disoriented— people who through no fault of their own need someone else's help.

Shocking?

I hope so.

This chapter isn't going to correct what's wrong. One person and one book can't do that. But one book *can* give Senior Americans and those who love them some real insight into nursing homes that can make a difference.

There *are* good nursing homes, managed and staffed by caring people who are as concerned as everyone should be about preventing abuse and preserving human dignity. And with some hard work and a lot of time these homes can be found. Not only will your work result in locating a good nursing home; it also will set up a circle of protection that is the result of someone caring enough to serve notice that *this* resident will be backed by another's knowledge and strength. It's a difficult and emotional task with complex considerations. However, if the job is done right, the payoff will be good care in a warm and friendly atmosphere for someone you love.

I got a lot of help developing this chapter from nursing home ombudsmen who work in every state in the nation acting as advocates for anyone who needs their help. The word "ombudsman" dates back to the fifteenth century. It's a Scandinavian word that literally means "for the people." As one woman who has been an ombudsman for a number of years said, "We're the people who everyone hiding something hates: The agencies who may not be doing their jobs, the institutions or facilities that have something to hide, and family members abusing someone inside or outside a nursing home." She went on to say that an ombudsman gets treated with a lot of respect when people discover that the law in some states includes the possibility of felony convictions that carry a $10,000 fine and/or a two-year prison term for those convicted of abuse. In one state, the law goes even further. The same fine and/or prison term can also be meted out for someone who observes but doesn't report abuse. And an ombudsman's authority isn't limited to nursing homes. It extends to hospitals, community group homes, home care agencies, families providing care, and state agencies. An ombudsman's intervention can cause a fine of $5,000 a day to be levied for every day a nursing home is out of compliance with state codes and regulations. He or she can cause a facility to be closed down entirely. The courts are used when needed, and literally no stone is left unturned.

There's a lot of misinformation about nursing homes. One of the most commonly held beliefs is that a home with plush accommodations and beautifully landscaped lawns admitting only private-pay patients is a guarantee of excellence. Not true.

Regulations that apply to nursing homes do not differentiate between private pay and payment through Medicare or Medicaid—by law, the care *must* be the same. The only difference is that if residents lose the ability to pay in a nursing home that doesn't receive public monies, they're out on their ear—no money, no bed. However, in a facility that *does* accept public monies, an inability to pay cannot be used to throw someone out or keep someone out.

Many homes have waiting lists and in some cases a charge that can vary between several hundred and several thousand dollars is charged just to get a name placed on it. The logical next question is, "Does this guarantee that when the name comes up the person gets in?" The real answer: "It guarantees nothing." In many states it's now illegal to collect a waiting list charge—but I'm also told that the game goes on under the table more often than not, regardless of the law.

If it appears that nursing-home care may be in the cards for you or someone close to you, investigation and selection should begin before an emergency demands immediate placement. And if it seems advisable to be placed on a waiting list, your name should be added to those nursing-home waiting lists that meet some critically important standards.

This is what initially needs to be done when you conduct an investigation into a nursing home:

- Schedule an appointment to meet with the medical director, administrator, and head nurse. Based on what I've learned, a nursing home will be as good or bad as its top administration. The medical director and head nurse will reflect the attitudes and skills of everyone else employed. Find out if the medical director is on call twenty-four hours a day and will be willing to talk to you if you have questions at a later date.

- Find out who owns the home and whether it's run on a for-profit or not-for-profit basis. Find out how many staff members are employed to care for what number of people. Find out whether or not the home employs a social worker, physical therapist, occupational therapist, or program director.

- Discuss costs. Find out whether or not the rates include supplies, services, and medications. Find out if the home accepts Medicare and/or Medicaid payment.
- Find out how the home manages services that may be needed, like dentistry, podiatry, ophthalmology, and audiology—do they make the arrangements and schedule appointments or is that up to you?
- Telephone your local Department of Health and Social Services and find out if the state has reported any violations at the home. If there have been violations, telephone an ombudsman and discuss what these violations mean and ask if he or she can tell you more about the facility in question.

Then once you've identified some nursing homes that seem right, it's important that you tour the facilities you're considering at several different times of the day. According to my ombudsmen advisers, scheduling appointments with the administration of the nursing homes and making a couple of unannounced visits at differing times during the day are the most effective way to really see for yourself. Above all, trust your instincts and your own judgment. These are the questions to ask and the observations to make during your visits:

- Look at the residents. Are they out of their rooms; are they well-dressed and well-groomed?

- Will a meeting between the staff, resident, and family be held if you request it?
- What are visiting hours—can a family member remain beyond visiting hours, or stay all night? Ask for a copy of the policy and visitors' rules.
- What are the room accommodations? Ask to see several different rooms in various areas of the home.
- Inspect the dining room and kitchen. Find out when meals are served and ask for a copy of the weekly or monthly menu. Then, on a return visit, compare what was scheduled to what actually is being served.
- Observe the appearance and conduct of the staff.
- Is the home clean and odor-free?
- Is it well-lighted and well-ventilated?
- How close is the nursing station to the rooms; how close are bathrooms?
- Find out what the medication and restraint policies are—ask for a written copy of the policy.
- Are the emergency call buttons easy to reach; does the home have smoke alarms, and rails to assist walking in hallways?
- Are religious services offered?
- What planned activities exist? If community rooms are provided, ask to see them.
- Listen to the manner in which the staff talks with residents and visitors—tone of voice, language, general attitude.
- Talk to residents and visitors. Ask them how they feel about the care, the staff, the administration, whether or not problems exist and what they consider them to be.

- Is there a resident council and does the home have a resident bill of rights? If yes, ask for a copy.
- Are residents allowed to bring personal possessions into the home?
- Are beautician and barber services available? What cost is involved?
- If a resident or member of his/her family has a complaint or other problem, how will it be handled?

There are two things I strongly recommend doing when someone you love becomes a resident of a nursing home. First, if the person is able to use the phone and has good vision, tape a copy of the telephone number of the regional ombudsman and the number of the State Division of Health and Social Services right on the telephone. Make certain there is a clear understanding that if anything happens, this is a number that can be called twenty-four hours a day. Most states have an 800 telephone number which can eliminate difficulty that could be encountered attempting to make a long distance telephone call and getting stopped at a switchboard. List the number exactly as it should be dialed: 1–800–000–0000, or 1–area code–000–0000.* If the person is unable to use the phone or

*For information about obtaining an American Security Card℠ like the one I carry, see page 440. Space is provided to list the telephone numbers of your regional nursing home ombudsman and your State Division of Health and Social Services.

doesn't have a bedside phone, the number should be put on a card that can be kept in a readily accessible place.

I recognize that this action may make others feel you're looking for trouble. *Take that risk.* A good nursing home is hiding nothing and has no reason to object to people feeling strongly about those they love and doing everything they can to protect their best interests. In fact, good nursing homes also call on ombudsmen to help when family members financially, mentally, verbally, or physically abuse residents. It works both ways. And even in the best-run hospital, nursing home, or group home, situations can occur that go unnoticed unless they are brought to another's attention.

The second thing I advise is to make unannounced visits at different times during the day. Many facilities discourage visitation—particularly visitation at unusual times. Don't be intimidated. This gives you a chance to see how the facility runs at times when residents' families usually don't show up.

No facility can run without rules, regulations, and policies. Providing care and managing the welfare of all residents requires considerable effort if it is done well. When a large number of people need to be fed, meals do have to be served on a schedule. And rules must exist to guarantee the welfare of everyone. Families have no right to capriciously manipulate rules for one person, and such actions are as out of order as mistreatment. However, there is a marked difference between rules, regulations, and policies that are for the welfare of the entire resident population and those that are deliberately restrictive.

If you would like more information about the rights of patients in nursing homes, I suggest you contact your local or state department of health and social services and ask for a copy of the Code of Federal Regulations governing skilled-nursing facilities.

3
The Right to Health Care

In all instances where decisions governing personal health are concerned, Senior Americans have the right to complete and accurate information necessary to ensure freedom of choice in selection of health care services. They have the further right to expect medical treatment from persons whose knowledge is strengthened with compassion and whose judgment is governed by moral restraint.

"Where health is concerned, tell the unvarnished truth in language we can understand and we'll make our own decisions. If we're seriously ill be gentle and . . . spare the heroics." —Art Linkletter

Understanding what today's health care system really means isn't just a challenge for Senior Americans. What once were clear-cut and uncomplicated decisions have become much more difficult. The Marcus Welby–type doctor is long gone, and many Americans are confused about health care and concerned about what might happen on a foggy horizon loaded with unclear choices. Out of the blue, combinations of initials like HMO, PPO, and DRG became part of our lives and we were automatically expected to understand what they mean. Who really knows if second medical opinions are needed, whether they're good or bad, a waste of time, or will make any difference in the final analysis? Who knows—or prepares for—what he or she would do if faced with a catastrophic medical dilemma?

We spend more on health care each year than we do on national defense. It has become a $425-billion-a-year industry. Hospitals that once were jammed to the rafters are now half empty and underused. Instead of asking patients to wait for an available bed, hospitals fiercely compete to fill those beds. We have urgent care centers, walk-in clinics, surgery centers, and every other form of quick-stop, quick-shop medicine. Are they good or bad? Are they right for you? Generic drugs may be advertised at fifty percent less than their brand-name equivalents. Are they equivalents or dangerous substitutes? What about outpatient surgery? Are people being released from hospitals quicker and sicker because of the DRG system which now governs Medicare? (See p. 244.) What about HMOs (see p. 246) or PPOs? Does joining one eliminate your guarantee of quality when it might count most? Does "medigap" insurance, which promises to alleviate all your worries, back its promises or are you in for a surprise when you most need the coverage it promised?

I believe American doctors are the best in the world today. But like everyone else, doctors are concerned about the shifts and changes occurring in medicine. And patients aren't certain whether they should sympathize with their doctors or blame them because they believe their first concern is protecting high incomes.

In the eye of this hurricane is the Senior American—one of us in ten is now older than sixty-five and in the next forty-five years that number will grow to one in five. We're active, healthier, and willing to spend our money to maintain our independence and have fun. We're often more carefree than people younger than us and more satisfied with our lives. The good news is that the nation is finally learning we aren't decrepit, senile people who need to be tolerated. We're a national resource with minds of our own, and we're well able to make our own decisions—when we choose to do so.

I'm against Senior Americans blandly sitting back watching life pass while handing over decisions that belong to them. I'm for encouraging every Senior American to assume control and manage the future wherever possible. Where health care is concerned, nothing could be more important.

I've provided a list of questions for you to ask your doctor, hospital, and pharmacist—the key players in your health team. You may think, "Ask questions of these people?" You bet. Exercise your right to choose; trust your ability to make judgments you've made all your lives; remember that it *is* your life and you *are* paying the bill. What happens and how it happens can, to a large extent, be controlled if you choose to exercise that control.

Think for a moment about your rights. Don't

you have the right to know the answers to questions about your own health? Since when, if you're paying any bill, don't you have a right to ask what you're buying, and what qualifies the product and the seller?

We do have the right to complete and accurate health information, but getting it is up to us. I'll grant that this is a new way of thinking. Traditionally, doctors and everything related to medicine have been considered hallowed ground. But in today's complicated world, sitting in a doctor's office nurturing concerns and questions we're afraid to ask, questions we fear are unimportant, or questions we think may be a waste of the doctor's time just isn't smart.

We also have the right to be told the unvarnished truth in language that can be understood. And that's not unreasonable or out of order. All professionals have their own confusing language, but they must speak to us in words we can understand.

When I was discussing this right with a group of Senior Americans one lady began to laugh as I compared the confusing language of doctors to the equally confusing language of plumbers. The more she thought about it the harder she laughed. Now you know me. There was no way I could let her get away without knowing why.

This small, wiry, attractive, white-haired lady had attended a session in northern California wearing a running suit. Her sparkling eyes and hearty laugh made her recounting of what had happened even funnier. She said she called a plumber after

she'd discovered a problem with a drain in an upstairs bathtub. When he arrived she took him upstairs and showed him the problem. As he struggled
trying to free a connection without any luck, she
stood over him and watched. "First he tried kneel-
ing on the floor next to the tub using a wrench to
loosen a rusted part," she said. "Then he got in
the tub and knelt down and tried the wrench again.
But he kept sliding backwards in the tub. All of a
sudden he turned and looked angrily at me and
said that instead of just standing there I could do
something to help if I ever expected him to get to
the 'nipple.' I was so startled, I did what he told
me."

The plumber ordered her to get into the tub, sit
down, and pull her feet up so he could brace his
feet against hers to get the leverage he needed to
turn his wrench. "Then," she said, "all of a sudden
the thing came loose and he changed from talking
about nipples to talking about other parts that he
referred to as male and female and—we were still
in the tub together." When the phone rang a few
seconds later, she described struggling to her feet
and climbing over the plumber to get to the phone
before it stopped ringing. On the other end, her
husband could sense her agitation when she answered the phone and asked why she was out of
breath. "Because I was in the upstairs bathtub with
the plumber helping him fix a nipple and nearly
killed myself getting to the phone—that's why,"
she blurted out.

"Don't tell *me* about confusing language, Art," she said. "My husband still has doubts regarding which nipple was the real target of that plumber's wrench."

The language of health care is every bit as intimidating as the language of plumbing. It's been suggested that "medicalese" is deliberately used to tune patients out or discourage questions. It's not difficult to conclude that what's being said is so lofty it can only be understood by another doctor, and patients often decide that it's better to pretend they understand than appear to be stupid. My advice? When anyone in the health care profession switches to medicalese it's time to say, "Sorry, I haven't understood a word you've said." And if it happens again, repeat your statement and keep repeating it until you get an answer you *do* understand.

Always remember that your life could depend on the amount of information you're given with which to make a decision. There should be no hesitation on anyone's part at asking whatever questions come to mind. *When it's your life there isn't any such thing as a stupid question.* Nor should anyone hesitate to ask on what basis he or she can be assured that all complete and accurate information has been furnished. It is up to the doctor or other health professional to tell you what you need to know that will put your mind at ease. Example: A doctor should have no objection to explaining fully what tests will be involved, why they're being ordered, what they will or won't contribute regarding your diagnosis, or what will be gained by referring you to someone else.

People who are old, infirm, and alone are vulnerable and don't always bring out the best in others. Elderly abuse isn't a problem I cite for the first time. Hundreds of others have said it before me and, like it or not, it exists in families, nursing homes, hospitals, and many other places. People who are alone and without family or friends literally are at the mercy of those providing care, offering advice, or in a position to help. It's all well and good to talk about the agencies that exist to redress abuse. But what do people do who are physically or mentally unable to ask for it? Where members of Senior Americans' families are concerned, compassion means doing whatever it takes to make certain people they love are being treated as they should be. It also means that if mistreatment or abuse is uncovered, they do whatever is necessary to bring about change. Compassion finds its roots in an understanding that results in patience, tolerance, willingness to explain or care, take time, or recognize when a little extra care is needed.

Since no one has the ability to guarantee what the future holds, the best insurance is a Living Will outlining one's real wishes—just in case. However, that's only part of it. The other part is letting everyone who might be in a position to act or speak for you know what your wishes really are. This is especially important when the issue is whether or not life should be sustained by artificial means, which could result in someone other than us making the decision.

Judgment and moral restraint are almost impossible to define when they involve the care and treatment of people in nursing homes or other situations where people are entirely dependent. Without compassion and respect for human dignity, neither judgment nor moral restraint is possible. We can't see inside every household, but we can demand that health providers back up the dedication they advertise by maintaining an environment and employing the kind of people who will assure the most basic of human rights for those who cannot help themselves.

Health Security: Later Won't Work

A real sense of security surrounding your health and the unknown can be established. Although no one ever will be able to foresee and protect against everything that could happen, Senior Americans do have a better choice than remaining silent and hoping for the best—they can take some specific actions to help prevent future problems from occurring.

Later won't work.

Before it happens is when Senior Americans must take action. If some of what really could happen is to be prevented or controlled, the time for action is now.

As Senior Americans, we've lived long enough to have witnessed incredible change in nearly everything that touches our lives. Where health care is concerned, we've seen our image of country doctors traveling in howling snowstorms to the bedsides of the ill and injured replaced by sick people who drive to doctors' offices or—when illness strikes after office hours—to the closest emergency rooms. We've seen uncomplicated testing and armchair diagnoses replaced by highly developed technologies and specialized levels of knowledge and skills. The impact of this change has made a weighty contribution to changing the average American's expected lifespan. In 1900, life expectancy was forty-seven years of age. Today, it's seventy-four.

We've also seen health costs continue to climb, with no apparent end in sight. In 1937, one Midwesterner was billed thirty-eight dollars for a fourteen-day hospitalization. The invoice wasn't itemized and it was written by hand. Today, thirty-eight dollars might—or might not—cover the cost of a two-minute visit from a doctor stopping to ask how a patient is feeling the day before discharge. There's no doubt about it—change and progress in health care have been phenomenal.

Yet in all my discussions with Senior Americans, the number-one concern expressed relates to health care. Regardless of available technology, skill, and resources, those fears and concerns center around a single word: care.

This is some of what I've heard: "When it really comes down to it, Art, *they* don't give a damn— all *they* want is their money." . . . "My doctor make a housecall? He'd think I was crazy if I ever asked." . . . "Why didn't I complain when I was in the hospital about what happened? I was afraid of what *they* might do to me." . . . "When *they* look at old people, *they* don't think we matter." . . . "How do I define care? That's easy. If you can prove you've got the dollars, *they*'ll prove they care." . . . "I'd like to tell every person in the country that if they care about someone who is old and sick, they'd better not leave 'em alone in the hospital."

The word "care" can be interpreted a lot of ways. But when it relates to health it's as simple as having the people who say they care back up their words with caring actions. That's what seems to be missing. Senior Americans don't really feel a sense of security in knowing that if and when the chips are down, the health care system will come through. The best they'll allow is even odds depending on which hospital, which doctor, time of day, whether or not one has the support of family or friends, and, most of all, what kind of insurance coverage exists. If it's only Medicare, it had better be backed by a guaranteed ability to pay what isn't covered.

There isn't enough time or combined energy

available to find solutions that will correct everything that's wrong within the health-care delivery system. And I don't think it makes sense to spend time searching for the problems' roots in order to discover who or what is or isn't at fault. The only purpose served is the waste of time and energy. What is needed is informed Senior Americans who'll take some positive steps to help ensure a positive result if and when a real problem occurs.

The Good Old Days

Health care has come a long way in a hundred years. Doctors once were described as men with "an elementary education who could take a course of lectures for one or two winters, pass an examination and thereby automatically achieve the right to practice medicine by state law." One turn-of-the-century writer said nurses were "profane, ignorant, careless, heartless and in most cases utterly unfitted for their positions." In the same era, a charity hospital was described as a place where "there are no luxuries, not much gentleness, and many of the patients lie for months without receiving one friendly call except from the colporteur, the priest, or the ladies of the Flower Mission . . . the wards are filled with wasted souls drifting through the agonies of disease toward unpitied and unremembered deaths." And the ominous clang of the "surgeon's bell" signaled volunteers to rush to the hospital and assist in holding a patient down while a surgeon operated. Those were "the good old days"?

It's no wonder that people often put their trust in home remedies, hypnotism, electricity, faith-healing and patent medicines. In fact, one ad promised "Riches, Titles, Honour, Power and Worldly Prospects" to anyone who had regular bowel movements induced by using a product called Eno's.

In John Camp's book entitled *Magic, Myth and Medicine,* he told how a famous advertiser's ads were "everywhere—on trams, on buses, on every bathing-hut and in every newspaper and maga-zine." The advertiser was Thomas Beecham, and Camp tells a funny story about his offer to supply a poor parish in the east end of London with hym-nals. The vicar was grateful but leery that Bee-cham's Pills would be advertised on every other page.

Beecham promised that wouldn't happen and sure enough, when the books were delivered no advertising appeared anywhere.

"It was not until the carol service later that year that the vicar realized he had been outwitted when, to his rage and mortification, he heard his congre-gation singing:

> "Hark, the herald angels sing
> Beecham's Pills are just the thing.
> For blessed peace and mercy mild
> Two for mother, one for child!"

The contrast between yesterday's practice of medicine and today's advanced technology and highly trained, skilled people is nothing less than astonishing.

Until I was hospitalized for surgery a few years ago, I'd never really given much thought to what really was available. After a battery of tests and a lengthy discussion with my doctor, I was told I needed surgery. My doctor said he'd make arrangements for my admittance to the hospital whenever we could agree on a day that was mutually convenient. Although I wasn't looking forward to an operation, I listened carefully, agreed to check in at the hospital on the scheduled day, and promised not to deviate from the restricted diet I'd been directed to follow. A minor detail like the hospital where the surgery would be performed seemed pretty unimportant in the scheme of things. After all, a hospital is a hospital, isn't it? The answer is no, it's not—there are many differences.

There are two kinds of hospitals: *community hospitals* and *medical centers*. A medical center usually is considerably larger than the average community hospital, and it may be affiliated with a medical school. House doctors (doctors on staff) are available twenty-four hours a day, as they are in some of the larger community hospitals. Generally speaking, patients who need highly specialized treatments, complex surgeries, or sophisticated diagnoses probably belong in medical centers. That's where the latest equipment will be housed, as well as the personnel trained to perform special tests and procedures. In a community hospital without a house staff, patients see only their private doctors or whichever doctors cover for them when they are unavailable. If emergencies arise, their doctors have to be contacted.

Community hospitals and medical centers can be *public,* which means they are government supported, or *nonprofit* (voluntary), which means they are dependent on insurance payments, contributions, and endowments. An increasing number of community hospitals now come under a third form of ownership and financing: They're owned by individuals or investors, are run for profit, and are called *proprietary* hospitals.

Patient care, however, has nothing to do with whether or not patients are admitted to public, nonprofit, or proprietary hospitals or whether they are community hospitals or medical centers. Patient care is a direct result of how well a hospital is managed and whether or not the hospital chosen is the right one for a particular medical problem or condition.

Like hospitals, there are differences in personnel who give care. Nurses are no longer "utterly unfitted for their positions"; they're professional members of a nursing team who together care for patients.

All hospitals employ twenty-four-hour-a-day nursing staffs that include registered nurses (RNs), licensed practical nurses (LPNs), or licensed vocational nurses (LVNs), and nursing assistants who are sometimes called orderlies and aides.

In order to be registered, an RN has had at least two years of training, has graduated from an accredited school, and has passed a state licensing examination. An RN is the person who is legally responsible for your care, who plans your care, does most of the consulting with your doctor about your progress, administers your medications, and does everything related to the management of intravenous (IV) solutions.

LPNs and LVNs have had at least one year of training and are licensed to perform many technical functions. They do some of the same things nurses do, like change dressings, make beds, and assist in keeping records and giving injections.

For the most part, assistants, aides, and orderlies are trained in the hospital. They help with baths, take temperatures, bring bedpans, give back rubs, and assist as much as their training allows.

Many hospitals no longer require nurses to wear starched white caps and, in some areas of the hospital, they don't necessarily dress in white. Figuring out who's who can be a real challenge. If you want to know for sure, read the name tags worn by all members of the nursing staff. In addition to the person's name, his or her title also is listed.

The Medical Mystique

I can vividly recall an evening when a friend and I talked through dinner—eating soup, salad, an entrée, and dessert without changing the subject. *We* didn't really talk; I listened as *he* talked about the car he'd decided to buy. I remember the extensive information he'd accumulated and the hours of comparative shopping that had gone into his choice. It was a tour de force in the presentation of facts he'd hoped would elicit responses from me, like "what a terrific choice . . . what a great car . . . what a super deal . . . what a smart man you are to have gone to such lengths before making such an important decision."

He had every fact and detail at his fingertips and had put considerable time into his decision. What did I think? Well, he'd done his homework all right and, in spite of hoping for three hours that the subject would change, I was impressed.

I find it fascinating that when the subject is the choice or purchase of a doctor's or hospital's services, the rules seem to change. Although patients *are* consumers (purchasers) of services, more often than not they refuse to exercise the same clout they automatically use when buying a car.

Medicine and all that surrounds it is cloaked with its own mystique and can be controlled with two words: "Trust me." This can imply that if someone doesn't have an equal base of medical knowledge, there is no basis for conversation. In order to make sure of that, what goes up like a shield is the "medicalese" language barrier. And patients are treated to officious attitudes and a parade of uniformed people who can't be identified without a program. The hospital atmosphere has effectively intimidated people for years. It's particularly noteworthy that the same people who routinely accept all this wouldn't permit similar treatment anywhere else. Can you imagine my friend putting up with an officious car salesman in a three-piece, pin-stripe suit talking down to him in technical language he didn't understand?

One of the ladies I interviewed before writing this book described her husband, an executive with a large corporation. From her description, I instantly knew his type. He's in control, has responsibility for an entire division of his corporation, hires and fires people, and is accustomed to giving orders. She said, "Believe me, Art, my husband scares the devil out of everyone . . . even the dog barks differently when he's home." Yet this same man managed to lie in a hospital bed in a less than flattering gown, rolled over when told, pulled up his gown to be examined when told, ate what was put in front of him, submitted to all the tests that had been ordered, and complained only in whispers to his wife. As she recounted the story for me months later, she still hadn't gotten over what happened. She laughed so hard she had tears in her eyes describing the morning that a stream of different people had come in, one after the other, to examine her husband. She said that because of his particular medical problem, a complete examination necessitated pulling up his hospital gown. Apparently he'd done it so often he assumed that when the last official-looking woman entered his room wearing a white lab coat, he was in for the same routine. Thoroughly annoyed, but without a question asked, this distinguished-looking man threw off the covers, yanked his gown up to his neck, and the president of the Memorial Hospital Volunteers nearly fainted.

Fair is fair. Granted, there is much that could be changed in hospitals. However, consumers of health care services must involve themselves and take more responsibility. A hospital isn't a hotel, it's a hospital. And much of the roughshod treatment patients experience and complain about is the result of their own silence. People who refuse to get involved, don't object, refuse to ask questions, and turn over complete responsibility for their health to someone else contribute to the problem. Silence can be golden but it can also license a continuing of something that needs to be corrected or stopped.

Most of the people who work in the health care industry, from doctors on down, are caring people. That opinion is heavily supported in many hospitals' opinion surveys, with consistent results. People who check into hospitals tend to have complete confidence in their doctor(s) and everyone in the hospital. They assume that people who provide care and treatments and who are involved in helping them get well know what they are doing. When asked questions related to care, people describe attitudes and perceptions, not the technical skills with which treatments or procedures were performed. For example: "The nurse on 4-West was so kind. She took time to talk to me." "I particularly liked the people in the therapy room. They seemed to understand how much it hurt." "From the moment the volunteer wheeled me to my room, everyone was so nice. They bent over backwards to be nice to my family, too." The key words are "kind," "understand," and "nice." As people are loyal to their doctors, they are loyal to their hospitals. It takes a great deal for those loyalties to be shaken.

Consumer silence in health care is finally beginning to disappear, and so it should. If we agree that old age is *not* for sissies, then we also agree that making choices where your own health care is concerned is something only you can do. Senior Americans need to muster courage, find whatever time is needed, and ask some commonsense questions before choosing a hospital. Like choosing a doctor, "later" won't work. It needs to be done now. Consumers of health care services make better choices when they're well.

We're Getting Older, But . . .

If there's anything I dislike hearing, it's recommendations that we be complacent about aging because it's the "mature" thing to do. Baloney. That's a philosophy of resignation and nothing is more deleterious. In all life situations, we have choices. We can choose to start an exercise program or change bad habits—not because we'll roll back the years but because we'll feel better and diminish the natural effects the years dish out. Like any well-designed machine, our bodies respond to being respectfully cared for and considerately used. But that doesn't mean that when we start to creak a bit, we've been given sufficient reason to throw in the towel and confine exercise to a rocking chair.

Misplaced keys, stiffness after a day's work in the yard, and the discovery of gray hairs aren't signs the end is in sight. In fact, some people exaggerate fears related to aging to the point that their overall attitudes become self-defeating. In my opinion, the smartest approach to aging is to accept those things that really are inevitable and to concentrate on the ones that aren't.

It's true. As we get older, the years do take their toll, but many of the things that cause mental and physical problems are a result of our own choices.

Our smoking, drinking, eating, exercise, and other habits have a direct bearing on how much we'll pay later on. We're never too old to change.

Experts tell us we age at different rates and that each person's organs and body system are affected differently. There are lots of theories offered as to why we age, but no one has all the answers. However, the following is a summary of some of the answers we do have.

- If we keep fats at less than twenty-five percent of our diet and watch the salt we consume, we'll help our hearts stay healthy.
- Exercise can thwart, or slow down, what tends to age us—it strengthens our heart and lungs, keeps muscle and joints in shape, and it slows the progress of osteoporosis.
- Ears lose some sensitivity to higher frequencies as we grow older, and thirty to fifty percent of people older than sixty-five have some hearing loss. The greatest contributor to a hearing problem resulting from nerve damage is noise we've been exposed to all our lives. If you have a hearing problem, your doctor can determine its cause and whether or not you need to see a specialist. Many hearing problems can be helped with a hearing aid or a device that amplifies a TV or telephone.
- Bones do weaken and gradually lose calcium. They also tend to fracture more easily. Because of decreasing hormone levels, insufficient calcium in the diet, and a lack of exercise, one

woman in four—older than sixty—suffers from osteoporosis, the bone-thinning disease.

- We get shorter as we grow older because the disks between vertebrae become narrower and compress. Bones in our hips gradually widen, our shoulders narrow, and the joints in our knees, hips, neck, and lower back can become stiff and painful, causing difficulty in walking. It's estimated that half of all Senior Americans older than sixty-five have some arthritis or joint pain. If joint pain persists, you need to see your doctor.

- As we get older, the lenses in our eyes get more opaque and many Senior Americans develop cataracts. There are other vision problems that can also occur. However, when detected early, they can often be treated. It's advisable for everyone to have regular eye examinations. Where Senior Americans are concerned, it's particularly important.

- Because of wide exposure in the media, Alzheimer's disease is widely feared. However, it's not inevitable and it isn't a normal part of aging. Most people think the disease is much more prevalent than it really is. It strikes only five percent of Senior Americans over sixty-five and rarely shows up before the age of seventy.

- Kidneys get smaller as we get older and their function becomes less efficient. Bladder capacity also decreases, and because the bladder becomes less sensitive, it may not give ample warning that it's full. Aging kidneys are unable to keep as much water in the body. Consequently, dehydration can be a real problem in older people, especially if fluids are lost because of fevers or diarrhea. Experts recommend drinking six to eight glasses of water every day if we want to keep our kidneys functioning smoothly.

- Older skin wrinkles because it loses elasticity and the underlying layer of fat diminishes. And sun damages the elastic fibers beneath the skin's surface. Stay out of the sun or use a sunscreen.

- Although normal aging doesn't affect the function of our hearts, approximately half the people older than sixty-five have some evidence of heart disease. And many Senior Americans develop some degree of arteriosclerosis—hardening of the arteries. This can cause chest pain and panting when a person exerts himself/herself strenuously. An aging heart becomes thicker and weaker, but it can still meet normal demands and will continue to be strengthened with regular exercise.

- Lungs usually show more effects of wear and tear than hearts. With advancing age, the chest wall hardens and lungs become stiffer and more difficult to inflate, making it more difficult to take deep breaths. Older lungs are much more susceptible to infections like pneumonia; consequently, respiratory infections in older people need to be closely monitored medically. If you smoke, stop. Lungs can repair themselves over a period of time after you quit.

- Chronic constipation is one of the most common

complaints among Senior Americans. Because the large intestine becomes less active with age, food tends to collect and dry out, making it harder and more difficult to move along. "Home remedies," such as regularly using laxatives, increasing the consumption of soft foods, and decreasing fluids only make things worse. Eating foods rich in fiber should help, but when constipation doesn't improve, you need to see your doctor. It can be a sign of a medical problem.

• Memory doesn't have to fade. Forgetting names and faces or misplacing keys are normal occurrences. When we're young, we think nothing of them. However, as we get older, we're tempted to worry that they're signs of senility. Experts tell us that our minds need to be intellectually stimulated if they are to remain sharp. In fact, memory is a skill that can be improved with mental exercise.

Sexuality

Most Senior Americans will agree with me that sex is among the most private of subjects. But let's be candid about it: Many Senior Americans like sex as much as their younger counterparts. When a wife or husband dies, the reason we remarry isn't only to gain a bridge partner or have company watching TV. Nevertheless, the majority of Senior

Americans view the subject of sex as hush, hush— "If it really does go on, keep it quiet." It's the quickest of subjects covered in conversations with Senior Americans, because everybody clams up. A lot of snickering takes place and a few faces turn pink, but all in all, we moved on to talk about something else with record speed every time I approached the subject. When I said, "So what if it *takes* all night to do what you used to *do* all night," I got a roaring laugh but no information.

Almost every doctor thinks sex is good for Senior Americans. They tell us it's good for one's general physiology and that it takes place the way it always did when we were younger. Only one problem—according to my expert clinical psychologist advisers, more doctors than not refuse to open the subject with their Senior American patients. And there's a lot they could do to help. They could begin by letting older patients know they aren't abnormal when they want "sleeping together" to mean more than sharing the controls on the electric blanket.

Why shouldn't Senior Americans have the right to be attracted to others, as they always were, with the expectation that, at some point, intimate sex may be part of the package? Is it necessary to explain one's actions or expect to have children look at you or ask questions as though you're slipping into your second childhood? Frankly speaking, it's none of their business—tell them to go to a video store, rent a copy of *Cocoon,* and watch Jessica Tandy's jealousy erupt when Hume Cronyn has a fling with a waitress. If that doesn't work, tell them to rewind it, and watch again for the look in Don Ameche's and Gwen Verdon's eyes as they're being married. They aren't thinking about playing checkers.

Sexual dysfunction isn't something that occurs automatically when one passes a certain age. Healthy older Americans enjoy sex as much as younger Americans. In fact, sexuality, which includes looking good, dressing well, and appearing attractive to the opposite sex, is important to healthy Senior Americans. As one clinical psychologist said, "It's the last thing to go."

The same psychologist described a woman who'd scheduled an appointment to see her. She had just gotten through a divorce after a six-month marriage to a man who was seventy-nine years old. They had "gone together" for several years and had enjoyed each other's company and made many mutual friends. They finally decided to get married. Now, six months later, the seventy-eight-year-old divorcée was sitting in her office in need of divorce counseling. The reason she gave for the divorce was sex: "That's all he wanted," she said. "Twenty-four hours a day . . . sex, sex, sex. I couldn't take it anymore!"

Regardless of how far we think we've come in the twentieth century in addressing certain subjects, sex is one that still is considered—by much of our society—as "not nice" after a certain age. And there are reasons for that. When an older parent dies, children often feel that a mother or father cannot be replaced, which results in misguided and unrealistic attitudes toward the surviving parent. Other children are concerned that if an older parent remarries, their inheritance may be affected. Yet others determine that since Mother or Dad "certainly doesn't do that anymore, why bother remarrying?" As one younger woman said when asked about her widowed mother and sex: "Oh no. I know my mother wouldn't do that . . . but my mother-in-law would!"

I've been told that women are more aggressive about wanting to remarry following death or divorce of a spouse than men. And they most often fall into two distinct groups—one that says "no marriage, no sex," and the other that thinks that sex without marriage is all right. In fact, in the second group, the reason for sex without marriage may well be because of children who don't think a parent should remarry, fear of having to nurse another spouse through an illness, risking another spouse's death and having to grieve a second time, or fear of the opinions of friends and peers.

Senior Americans are quiet on the subject of their sexuality because the Victorian view of sex as a "dirty secret" continues to this day. Nevertheless, secret or not, there are a few points that need to be made. When people marry in later years, intimacy *can* stop at a level that doesn't include sexual intimacy—particularly if the primary objective for marrying is companionship. And there are medical problems affecting sexual desire that can be related to the increased number of medications Senior Americans take, including those for blood pressure, sedatives, and tranquilizers. If there *is* a problem, your doctor may be able to help, but you'll have to let him or her know. Physicians—particularly if they're younger than their patients—aren't likely to open the subject.

Experts say that for the most part, whatever one's sexual practices have been before, the same expectations and desires continue in later years. Simply stated, Senior Americans who want sex to remain a part of their lives aren't abnormal. Regardless of any societal image, misinformed children or friends, or the pervasive attitude that keeps people from seeking medical help because "sex isn't nice" when you pass a certain age, the choice is as much in your hands now as it's ever been.

What do I think about sex for Senior Americans? I'm for it.

HEALTH CHOICES

Is There a Doctor
in the House?

Yes, there is—me—Arthur Gordon Linkletter—*I'm* a doctor! But you'd better hope that if your life hangs in the balance, my face isn't the "doctor's" face you see first in an emergency room. The fact that I could legally sign my letters "Dr. Linkletter" if I wanted to doesn't qualify me to remove tonsils. My doctoral degrees were honorarily awarded for many reasons—not one of which has anything to do with medicine.

In the world of doctors there are a lot of people entitled to call themselves "doctor." But there are doctors and *doctors*. A "doctor" can be a medical doctor, a doctor limited to doing eye examinations and fitting glasses, a doctor limited to treating or operating on everything below the ankle, a doctor of chiropractic, a doctor of psychology, and so on.

Trying to figure out who's who is no task for a layman. Rather than risk misinformation, I went to *Taber's Cyclopedic Medical Dictionary* and am including the definitions exactly as published.

Physician (M.D.)—a person who has successfully completed the prescribed course of studies in medicine in a medical school officially recognized by the country in which it is located and who has acquired the requisite qualifications for licensure in the practice of medicine.

Intern (M.D.)—physician or surgeon on a hospital staff, usually a recent graduate receiving a year of postgraduate training prior to being eligible to be licensed to practice medicine.

Resident (M.D.)—a physician who is obtaining further clinical training after internship. Usually this is done as a member of the house staff of a hospital.

When a man or woman graduates from an accredited American medical school, a doctor of medicine degree (M.D.) is awarded. But that degree does not include a license to *practice* medicine. That comes later during practical training in a hospital-based intern or residency program. Licenses are granted by individual states after written and oral examinations are completed successfully.

Taber's Cyclopedic Medical Dictionary defines other doctors commonly found on the menu of health care choices as follows:

Osteopath (D.O.)—a practitioner of osteopathy.

Osteopathy—a school of medicine based upon the theory that the normal body is a vital mechanical organism in which structural and functional states are of equal importance and that the body is able to rectify itself against toxic conditions when it has favorable environmental circumstances and satisfactory nourishment. Therefore, it is the osteopathic physician's responsibility to remove any internal or external peculiarities to the system. Although using manipulation for the most part to restore structural and functional balance, osteopaths also rely upon physical, medicinal, and surgical methods. Osteopathy, founded by Dr. Andrew Taylor Still (1828–1917), is recognized as a standard method or system of medical and surgical care.

Optometrist (D.O.)—a person specifically trained and licensed to examine the eyes in order to test visual acuity and to prescribe and adapt lenses to preserve and restore maximum efficiency of vision. The optometrist's professional degree is Doctor of Optometry (D.O.).

Podiatrist (D.P.M.)—a health professional responsible for the examination, diagnosis, prevention, treatment and care of conditions and functions of the human foot. A podiatrist performs surgical procedures, prescribes corrective devices, drugs, and physical therapy as legally authorized in the state in which he or she practices. (A synonym for a podiatrist is a chiropodist.)

Chiropractor—a person certified and licensed to practice chiropractic care.

Medical doctors share a number of common links. They use the same initials (M.D.) after their names and have comparable medical knowledge. They talk the same language regardless of specialty and are medically educated to understand the entire human system. They must be equals in this sense before deciding on a specialty, such as orthopedic surgery, internal medicine, pathology, psychiatry, neurology, obstetrics and gynecology, ophthalmology, cardiology, anesthesiology, emergency medicine, general surgery, etc.

Regardless of the stringent requirements that must be met before any doctor enters practice, it is still no easy task to figure out who's who. There is an additional benchmark a doctor voluntarily can obtain—board certification. In order to pass the "boards" a physician has had to practice at least a year in his or her chosen specialty and then pass comprehensive written and oral examinations over a period of several days. Each specialty has its own requirements for board certification.

Wading through this complicated arena of physicians and nonphysicians—all of whom are called "doctor"—is so complex an entire volume would be required to explain the differences and be fair to each. There are good psychiatrists and good psychologists, good ophthalmologists and good optometrists, good anesthesiologists and good anesthetists, good orthopedic surgeons and good podiatrists, etc. In each case, one is a medical doctor and one isn't. The key word in determining what's right for you is *risk*. And the person best qualified to determine that risk is your primary doctor. He or she knows *your* medical history and which doctor is best suited to provide whatever specialized care is needed.

In order to illustrate the confusion we experience among those we commonly refer to as doctors, consider "eye doctors"—ophthalmologists and optometrists.

Ophthalmologists are medical doctors who have completed three or more additional years in a hospital-based residency program studying medical and surgical conditions affecting the eye before they became licensed specialists in all aspects of eye and vision care. Consequently, their licenses permit them to diagnose; treat; prescribe medicine, glasses, and contact lenses; and perform eye surgery.

The National Society to Prevent Blindness provides this definition of an optometrist: "An optometrist is a doctor of optometry. Such a professional is licensed to practice optometry and specializes in determining the need for glasses and screens the patient for abnormalities of the eye. His or her education consists of two to four years of college and four years in an optometric college. The optometrist treats visual disturbances with glasses and contact lenses and may also prescribe exercises for muscle imbalances."

Here's the difference. Because one doctor is a medical doctor and the other isn't, their licenses restrict what they legally may do. Medical doctors—regardless of specialty—have completed education and training that enable them to treat the whole person even though they may practice as specialists in one area, such as the eyes. So when ophthalmologists perform "routine" eye examinations, their complete medical training enables them to see more than the eyes. For example, an ophthalmologist looking through an ophthalmoscope during a routine eye examination may see symptoms indicating high blood pressure, diabetes, a brain tumor, or another medical problem. In fact, it's estimated that an ophthalmologist detects symptoms of other medical problems during routine eye examinations in as many as one patient out of twenty.

Or consider the Senior American with the painful bunion. Not only can he or she choose where the surgery will be performed; a choice can also be made between an orthopedic surgeon and a podiatrist, who are different kinds of "doctors" although both are licensed to perform bunion surgery. An orthopedic surgeon, like an ophthalmologist, is a medical doctor practicing as a specialist in orthopedics. In addition to treating bunions, he or she has the medical training to evaluate and assess a patient's entire medical history and any other related problems before making a decision regarding anesthesia, drugs, and whether or not the patient should be hospitalized or sent home to recover. A podiatrist is trained and licensed only to treat foot problems and perform foot surgery.

Deciding who is or isn't the right choice in doctors—physician or nonphysician—involves your life. *Before deciding the level of medical risk you are willing to or can afford to take, consult your primary doctor*. He or she is the center of your health care team and knows your medical history.

Choosing a Primary Doctor

I've discovered that in one very important area a lot of my peers have made the same choice I've made: They're working hard to maintain good health. They're involved in physical fitness programs, are conscious of eating nutritious meals, and are anxious to learn what can be done to make their health even better. As I meet people around the country and talk to them about health care, the same two subjects always come up: doctors and hospitals. Through these conversations and listening to what's said and asking a lot of questions, I've come up with a commonsense list of questions that I think all Senior Americans should ask—and have answered—by the doctors and hospitals they choose. The key word is "choose." If we agree that freedom of choice is a human right, why is it, then—when doctors and hospitals are involved—that so many people hand over the right to make decisions and choices without a question asked? Think of it this way—if it's important to obtain a warranty when you buy a new vacuum cleaner, doesn't it make sense to at least obtain a *limited* warranty before purchasing services on which your life may depend?

The answers to the ten questions I've listed in the next few pages will help you decide whether or not you've made the right choice.

Experts in the health care industry have told me that an interesting phenomenon occurs between a patient of any age and his or her doctor. Patients tend to view doctors in whom they place their trust as people who—short of a veritable disaster happening—are incapable of being wrong. These same experts prove that statement by pointing out what people often say before seeing a doctor for the first time: "I'm going to see *the* doctor," or "I have an appointment with *the* doctor." When that first hurdle is over, the new terminology becomes "*My* doctor said . . . ," or "I have an appointment with *my* doctor."

Choice of physicians is a very personal thing. It's viewed by most people as a direct reflection of an individual's ability to make a judgment call in a critically important area. That's fine and as it should be unless one is blindsided by a lack of information and misplaced loyalty.

A secure doctor-patient relationship is a two-way thing. Doctors should not be held accountable for reading the minds of people who refuse to talk openly or lay out their real concerns. On the other hand, doctors who push aside or never answer questions or who never return phone calls except through someone on the office staff shouldn't be surprised if patients find other doctors.

These are the ten questions that need to be asked by everyone of his or her primary physician. And,

by primary physician I mean the doctor you call
first—the one *you* refer to as "*my* doctor."

1. *Will you tell me what I can do that will help
   establish a good doctor-patient relationship?*

   Establishing a good relationship with a doctor
   is a two-way street. A doctor needs a clear
   understanding with patients governing what
   can be expected and what can't—for example:
   Doctors aren't clergymen and patients can't
   expect them to provide hours of time in the
   middle of busy professional schedules to talk
   about things that have no bearing on medical
   care. There is a fine line between telling your
   doctor all that's needed to provide a complete
   medical picture and assuming that he or she
   wants to know how the grandkids did on their
   last report cards. All the doctors I've talked
   to have told me they would welcome patients
   asking the questions I've listed. They agree
   that if you know what is expected of you, what
   your doctor needs and wants to know about
   you, and are familiar with routine office procedures, it's of mutual benefit.

2. *Can I expect that when I schedule an appointment with you I will receive your undivided
   attention and not be made to feel as though I
   am being rushed along so you can stay on
   schedule?*

   No one wants to ask questions or be examined
   in between telephone calls and other inter-

ruptions. The point here is that when you schedule and prepare for an appointment in advance and are charged for the visit, you're entitled to the time and advice for which you are charged.

3. *When I arrive on time for an appointment, what do you consider a reasonable time that I should have to be kept waiting if you're running late?*

This is a question that doesn't have a precise answer because, depending on what the doctor encounters, that time could vary. Keep a couple of things in mind. It could happen that you will also need more of the doctor's time if a special problem or circumstance arises. Since doctors cannot foresee when this may happen, they schedule time to be as fair as possible to everyone. Coming prepared to wait longer than you planned is a consideration I recommend. However, if you have to wait a long time *every* time you go in for an appointment, then you can assume the doctor is over-scheduling and have a right to object.

4. *How do your doctor's fees for services compare to what is reimbursed by Medicare?*

It is very important that you know the answer to this question. If your doctor's fee schedule—compared to the state and national averages—falls way above or way below the averages, you should know why before establishing a relationship. Since 1983, the DRG

(Diagnosis-Related Groups; see p. 244) system has put a limit on what Medicare will pay for hospitalization. However, there is no system that limits what a physician can charge.

5. *Do you have medical privileges at (your choice) hospital, which, in the event that I need to be hospitalized, is where I want to be admitted?*

The choice of hospitals should be considered carefully. In a community where there is only one hospital there is no problem. However, when more than one hospital is available, your doctor should know the one you prefer. You need to know if he or she has staff privileges to practice there.

6. *When I have questions that concern me about my health, can I feel free to telephone you and expect that you will return my call at a time that is convenient for you?*

This is a very necessary question. Patients do *not* have the right to assume that their doctors will drop everything to talk with them whenever calls are placed. The only exception would be in an emergency. Other patients are as concerned as you are about having their medical appointments unnecessarily interrupted. What you *are* entitled to is knowing that when the doctor has available time, your call will be returned.

7. *What would you like me to do if I telephone and your office help refuses to let me talk with*

you even though I consider the problem to be urgent?

I often wonder if there is a doctor in the country who understands how important people who answer telephones are. I only wish I could demonstrate the high percentage of people who say their doctors are unreachable and describe second- and third-hand information passed through receptionists. In my opinion, you have every right to make it very clear that unless your call is routine, you expect that medical questions will be answered by the doctor when he or she has available time.

8. *I would like to choose specialists to whom you would refer my care in the event that a particular medical problem occurs. Will you advise me in making those choices?*

If you are unconscious when admitted to a hospital through an emergency room, any choice governing which specialist will be called to care for a heart attack, a broken hip, head injury, etc., is out of your hands. The only way your doctor can honor your wishes is by knowing in advance whom you want. And if the physician in the emergency room has no way of knowing who your primary physician is, he or she will telephone whoever is on call and you may or may not get the doctor you want. I strongly recommend that, in addition to establishing your specialist choices with your doctor, you also carry a medical information card that identifies your primary physician and specialist choices. See p. 440 for information about how you may obtain a medical information card like the one I carry.

9. *If an exceptional situation occurs where I am too sick to drive safely to your office but not sick enough to need an ambulance, will you make a housecall?*

All people don't have a member of the family or friend to whom they can turn when they are too sick to drive a car safely. And it's worthy of notation that not everyone has a car. The question of housecalls is a legitimate and reasonable one to ask and, in an exceptional circumstance—exceptional should be defined by your doctor—requesting that he or she make a housecall is, in my opinion, not outside the bounds of all that is good and decent.

10. *I would like to discuss how I feel about prolonging my life in medical situations that could occur. If I am ever unable to speak for myself, what can you do to help assure that my wishes are upheld?*

Although your doctor cannot legally guarantee that your wishes will be upheld, he or she must be told how you feel. Without doubt, an informed doctor has considerable credibility with family and/or friends who, for whatever reasons, may want to authorize something you don't want. And your doctor will have a far easier time speaking on your behalf knowing that what he or she is saying really *was* established between you and that what's being said represents your true choice.

When you've asked and received answers for the questions listed, you need to do one other thing. Your family or significant friends must be told. They need to be fully aware of the fact that what you've discussed with your doctor is what *you* want—that you expect them to respect your wishes if and when they must make such a decision for you.

Solidly establishing your primary-physician relationship *now* is just plain smart. The level of confidence you need in your doctor and your doctor needs in you can be achieved.

Getting there is a two-way street.

Choosing a Primary Hospital

I'm going to suggest some questions that need to be asked of the hospital you consider your first choice if and when you should need to be hospitalized.

Before you ask them, however, there is a preceding question to ask: Who can answer your questions? In my opinion, that can be one of several people: The director of admissions, the hospital's patient representative, or someone in the Department of Social Services. The first thing to do is telephone *your* hospital and ask for the director of admissions. Explain that you'd like an appointment at his or her convenience and explain its purpose. If this person isn't the one with whom you should meet, the director of admissions will tell you. Make certain that you let whomever you are going to meet with know that you won't need an excessive amount of time. Thirty minutes should be more than sufficient.

Now, here are some essential questions to ask:

1. *Can you tell me what I can do to help establish a good relationship with this hospital?*

   As with your doctor, a good relationship with a hospital is a two-way street. All the hospitals I've talked to are very receptive to people coming in to talk about the hospital and what might be involved during a hospitalization. Although one or two said a few people actually have done this, most admit that this isn't standard procedure. It is your task to let the hospital know that you will cooperate and that you want specifics of what the hospital needs from you clearly outlined.

2. *If I'm admitted, I want to be able to see my medical record and keep a copy of it when I*

am discharged. What is this hospital's policy where my medical record is concerned?

Doctors who are resistant to patients seeing their records contend that patients will needlessly be upset and can't understand them anyway. However, your medical record is a valuable part of your continuing health care. It provides a clear picture of your medical condition, and the truth is that not much effort is required in explaining it to you. Either you or whoever might be in charge of your care will be helped considerably by having this record in the event that you move, have a recurrence of illness, have to go to the emergency room, or are referred to another doctor. Your medical record can also eliminate repeating expensive lab tests and examinations that have already been performed.

Because all states are different, your hospital will know whether you are legally allowed direct access to your record. Regardless, the information in the record belongs to you even though the piece of paper on which it's written legally belongs to the doctor or hospital.

In my opinion, the strongest reason for having your own record in your own possession is to make you more responsible for your own health and health care.

3. *My primary doctor is (your choice). If I am hospitalized in an emergency situation and am*

unable to state my preferences, what can the hospital do to assure me that my doctor will be notified as well as any specialist(s) I prefer if and when they are needed?

This is a key question. A hospital can enter information like this in its computer or files. In an emergency, these files are pulled and the information comes up. If you've been hospitalized in the last several years, chances are good the information already is there. If you haven't, what you are asking the hospital to do is open a file for you that includes the name of your primary doctor and specialists you've selected in the event they are needed, your insurance information, names of persons you wish to have notified if you are admitted, and the person you've chosen to act on your behalf if it is required. In addition, I believe everyone should carry a medical information card that also contains this information. Regardless of how well you prepare, illness and injury can also happen when you are out of town. See p. 440 for information about how you may obtain a medical information card like the one I carry.

4. *If I am hospitalized, will the hospital make someone available to explain my Medicare DRG and my hospital bill before I am discharged?*

Medicare DRGs are confusing to understand. You have every reason to want to know where and how the Medicare DRG that applies to your medical problem will affect your length of stay, treatments, and procedures. And before paying the bill, you are entitled to an explanation of charges and any codes that may be used that you don't understand. The bill shouldn't be in summary form; it should be itemized. You want to make certain you weren't charged for a procedure that was scheduled and then canceled and that you weren't charged for equipment that was used for a short time and then discontinued. And you should be especially careful about room charges.

5. *Does this hospital have a patient representative on staff?*

Many hospitals employ a patient representative whose sole job is to act as liaison and troubleshooter between patients and the hospital staff. This person can literally move a mountain if one needs to be moved. He or she can move freely in the hospital and has access to all those areas that can bring an immediate resolution to a problem. Conversations with the patient representative can be kept entirely confidential—unless you choose otherwise—and problems get immediate attention. This person can eliminate a stressful encounter between you and a member of the staff, a physician, troublesome visitors, and so on.

If no patient representative is on staff, ask

what procedure should be followed and the name of the person to contact in the event you are hospitalized.

6. *Does this hospital support the American Hospital Association's Patient's Bill of Rights? (See p. 199 for complete Patient's Bill of Rights.)*

California, Colorado, Massachusetts, Michigan, Minnesota, Pennsylvania, and New York have made compliance with this bill mandatory. If your hospital does not support the bill, you should ask for a complete explanation of reasons. If it does, ask for copies of any literature the hospital provides which includes the bill.

7. *What are the rights of my family and friends regarding timely information about my medical condition and special visiting hours?*

If you are admitted for surgery and there is a delay in the schedule, family and friends can become upset or very angry when hours pass without information. And they are entitled to information. This question is intended to establish the hospital's procedure in the event this should occur. Where visiting hours are concerned, what you want to know is what the hospital's policy is in an exceptional situation where a family member or friend wishes to stay at your bedside all night or at other times outside the standard visiting hours.

8. *Will this hospital support my right to be told I am dying?*

Generally speaking, members of the hospital staff take their clues from the patient. However, if it is your express wish to be told, you are entitled to an honest answer. In my opinion, you have the right to prepare for your death any way that you choose to do so. If the answer is yes, you can ask to have this information entered in your medical record.

9. *Will this hospital respect my wish to die with dignity?*

This question involves respecting a person's specific wishes in the event they are known. The best way to make sure they are known is to sign a Living Will, which specifies that it is your wish that no "heroic" measures be used to sustain your life when all hope of recovery is gone. Although I believe it is essential for Senior Americans who subscribe to the concept of a Living Will to obtain and sign one, it is important to know that if a family member were to overrule your request, the doctor and hospital probably would not uphold it. Therefore, it is of critical importance that your Living Will be discussed with anyone who might be responsible for your care, with your primary doctor, and with your attorney if you have one. You can also ask the hospital to make this information part of your legal medical record.

If you wish to obtain a copy of the Living Will, write to: Concern for Dying, 250 West 57th Street, New York, New York 10107.

10. *Is this hospital accredited?*

The JCAH—Joint Commission on Accreditation of Hospitals—was founded by the American Hospital Association. It consists of members of the medical profession who are hired to inspect hospitals and grant accreditations. Most major hospitals are accredited. However, if a hospital is *not* accredited, it *cannot receive Medicare payments*.

When you've asked and received answers to the questions listed, request that you be placed on any hospital mailing lists that will provide health, wellness, other information, and any newsletters published. I also recommend that you find a time to tour the hospital and become familiar with the location of the after-hours entrance and the entrance to the emergency room.

Tell your family and/or significant friends about your visit and discussion at the hospital. If you want to sign a Living Will, send for it today.

The Patient's Bill of Rights

Before I was admitted to the hospital for surgery, I received a thick packet of information from the hospital that included a copy of the Patient's Bill of Rights. I'll confess to never having realized it existed or ever having encountered it before then and, as it turns out, I'm not alone. The majority of people I've talked to since then don't seem to know any more than I did. In my opinion, it would make a big difference if everyone who was—or might be—hospitalized knew it existed. It's an important document that covers a number of the problems encountered in hospitals.

The Patient's Bill of Rights was adopted by the American Hospital Association in 1973, but is mandatory policy in just seven states: California, Colorado, Massachusetts, Michigan, Minnesota, Pennsylvania, and New York. Many hospitals include a copy of the Patient's Bill of Rights in patient information packets. On the other hand, many hospitals do not provide patients with a copy of the Bill of Rights. They do not want it to appear as though the Bill has been adopted officially because it could be introduced in a court of law as evidence against that hospital.

Following is the ten-point Patient's Bill of Rights defined and passed by the American Hospital Association. It covers a patient's right to courteous treatment, confidentiality, and informed consent.

1. *The patient has the right to considerate and respectful care.*

Although this isn't a legal right, you have a right to expect common courtesy. People who care for you don't have the right to call you by nicknames like "honey," "sweetie," "gramps," "grandma," "dear," or by your first name unless *you* establish that familiarity. It also means that you are entitled to personal privacy—for example, like having the curtains drawn around your bed—or the door closed—while being examined, bathed, or while using a bedpan.

2. *The patient has the right to obtain from his physician complete current information concerning his diagnosis, treatment, and prognosis in terms the patient can be reasonably expected to understand. When it is not medically advisable to give such information to the patient, the information should be made available to an appropriate person on his behalf. He has the right to know, by name, the physician responsible for coordinating his care.*

This legal right means that you—or someone you've chosen to be responsible for you—has the right to know what medical treatment you are getting. Unfortunately, many doctors and other medical personnel won't take the time to talk to patients. Others speak in language which can't be understood by a layperson, or they don't answer your real questions because they resent patients' questions. Your doctor has no reason to resent questions—if anyone has a right to information about the status of your health, you do.

3. *The patient has the right to receive from his physician information necessary to give informed consent prior to the start of any procedure and/or treatment. Except in emergencies, such information for informed consent should include but not necessarily be limited to the specific procedure and/or treatment, the medically significant risks involved, and the probable duration of incapacitation. Where medically significant alternatives for care or treatment exist, or when the patient requests information concerning medical alternatives, the patient has the right to such information. The patient also has the right to know the name of the person responsible for the procedures and/or treatment.*

This legal right states that before agreeing to certain procedures, you must have a complete understanding of what is involved, what the consequences may be, and whether or not alternative treatments and procedures are available. Although the benefits of a given procedure cannot always be guaranteed ahead of time, you have a right to know what benefits can be expected as a result of the procedure you are agreeing to. If you give your written consent and then change your mind, consent can be withdrawn by asking to have the original form returned so you can destroy it.

4. *The patient has the right to refuse treatment to the extent permitted by law and to be informed of the medical consequences of his action.*

You have a legal right to refuse any treatment if you are not completely convinced it's necessary. You also are entitled to a complete explanation of what the treatment is and what might happen if you don't consent. However, you should understand that even though you can refuse treatment just because that's what you want to do, the hospital may ask you to sign a form that releases it from any liability which may result because of your refusal.

5. *The patient has the right to every consideration of his privacy concerning his own medical care program. Case discussion, consultation, examination, and treatment are confidential and should be conducted discreetly. Those not directly involved in his care must have the permission of the patient to be present.*

Although not a legal right, this relates to the invasion of your privacy. It covers situations like examinations by medical students or others accompanying your doctor while he or she examines you. Before either situation occurs, your permission should be obtained. If a student insists on the need to examine you even though you refuse, use the button that calls your nurse and ask to talk to the head of the department. Hospitals and attending physicians are liable for unauthorized examinations or treatments, and medical students are not allowed to represent themselves as doctors. They must identify themselves as students. A point needs to be made here: Although what I've explained is your right, students who will go on to become excellent doctors do need to learn. There's a fine balance between being cooperative and having your right to privacy invaded. As in almost all situations, courtesy goes a long way in encouraging cooperation. Most patients are receptive to someone who explains the purpose of the visit and asks permission.

6. *The patient has the right to expect that all communications and records pertaining to his care should be treated as confidential.*

As I have already advised, discuss your feelings with your doctor regarding confidentiality where information about your health is concerned *before* you end up in the hospital. A doctor-patient relationship is confidential, and the hospital does not have the right to release any information about you without your permission.

7. *The patient has the right to expect that within its capacity a hospital will make reasonable response to the request of a patient for services.*

The hospital must provide evaluation, service, and/or referral as indicated by the urgency of the case. When medically permissible, a patient may be transferred to another facility only after he has received complete information and explanation concerning the needs for and alternatives to a transfer. The institution to which the patient is to be transferred must first have accepted the patient for transfer.

Although this is not a legal right, it means that if a hospital does not have the equipment or personnel to perform a certain procedure, it should make arrangements for you to be admitted or transferred to a hospital that is able to do what's needed—unless your condition makes it medically unsafe.

8. *The patient has the right to obtain information as to any relationship of his hospital to other health care and educational institutions insofar as his care is concerned. The patient has the right to obtain information as to the existence of any professional relationships among individuals, by name, who are treating him.*

This is a courtesy, not a legal right. The relationship between the hospital where you've been admitted and any other hospital, medical school, skilled care or other facility is something you have a right to know. You have the same right to be informed of any existing relationships between your doctor and other doctors who may provide consultation about your care. If you want a doctor who isn't affiliated with your doctor, discuss this with him or her and state your request.

9. *The patient has the right to be advised if the hospital proposes to engage in or perform human experimentation affecting his care or treatment. The patient has the right to refuse to participate in such research projects.*

This has been a legal right since 1966. Your best protection is to be fully aware of what your treatment is and to ask all the questions needed to help you remain completely aware of everything related to your care. If you are asked to participate in an experimental program—as some patients are when chemotherapy is involved—be certain you understand all the risks, possible side effects, and possible benefits before making the decision.

10. *The patient has the right to expect reasonable continuity of care. He has the right to know in advance what appointment times and physicians are available and where. The patient has the right to expect that the hospital will provide a mechanism whereby he is informed by his physician or a delegate of the physician of the patient's continuing health-care requirements following discharge.*

This is a courtesy, not a legal right. It means that when you are discharged you should leave the hospital with any needed medications and prescriptions, be advised about when to schedule an appointment with your doctor, be fully instructed about caring for yourself, and be instructed about the proper use of prescribed medications. If you are not going home to recover but to another facility, the hospital's Department of Social Services should make those arrangements for you. If assistance with home care is required, you or someone responsible for your care should be informed about available services.

Outpatient and Ambulatory Surgery

Most people don't look forward to being patients in hospitals in spite of the fact that there *are* times when a hospital is the best place to be. Now, compounding the problems of choosing a hospital, there are other choices that at best are poorly understood—if they are understood at all. Supposing you need a surgical procedure that you've been told can be performed on an outpatient or ambulatory basis. Do you know what this means and understand why Medicare and other insurances may require that the procedure be done this way? Remember, there's more to surgery than where it's performed, whether or not you get home the same day, and finding the lowest possible price. The real considerations should be how well qualified the surgeon is and how safe it is to have surgery outside the confines of a hospital.

Outpatient surgery began to emerge in the United States in the early 1970s and grew in popularity because of the nationwide shortage of hospital beds. In the beginning, hospitals lost money because the extra days that once were billed for patients recovering in the hospital were lost when they went home the same day. But as hospitals became more sophisticated, the tables turned and most hospitals learned how to make outpatient surgery financially beneficial. It's estimated that as many as forty-five percent of all surgeries performed today are done on an outpatient basis.

In the fledgling days of outpatient surgery patients literally said, "No way. Not me." They preferred checking into hospitals if only because surgery conjures up images of pain, incapacitation, and general misery. The medical profession was equally unsure and skeptical about which procedures could be done safely. Doctors weren't any more eager than patients to jump onto the outpatient-surgery bandwagon. But all that has changed. Outpatient surgery worked and patients became supporters when they found out that they could have surgery, go home, and still get well. And patients liked outpatient surgery's lower co-payments compared to an expensive stay in the hospital.

Predictably, after hospitals proved the success

of outpatient-surgery programs, physicians caught on and decided a number of procedures could be done inside their own offices and clinics, thereby bypassing hospitals entirely. This alternative became known as ambulatory surgery.

Outpatient and ambulatory surgery are *not* the same. The one thing they both promise is to get you in and out and back home in one day. The difference is that outpatient surgery is performed *inside* a hospital and ambulatory surgery is performed *outside* a hospital at a freestanding ambulatory surgicenter, a physician's office, or a medical clinic.

Most people assume that there is some official organization somewhere that is the watchdog or overseer that makes certain doctors practice medicine according to some set of rules and regulations. The truth is that there is almost none of this kind of regulation. If you talk to two doctors about a sprained wrist, one might suggest using it as quickly as possible and the other may direct you to not use it at all and to keep it in a sling. And when we're advised that we need surgery, there is no final authority to turn to for answers—we're on our own.

There also is no official organization that specifies how operations should be performed and what should or shouldn't be removed or the best way to do the procedures. Consequently, who the surgeon should be and how qualified he or she may be is one mighty tough question to answer. The same is true about the facility where a surgical procedure is going to be performed.

Hospitals and ambulatory surgicenters don't *perform* surgery—they're places where *surgeons* perform surgery. Both employ the people needed to assist surgeons and help patients recover. They also purchase and supply technical equipment, medications, operating rooms, postoperative recovery rooms—everything needed to take patients from admittance to discharge. A not-too-subtle difference separates them, however. If something goes wrong, a patient having outpatient surgery in a hospital doesn't have to worry about whether or not super-expensive equipment generally housed only in hospitals will be available. Fully staffed and equipped hospitals back outpatients with everything they provide for inpatients. And if a hospital stay *is* required, being admitted isn't necessary—an outpatient simply becomes an inpatient.

People checking into ambulatory surgicenters or hospitals for outpatient surgery can expect to have surgical procedures performed, to be taken to postoperative recovery, and then returned to a holding area until well enough to be released—often before noon the same day. Procedures being performed on an outpatient and ambulatory basis include cataract removals, foot surgery, hernia repair, cosmetic surgery, arthroscopy, and various gynecological procedures, to name but a few.

Perhaps the greatest concern governing an ambulatory surgicenter—sometimes called a "doc-in-the-box"—is accountability. Think about it. If we have trouble choosing among three hospitals that are governed by codes, regulations, and laws that are very stringent, how do we choose among ambulatory surgicenters? One means of determining a hospital's accountability can be accomplished with a telephone call or visit to find out if it is accredited. (See p. 198, Choosing a Primary Hospital, Question 10.) But deregulated, ambulatory surgicenters can vary from those that are small and intimate to those so large they have every appearance of being a hospital. And then there's the accountability of the doctors. In order for a doctor to be able to perform surgery in a hospital, he or she must be granted that privilege and be a member of the staff. That alone is no guarantee that he or she is the best there is; it simply tells you that by the standards set by that hospital the doctor is qualified.

Some ambulatory surgicenters are owned by doctors and others are owned by investors who employ doctors. And since most do not have to worry about certificate-of-need regulations that apply to hospitals, they have greater flexibility in being able to respond to changing market trends. There also are strong financial incentives for opening them. Although doctors fees are about the same regardless of where the surgery is performed, ambulatory surgicenters eliminate the inconvenience of doctors wasting time driving to visit patients in hospitals—time, incidentally, that can't be billed. And the surgicenter also profits from X-rays, blood tests, supplies, and other highly marked-up products. To be fair, these services are not only "cash cows" for ambulatory surgicenters; the same is true for hospitals.

So now we come to the Senior American whose bunion has become so painful he's finally decided to have something done about it. Where does he go? Does he choose the well-advertised ambulatory surgicenter specializing in foot surgery that promises the best prices in town, assuring him he'll be well enough to be driven 100 miles home in the late afternoon? Does he find a surgeon in the Yellow Pages and call to find out if the surgery can be done on an outpatient basis in the nearest hospital—or does he let a toss of a coin make the decision for him?

If you've read the section "Choosing a Primary Doctor," you know the answer. You call your primary doctor and schedule an appointment—whether the problem is bunions, cataracts, arthroscopy, or anything else. Your primary doctor should always be your point of reference—the person you talk to first. He or she knows *your* medical history and is in the best position to anticipate another medical problem that could occur. Most important, he or she knows—or can find out—the qualifications of the surgeon being recommended, as well as the best and safest place for you to have the surgery performed.

Like everything else, there are good and bad doctors, good and bad hospitals, good and bad outpatient surgery programs, and good and bad ambulatory surgicenters. Choosing among them is the tough job. Any decision regarding an outpatient or ambulatory surgical procedure should always be made with the help of your primary doctor.

Choosing a Pharmacist and Drug Store

Pharmacists are key members of every Senior American's health team. Just as I strongly recommend choosing a hospital and primary doctor, I feel the same way about selecting a pharmacist who understands you and your medical history. It makes no difference if the pharmacist works in a large drug store located in a shopping mall or two blocks from home—what is important is that he or she knows you and is interested in your well-being. Although I believe it is everyone's responsibility to know exactly what drugs have been prescribed, what they are for and any possible side effects, a pharmacist can be the key in making certain drugs are used as they should be.

Tragically, many Senior Americans needlessly suffer from misuse and unintentional abuse of prescription and nonprescription drugs that could contribute to increased longevity and to an improvement in the quality of life. This happens for a number of reasons:

- Prescription and nonprescription medications—intentionally or unintentionally—are used improperly.
- Senior Americans are more likely to be taking more than one drug—often simultaneously. This makes them more likely to experience adverse side effects and dangerous drug interactions. *The greater the number of drugs being taken, the greater the risk.*
- Changes in the body related to age diminish a person's ability to tolerate drugs and can increase the likelihood of adverse reactions.
- Poor communication between doctors and patients, as well as between patients and pharmacists, prevents the kind of understanding people need to use prescribed drugs and other medications safely and properly.

When people intentionally misuse drugs, it is usually because they lack proper information. If Senior Americans deliberately ignore directions governing how the drugs should be taken, it is usually because pills or capsules are hard to swallow, the medication tastes bad, the medication or prescription is unpleasant to use, or because it has unpleasant side effects. Directions for taking medications are important and deliberate misuse can have serious effects.

In each case, a pharmacist may be able to help with whatever causes the deliberate misuse of the drug. For example: Capsules can be easier to swallow than pills—they often can be opened and the contents sprinkled on food. Some pills—*not all*—can be cut in half or chewed. Bad-tasting medicines often can be diluted in fruit juices. Your pharmacist may know of one drug manufacturer producing a better-tasting medicine than another. Sometimes dosages can be made easier to use. Although unpleasant side effects may be unavoidable with some drugs, others can often be relieved. In any case, your doctor or pharmacist can advise you.

10 Questions to Ask Your Pharmacist

After talking with a number of pharmacists, I've developed a list of questions that they agree are important for each Senior American to ask—and have answered—before choosing a pharmacist.

1. *What can I do to establish a good relationship with you and this pharmacy?*

   A good relationship with anyone is a two-way agreement. All the pharmacists I talked to welcomed the idea of Senior Americans asking questions and volunteering forthright and honest information about medical histories. And they recommend always asking the following questions when drugs or medications are purchased:

 • What times during the day should I take this drug?

- Should I take this drug with food or on an empty stomach—should I avoid alcohol or certain foods?
- Are there any possible side effects I need to know about?
- Will you explain the label directions to me?
- Is it safe to take this drug with other drugs I am taking? (This includes prescription and non-prescription drugs and medications.)

2. *As my pharmacist, how accessible will you be?*

You want to be told that it isn't necessary to go through channels that can include a cashier or clerk. If you need to talk to a pharmacist, he or she should be readily accessible. You also want the assurance that important information about proper use of medication will be voluntarily provided and that you are encouraged to call any time you have questions. A pharmacist is a professional who should be genuinely interested in you. If answers to your questions are provided with any annoyance or hostility, think twice. *Note:* If you have an American Security Card℠ screening of your drug information can be done quickly by a pharmacist to determine possible drug interactions or side effects that could occur. Ask your pharmacist if he or she will screen your card each time you purchase prescriptions or other medications.

3. *Will you advise me before substituting a generic drug for a brand-name equivalent?*

In some states generic drugs can be substituted at the discretion of your pharmacist without a physician's knowledge. Therefore, you should always ask whether or not a generic drug is being substituted, whether or not the generic and brand-name drug are equivalent, and what the difference is in price between the generic and brand-name drug. The decision to switch to or accept a generic drug should always be done with the advice of your doctor or pharmacist. Generic drugs that most often are equivalent include cold and allergy products, nonprescription drugs, antibiotics, painkillers, arthritis and high-blood-pressure medications.

4. *What are the normal business hours?*

This question is important because it establishes whether or not the pharmacy hours will accommodate your needs. For example: If you are dependent on someone having to drive to pick up prescriptions and he or she can only do that after work, a pharmacy that closes at 5:00 P.M. won't work for you.

5. *Do you provide emergency prescription services after hours and on holidays?*

This is a very important factor to consider in the selection of a pharmacy. Since no one can control when illness occurs, it's necessary to know if a prescription can be filled in an emergency that happens after hours or on a holiday.

6. *Does the pharmacy deliver?*

Many pharmacies will deliver and some charge a nominal fee for the service. For the person who lives alone or who doesn't have access to transportation, this service is a very good buy for the money. The pharmacists I talked with told me that although many drug stores don't advertise delivery service, it's often available on request.

7. *How competitive are your prices?*

Here is where I recommend you do some homework. Compare the price of one or more prescriptions by calling several different drug stores and asking prices of a specific quantity of a drug. If one drug store charges more, ask why. *Some drug stores advertise lower prices on commonly dispensed products to create a low-price image. Then, when the more unusual products are needed, consumers discover they are priced as high or higher than in other drug stores.*

8. *Are drug records readily available for insurance claims or do I have to keep track of them myself?*

The reason for this question is obvious. You need to choose a pharmacy that keeps your records up-to-date and available. In spite of most people's belief that all pharmacies keep such records, all pharmacies don't.

9. *Will the pharmacy prepare and submit insurance billing for me?*

If available, this is a wonderful service to find. Bear in mind, when increased services are offered, costs of drugs purchased may be higher as well. In my opinion, the choice of pharmacy shouldn't be based on the prices of the drugs alone—additional and important services can well be worth the added cost. As one pharmacist said, "There are no free lunches in drug stores either."

10. *Can I feel free to ask you about minor health problems?*

A pharmacist is a busy professional, not a substitute for your primary doctor. So this question isn't meant to imply that people have the right to ask frivolous questions or misuse a pharmacist's willingness to help in reasonable situations. Your pharmacist can be asked about over-the-counter cold medications, vitamins, products for insect bites, minor cuts, and so on. And if he or she suggests that you see your doctor, it means that in his or her professional opinion your illness or injury is severe enough to require medical attention. The better your pharmacist knows you and your medical history, the better able he or she will be to advise you.

Common Drug Sense

Certain drugs cannot be refilled legally in all states. All pharmacists recommend the same thing: plan ahead. If you're planning a trip and a specific quantity of a drug will be needed, purchase it before you leave. If you will need a prescription, ask your doctor to write a new one for you to take with you. And if you are traveling with needed drugs, don't put them in a suitcase that will be checked as baggage. Carry them with you. Needed medication won't do you much good if your baggage is delayed or lost. If you should be in a situation where a drug is needed and you've lost it, the importance of having established a relationship with your pharmacist becomes even more significant. If a pharmacist in another part of the country can telephone your pharmacist and be assured that what you've said is true, you'll probably be able to obtain a sufficient emergency supply of the drug to get you through.

Medicines never should be stored where they will be exposed to sunlight. They should be kept in a location that has a constant temperature and moisture level. The upper drawer of a bedroom dresser or on a closet shelf is a good choice—and also keeps them out of the reach of curious children.

Although we refer to the bathroom wall chest as the medicine chest, this is one of the worst places to keep medications. Steamy showers and concentrated heat are bad for drugs and can cause tablets and capsules to change color, fade, or stick together, and liquids can become cloudy. Some medications may lose potency and others can become toxic.

A cold place can be just as bad as a hot one. Unless your pharmacist specifically instructs you to keep medication refrigerated, never put it in the refrigerator.

- Keep all medications in their original pharmacy vials—this protects drugs from deteriorating, and their labels contain important identification information.
- Carry a list of your medications with you. Show it to each doctor, dentist, or pharmacist who treats you or fills prescriptions.
- Read labels each time you take your medications. Prescription vials tend to look alike.
- Ask your pharmacist to explain labels to you.
- Make certain you are fully awake before taking medications at night. Turn on a light so you can see.
- If you have poor vision, mark prescription vials with different color dots or other symbols.
- Measure liquid medications exactly.
- Ask your pharmacist to tell you how and when to take medication.
- Keep sleeping pills or capsules away from your bedside—it's easy to take too many accidentally.

- Never give drugs to anyone else and never take someone else's medication.
- Know which nonprescription drugs you shouldn't take.
- Observe all warnings about nonprescription drugs. If you have any questions about whether or not the drug is safe, ask your doctor or pharmacist.
- If you have difficulty opening childproof caps, your pharmacist can remove them from non-prescription or prescription drugs.
- Don't use a nonprescription drug for longer than two weeks without consulting your doctor.
- Become familiar with the ingredients in each product you may be taking. If you take more than one medicine that has the same ingredient, you could be taking an overdose.
- Throw away unused medications that are no longer needed.
- Dispose of unused medications by flushing them down the toilet.

Medicare

Sixty-one industrialized and semi-industrialized nations preceded the United States in offering some form of nationally sponsored health insurance. It wasn't until 1965 that the United States Congress passed legislation enacting Medicare. Before its enactment, millions of retirees had no insurance protection at all and were unable to get needed care. Other Senior Americans spent life savings paying for care or were forced to rely on children and other relatives when serious illness struck.

Medicare is a federal health insurance program for people sixty-five or older and certain disabled people. It is run by the federal government through the Health Care Financing Administration (HCFA) of the Department of Health and Human Services. It has two parts: Medicare Part A—hospital insurance and Medicare Part B—medical insurance.

Medicare Part A—hospital insurance helps pay for inpatient hospital care, inpatient care at a skilled nursing facility, home health care, and hospice care (also see p. 134, Assisted Independence, Hospice). Since 1965, approximately one percent of an employee's salary—an employee paying Social Security taxes—has gone to pay Medicare tax, which goes into the Hospital Insurance Trust Fund to pay the cost of this insurance. This is part of the money withheld for Social Security payments. Senior Americans who are sixty-five or older and *fully insured* under Social Security qualify for Medicare hospital insurance and are entitled to receive it as long as they live. Disabled widows and children, as well as anyone on renal dialysis or who has been the recipient of a kidney transplant are also entitled to Medicare hospital benefits. Although Medicare will pay for many health expenses, it won't cover every expense or eventuality. In addition, there is an annual hospital insurance deductible. This means that before Medicare will begin to help pay hospital bills, you have to pay the first $540. It's important to know in advance which expenses are covered and which are not.

Medicare Part B—medical insurance helps pay for necessary doctors' services, outpatient hospital services and a number of other medical services, as well as some supplies that aren't covered by Part A. It can also pay for home health services. Medicare Part B—medical insurance is not free and it is optional; you have to select this insurance and pay a monthly premium of $24.80 as of 1988. In addition, you must pay a stipulated amount of money (deductible) for medical expenses before Medicare begins to pay medical bills. The rate in 1988 is $75 and has to be paid only once each year. After that, Medicare will pay eighty percent of *approved charges*.

Part A—Hospital Insurance

1. *What is a benefit period?*

   A benefit period begins when you enter a hospital and ends when you have been out of the hospital or skilled nursing facility for sixty consecutive days. There is no limit on the number of benefit periods you can have. If you should have an extended illness that extends longer than ninety days, Medicare Part A hospital insurance includes an extra sixty hospital days that are called lifetime *reserve days*. The decision to use these days is up to you. However, they can be used *only once in a lifetime*. If you do not want to use your reserve days, you are required to notify the hospital in writing of your decision. If you do not notify the hospital, it will automatically use your reserve days. The point is, when the reserve days are used up, they are gone forever.

2. *What are the hospital (Part A) and medical (Part B) deductibles and what do they mean?*

These are amounts of money that you must pay in addition to what Medicare Part A and Medicare Part B insurance will pay for hospitalization and medical bills.

During 1988, from the first day of hospitalization through the sixtieth day in each benefit period Medicare Part A—hospital insurance will pay for all covered services except the first $540. Hospitals may charge you the deductible only for a first admission in each benefit period. If you are discharged and then readmitted before the benefit period ends, you do not have to pay the deductible again. However, what is most misleading about a benefit period is this: Although the benefit period doesn't end until you've had sixty consecutive days without inpatient Medicare coverage, the $540 deductible isn't the only amount of money you may be charged. Should you be hospitalized longer than sixty days in a benefit period, you will have to make a co-payment of $135 a day between days sixty-one and ninety. If you are hospitalized 91–150 days, that rate climbs to $270 a day. Medicare coverage stops at 150 days (unless you choose to begin using your sixty lifetime reserve days) and cannot begin again until a new benefit period begins—that can't happen until there have been sixty consecutive days without Medicare coverage.

Medicare Part A—hospital insurance works differently in an approved skilled nursing facility. From day twenty-one through day 100, you will have to make a co-payment of $67.50 per day.

Medicare Part B has a $75 deductible that is paid only once each year. This deductible can be met with a combination of covered expenses. You do not have to meet a separate deductible for each different covered service you might receive.

3. *Is enrollment in Medicare Part A—hospital insurance automatic? What about Medicare Part B—medical insurance?*

As long as you have applied for Social Security and are in the system, enrollment is automatic. If you are still working, you should apply for Medicare three months before you will need its coverage. Remember that enrollment in Medicare Part B is automatic but it isn't free. There will be a monthly premium charge of $24.80/month deducted from your Social Security check unless you decide you don't want the coverage and check "No" on the form you receive from the Social Security Administration.

4. *Can other hospital insurance coverge be continued along with Medicare hospital insurance?*

The quick answer is "Yes." However, I strongly recommend that you consult with your employer's insurance office before making any decisions. There are some complicated requirements that make this a question that requires close review on an individual basis.

I also suggest that you call the Social Security office and request a copy of the *Medicare and Employer Health Plans—A Special Rule for People Age 65–69* brochure. If you are age sixty-five through sixty-nine and either you or your spouse is working, there is a special rule that may affect you. This rule, which is administered by the Equal Opportunity Commission, says that an employer with twenty or more employees must offer workers and their spouses in the sixty-five-through-sixty-nine age group the same health insurance plan that it provides for younger workers. If you are not employed and qualify for Medicare insurance, you'll probably join the eighty percent of other Senior Americans and purchase what has come to be called medigap insurance. It is so called because it's presented as being insurance that "fills the gaps" not covered by Medicare.

A note of warning: Even though there are

medigap insurance plans offered by reputable insurance companies that provide needed coverage, it's been estimated that Senior Americans spend more than $3 billion a year on useless medical insurance.

Even with Medicare Parts A and B coverage, you may have to pay almost half of your health-care costs out of your own pocket. Eighty percent of all retirees purchase the additional coverage to fill in those gaps. Private medigap insurance can help pay for the deductible and co-payments applied to hospital charges covered by Part A and the twenty percent of Part B's approved charges that are not covered, as well as for other services and supplies not covered by Medicare. The problem is that there are a bewildering number of policies for sale—many that are bad investments that don't offer adequate supplementary coverage and include only a comparatively few number of benefits for the price.

I recommend that you do two things before purchasing any medigap policy: Call your local Social Security office and request the free pamphlet, *Guide to Health Insurance for People with Medicare*. It's published by the Health Care Financing Administration and describes the many kinds of available supplemental insurance and explains how differing policies relate to Medicare.

Then consult an insurance agent you know and trust and closely examine a number of supplementary plans. (Also see p. 246 and p. 250: HMOs, PPOs.) He or she will be able to make certain the policy you purchase doesn't contain hidden loopholes in the fine print that relate to pre-existing medical conditions, coverage if you are away from your own home longer than three months in a single year, or coverage that is a duplicate of Medicare, etc.

Forty-six of our United States and Puerto Rico have adopted federal minimum standards to govern medigap policies. Although Massachusetts, New York, Rhode Island, and Wyoming haven't adopted these standards, they ask insurers to submit their policies voluntarily to the federal Department of Health and Human Services for review. If the policies are approved, they will display an emblem certifying compliance with federal standards.

5. *Do you need to carry your Medicare card?**

Yes. The card outlines your Medicare protection (hospital, medical, or both) and the date your protection started. It also displays your health insurance claim number. If your spouse is covered by Medicare, he or she will have a

---

*For information about obtaining an American Security Card® like the one I carry, see p. 440. Space is provided to list your Medicare health insurance claim number, as well as the numbers of any medigap or supplemental policies you may have purchased. It also provides a space that indicates the date your Medicare protection began.

separate card and a different claim number. Remember to show your Medicare card to any health-care facility or health-care provider when you receive services for which Medicare benefits apply.

6. *Will Medicare Part A—hospital insurance pay for surgeons' fees, private rooms, private nurses, TV, and telephone service?*

No. Medicare Part B—medical insurance does pay for surgeons' fees. However, private rooms, private nurses, TV, and telephone services are considered personal conveniences and are not covered by Medicare Parts A or B.

7. *When you need skilled nursing care do you have to be hospitalized first?*

Yes. You have to be hospitalized for at least three consecutive days (not including the day you are discharged) and then Medicare Part A—hospital insurance can help pay for care in a skilled nursing facility. The following conditions must be met in order for you to qualify for coverage:

- Your doctor must certify that you require skilled nursing or skilled rehabilitation services on a daily basis for treatment.
- Your admission must be approved by the skilled nursing facility's utilization review committee (a group of the facility's doctors), or by a Professional Standards Review Organization (PSRO).

- The facility must be certified by Medicare to have the staff and equipment necessary for Medicare's reimbursement. (See p. 130, Nursing Homes.) If the facility is not Medicare-certified, you are not covered.
- Your care cannot be custodial. Care is considered custodial if it consists mainly of assistance getting in and out of bed, dressing, eating, walking, or meeting personal needs that could be provided by persons without professional skills or training.
- You are transferred to the skilled nursing facility because you require care for a condition that was treated in a hospital.
- You are admitted to the skilled nursing facility within a short time (generally thirty days) after you have left a hospital.

Bottom line? Medicare Part A—hospital insurance will help pay for your care in a skilled nursing facility if it is considered reasonable and necessary in the treatment of your illness or injury.

8. *How many days of care in a skilled nursing facility will Medicare help pay for?*

Medicare will pay all your covered bills for the first twenty days. It will pay all your covered bills for up to eighty additional days except for a co-payment of $67.50 a day.

9. *If you need a home-health-care plan, physical therapy, speech therapy, etc., will it be covered under Medicare?*

Yes. Medicare can pay for an unlimited number of home health visits if you need part-time skilled care in your home for an illness or injury providing these four conditions are met:

- The care you require must include part-time skilled nursing care, physical therapy, or speech therapy.
- You must be confined to your home.
- A doctor must determine that you need home health care and set up a home health plan for you.
- Services must be furnished by a participating home health agency approved by Medicare.

Medicare Part A or B will pay the full, approved cost of covered home health services without a deductible or co- payment on your part. Medicare will not pay for general household services, meal preparation, assistance in bathing or dressing, or other nonmedical services.

Four Things to Remember about Home Health Care:

1. Part A will not pay for doctors' services but Part B can.

2. Medications are not covered.
3. Check with your doctor or local Social Security office to make sure the home health agency you select is Medicare-approved.
4. There are no co-payments or deductibles for home health-care services.

10. *Do you have to file claims for hospital, skilled nursing facility, or home health-care bills?*

No. Hospitals, skilled nursing facilities, and home health agencies send their bills directly to Medicare. You will be billed by the providers only for the deductible and co-payments, if any, plus charges for services not covered by Medicare hospital insurance. Medicare will send you a Medicare Benefits Record that explains the decision made on your claim and shows the services paid for. Be certain to keep copies of all your hospital and other health-care receipts. If Medicare should make a mistake in the handling of your claim, you will need documentation to prove exactly what you've paid for.

Part B—Medical Insurance

1. *Will Medicare Part B pay for routine care in a doctor's office?*

It will help pay for medical costs caused by illness or injury, but not for routine physicals.

2. *Will Medicare Part B pay for diagnostic tests ordered by your doctor which are not part of treatment?*

No. It will only pay for diagnostic tests ordered as part of the treatment for an illness or injury.

3. *What immunizations will Medicare Part B pay for?*

It will pay for immunizations that are required because of an injury or immediate risk of infection. It will also pay for the pneumococcal vaccine—a preventive pneumonia immunization particularly recommended for the elderly.

4. *Will Medicare Part B help pay for physician-prescribed drugs?*

Yes. Medicare Part B pays for prescription drugs ordered by your doctor as long as you are a patient in a hospital or nursing home.

5. *Will Medicare Part B pay for routine foot services?*

No.

6. *Will Medicare Part B help pay for a second surgical opinion?*

Yes. As a result of the increasing evidence that many conditions can—in some cases—be treated without surgery, a second doctor's opinion is recommended and may become a mandatory Medicare requirement. Medicare Part B helps pay for a second opinion. You can ask your doctor to refer you to another doctor, or you can call Medicare's Second Referral Center for the names and telephone numbers of doctors in your area who will provide a second surgical opinion. The toll-free number is 1-800-638-6833; in Maryland, 1-800-492-6603.

7. *What is the yearly Medicare Part B deductible?*

Seventy-five dollars. However, it is important that you understand that this is not the only cost for which you are responsible. After you've paid $75 in approved charges for covered services during each calendar year, Medicare Part B will pay eighty percent of approved services received during the rest of the year. You must pay the remaining twenty percent.

Approved charges most often are less than the actual charges billed by doctors and suppliers. Medicare Part B—medical insurance will pay only eighty percent of approved charges. You must pay twenty percent of the approved amount plus one hundred percent of any excess amount.

On July 1 of each year, the Medicare carrier in your area determines the approved charges for covered services and supplies. These charges are based on the charges made by doctors and suppliers during the previous year and weighted by a complex formula. When your Medicare Part B—medical insurance claim is submitted, Medicare will pay either the approved charge or the actual charge, whichever is lower.

8. *Will Medicare Part B—medical insurance pay eighty percent of the amount a doctor charges for a covered service?*

No. Medicare Part B—medical insurance will pay eighty percent of the approved charges, which most often are less than the actual charges for doctors' services.

9. *When a doctor accepts "assignment," will Medicare pay the doctor directly for eighty percent of the bill for covered services?*

Yes. If your doctor wants Medicare Part B—medical insurance payments "assigned" to him or her by Medicare, the doctor must agree not to charge you more than the Medicare-approved charge. NOTE: More than half of all doctors will not accept "assignment."

10. *If you join an HMO (health maintenance organization), do you still have to pay a Medicare Part B—medical insurance premium?*

Yes. Many HMOs make arrangements with Medicare to receive direct payments for services that aren't covered under Medicare Part B—medical insurance. Others have contracts with Medicare as HMOs and can receive direct payment for services covered by either Medicare Part A or B.

The Senior American "Health Margin"

You can get quality health care, but not without an understanding of what's out there to choose from and how to make it fit your needs. If you choose to be a Senior American who "plays it by ear" taking your chances, you may get lucky and die on a balmy day on the golf course after sinking a hole in one. Then again, maybe you won't.

It was just before World War I that the searing Flexner Report was published condemning medical standards, medical quackery, and medical education. Flexner's exposé has been credited with creating the wake that led to the beginning of the high medical education standards we benefit from today. After Flexner came the roaring twenties, which brought the licensing of physicians and denied "quacks" privileges to practice in hospitals. The reforms and uniform standards had been badly needed.

As Senior Americans, most of us have clear memories of what preceded the great depression. The national mood was euphoric and it wasn't just medicine that was progressing. All the facets of our lives were touched by rapid change, and the years that preceded Black Tuesday, October 29, 1929, were exciting—every day brought something new. Clara Bow, the elusive beauty with the incredible eyes, was exposed by the "talkies" as a sex goddess with a nasal Brooklyn accent. Babe Ruth was every boy's hero. Gertrude Ederle swam the English Channel and Red Grange carried the football for four touchdowns the first four times he had it in his hands. "Lucky Lindy" flew the *Spirit of St. Louis* to Paris and collected the unbelievable sum of $25,000 for a prize.

Stocks soared. RCA became 1929's glamour stock as the country clamored for radios, spending a billion dollars to buy them in one year. Bing Crosby, Paul Whiteman, and Kate Smith were household names and the nation gathered around its radios to laugh with Amos and Andy. Advertising crept into our lives and we learned that Coca-Cola was the "pause that refreshes" and how many people would "walk a mile for a Camel."

Thanks to the Model T and wonders like electric sewing machines and vacuum cleaners, traveling salesmen came into our lives.

The "feds" shot it out on the streets of Chicago with Al Capone. Barrels of illegal liquor were seized while speakeasies flourished—the country was having a wonderful time. "Flappers," with the metal clips "flapping" on their rubber boots, showed us how to dance the bunny hug and sing "Five Foot Two Eyes of Blue" in syncopated rhythm.

Who would have believed that the patriotism

that inspired millions of people from all walks of life to invest dollars in American business stocks would take such a turn on one terrible day? The spirit in the country was "nothing ventured, nothing gained," and in haste to climb on the money bandwagon, even shoeshine boys were enticed by easy money and bought stocks on "margin" at illegal "bucket shops." The days of "sitting on something that wasn't paid for" had begun and the country flocked to buy now and pay later.

The signs were all there, but no one wanted to listen or believe what might be coming. It was more fun to hear about John D. Rockefeller arriving at the New York Stock Exchange passing out pocketfuls of dimes to kids on the street. As the news of Black Tuesday spread across the country, radio waves became shock waves. It didn't take long for the country to recoil in disbelief as hopes for a rosy future were wiped out with "margin calls" that couldn't be met. While $7 billion went down the drain before noon the day of the "crash," panic continued to mount as reality set in. The day of reckoning was at hand. Time had run out. The dreaded "margin calls" drove people to banks and their savings hoping to find enough dollars to cover what was due and payable.

Nearly sixty years later, the "margin call" for health care has come—the bill is due and payable. Senior Americans, the people who thought they'd paid the bill when they paid into the system, are in the center of the melée. They must fill the "gaps" out of their own pockets to have a chance if the worst happens.

In spite of having greater purchasing power than any other block of people, Senior Americans face health "margins" that never before existed. It's all well and good to say that one can't compare today to yesterday when choices like kidney dialysis and bypass surgery didn't exist. But then, neither did the likelihood of cancer or Alzheimer's to the extent we face today. People whose kidneys no longer functioned died. Today, they may die or they may not, depending on available health care, getting to it in time, and being able to afford it.

So, eighty percent of all Senior Americans are hedging their "health margins" by purchasing medigap insurance hoping to plug the holes. The challenge is to find the right policy. The most important advice I can offer is that you find out everything that can be learned before parting with a single dime for a policy. Reputable insurance companies and insurance agents have no reason to object to your questions—regardless of how many or how extensive they may be. In fact, they welcome your questions. They're no more interested than you are in being linked to the low-quality insurance products I describe in the paragraphs that follow.

According to a recent report of the House Select Aging Subcommittee on Health and Long-Term Care, Senior Americans spend $12 billion on insurance annually, with three billion of those dollars purchasing worthless insurance. Sometimes I wonder if the word "billion" has become so common in our daily language that what it represents is lost. A billion is one thousand million dollars—a staggering amount of money. Now, when we think of twenty-eight million Senior Americans wasting 3,000 million dollars a year, the impact of those numbers takes on a whole new meaning. The subcommittee says Senior Americans are spending more per person on health care today than they did before Medicare was enacted and are getting less for their money.

The "scams" being perpetrated come in many forms. They can include misleading representation of coverage, scare tactics, physical intimidation, falsifying signatures on agreements, and passing Senior Americans' names back and forth between agents, resulting in the sale of unnecessary, worthless policies.

Many medigap insurers—including HMOs, PPOs, and IPAs—include "pre-existing condition" clauses in their policies that generally state that patients cannot be treated for a problem that was treated within the preceding two years. For whatever reason, Senior Americans don't seem to realize that "pre-existing" can apply to just about anything, including stomach pain, backaches, headaches—whatever.

The Subcommittee on Health and Long-Term Care was also told that the odds for persons over sixty-five spending more than ninety consecutive days in the hospital are one in 5,000, and for 120 days or longer, one in 500,000. According to Med-

icare's 1985 figures, the average length of stay in
a hospital under Medicare was 7.5 days. Yet many
medigap policies entice Senior Americans with
benefits offering thousands of dollars worth of coverage for long stays in the hospital. Other policies
offer insurance against dreaded diseases like cancer. Kathleen G. Gardner, a subcommittee staff
member, said, "It makes about as much sense as
insuring your car for various parts, the motor, the
headlight, and so forth. Cancer by its very nature
complicates other parts of the body. These conditions are not covered. The policies are fraught
with exclusions that often make it impossible for
people to collect."

Some insurance agents use a method called
"twisting," which refers to the manner in which a
person buying insurance is "twisted" and turned
from one insurance policy to another. An insurance salesperson normally earns a high commission on a policy during its first year—as much as
eighty percent of the insured's premium. During
the following years the commission goes down.
What an unscrupulous salesperson does is "twist"
the insured from company to company and policy
to policy to keep getting the high first-year commissions. Senior Americans being "twisted" between companies and policies not only lose money;
they can also lose coverage on pre-existing conditions that other policies included. Sadly, many
people confronted by smooth-talking agents telling
them to make a change or purchase an additional
policy do buy. Fear that "something could hap-

pen" is so great that they hand over their money "just in case."

Fine print in other plans states that Senior Americans who spend more than three months away from their homes aren't covered while they're away. You guessed it—now you can buy an additional policy that will provide coverage to fill this gap, too.

If I've convinced you that your primary doctor, hospital, and pharmacist are the key components of your health team, it stands to reason you'll want to make certain they stay there. Consequently, you need to know if the medigap policy promising peace-of-mind and the medical care of your fondest dreams includes *your* hospital and *your* doctor or has a clause requiring that certain problems be treated at a hospital fifty miles away with specialists included in the plan. If the plan locks you into a group of physicians, it means what it says. No matter that you want a doctor not included in the group, if it's a cardiologist that you need and the group includes one, that's the doctor you'll get— unless you want to pay all bills out of your own pocket.

If long-term care in a nursing home is a worry, there are thirty to forty reputable insurance companies that now offer coverage.

One more time I make my point—old age is not for sissies. You are the consumer who pays the bill. This alone gives you whatever rights you choose to exercise before purchasing anything. Medigap insurance not only entails a significant expenditure of dollars to pay premiums; it represents whether or not you can pay for "quality" care when you need it. An insurance agent needs complete information about what you are looking for, how much you intend to spend, whether or not you want to purchase long-term care, if you need coverage that will include travel away from your home for an extended period of time or out of the country. You need to know exactly what the coverage includes and the ramifications of any hidden clauses that may exist.

In 1980, Congress passed the Baucus amendment to the Social Security Act in an effort to reduce medigap abuses. Although it left the regulation of insurance up to individual states, it outlaws the sale of multiple policies and establishes a minimum standard for medigap policies. Make no mistake about it, insurance agents or companies involved in any of the abuses described can lose their licenses to conduct business entirely.

If you have any doubts about an insurance agent's reputability, the policy he or she is trying to sell, or the company offering the policy, get as much information as you can and ask for the telephone number of the company or plan represented. Then call the number and ask for someone you can talk to about your concerns.

If you think someone is trying to "twist" you or "rip you off" in any other way, call the Chamber of Commerce and ask for the phone number of your state's insurance commissioner. This office maintains a staff who will look into any complaint or concern you may have and answer your questions. Another office that can help is your county's district attorney's office. "Scams" that may be running in your area are reported here first.

If you'll take the time and put some effort into the search, you can locate the coverage that fits your need. Then, if your "health margin" should be called, you'll be in a position to pay the bill. It may be some of the most valuable time you'll ever spend.

What in the World Are DRGs?

A new system known as Diagnosis-Related Groups now governs how hospitals are paid for patients covered by Medicare. It began in 1967 when Yale–New Haven Hospital contacted Robert Fetter, a Yale management professor, to see if industrial quality control theory could be used to determine if the hospital was spending its budget wisely. After considerable research, Fetter and some graduate students suggested that the hospital classify its admissions by diagnosis—an idea that became known as Diagnosis-Related Groups, or DRGs.

Following a congressional panic in 1982 over

fear that Social Security was heading toward bankruptcy, DRGs became part of the Medicare system. The legislation to bail out Social Security
included a rider regarding DRGs that went through
committee in two months.

DRGs have no bearing on anyone younger than
sixty-five and they put a stop to hospitals billing
Medicare on a pass-along basis. However, they
have no impact on physicians who continue to pass
along charges.

Four hundred and sixty-eight DRGs have been
identified and a price that will be paid has been
established for each one. For example: Let's say
a man is hospitalized for hernia surgery. It makes
no difference whether he is hospitalized for two
days or ten days. The hospital will be paid a flat
fee. That fee has been based on what's been determined to be an average length of stay for that
diagnosis—in this case, hernia. When deciding which
group a patient falls within, age and other health
problems also are considered. Consequently, an
eighty-six-year-old woman with a heart condition
and diabetes won't fall in the same group as the
fifty-eight-year-old man with a hernia and no other
medical problems.

Hospitals must provide whatever length of stay
is needed to care for a diagnosed condition even
if it costs more than DRGs allow. In spite of this
fact, there is a mistaken belief among some people
that because patients are being discharged sooner,
they are also being discharged before it is safe to

send them home. Yet even though individual cases of such abuse are possible, a recent investigation by the Senate Committee on Aging uncovered no widespread evidence to support such charges.

It's too early to know exactly what long-term effect DRGs will have since the program has only been in existence since 1983. Consequently, it's important that Medicare beneficiaries understand their rights. If a patient or his or her family does believe that a discharge was improper, Medicare ombudsmen are available to help file an appeal for a hearing.

Health Plans

Health Maintenance Organizations—HMOs

Health maintenance organizations provide health insurance for members who agree to obtain all their medical care from doctors and hospitals that are included in the insurance plan. Some HMOs pay one hundred percent of the cost of care; others require a limited co-payment.

An HMO gets paid in advance, not following treatment, and premiums reflect an *average* cost instead of the *actual* cost for each member. At the present time, more than ten percent of the U.S.

population belongs to an HMO. HMOs are attractive to patients because no unexpected costs are encountered. The problems within an HMO, however, can be considerable. In the days before HMOs, doctors had an incentive to perform tests, take X-rays and run up bills because the costs could be passed along to insurers. However, when HMO profits are affected by higher costs, there is a temptation to delay treatment and reduce the number of diagnostic tests. Obtaining a referral to a specialist not included in the HMO can be difficult, and it's questionable how good the quality of care really is.

Recently, a scary new phenomenon has emerged in the managed health care scene, in the form of a doctor called a "gatekeeper." The gatekeeper's task is to screen patients for other doctors and to decide who needs a specialist or hospital and who doesn't. Obviously, it costs an HMO less *not* to refer patients to specialists and hosptials. To sweeten the pot, some "gatekeeping" doctors earn a percentage of the monies they save by *not* referring. Talk about an incentive!

An HMO has three characteristics:

• It includes a specific group of physicians who provide comprehensive health services. They agree to provide services for all medical needs. Hospitalization and referrals to outside specialists are coordinated and controlled by the HMO.

- HMO members are enrolled within a designated area and agree to receive all their care through the HMO.
- A prepaid premium amount is established for a specific period of time (generally one year), and payments are made on a regular basis, usually monthly. Some HMOs are supplemented by limited co-payments.

There are four basic types of HMOs:

- Staff—Health services for HMO members are provided through a physician group established to provide health services for members. Physicians are salaried staff of the HMO. Some staff HMOs own hospitals but most develop affiliations with one or more independent hospitals.
- Group—This type of HMO contracts with a physician group to provide health services. The "group" is compensated on a capitation or prepaid basis. Patients generally are hospitalized at a single hospital where the group physicians have staff privileges.
- Independent Practice Association (IPA)—This type of HMO contracts with an association of physicians—doctors practicing alone and groups of doctors—to provide health services. Physicians usually are paid on a fee-for-service basis. Patients often are hospitalized in more than one hospital because physicians are located throughout a given area.
- Network—This HMO contracts with two or more

group practices to provide health services. Physicians usually are paid on a capitation or prepaid basis. Large networks often use a number of different hospitals.

Health Care Plans—HCPs

An HCP can be organized in any way the participating providers wish as long as it offers comprehensive medical coverage. An HMO's premium is prepaid; an HCP's premium may or may not be prepaid. In addition to being organized in any of the four types of HMOs described, an HCP presents an alternative called a Health Care Alliance. In an Alliance, physicians continue to practice in their offices and are reimbursed on a risk-free, fee-for-service basis. The Alliance is like a regular insurance plan except that members agree to receive their care only from Alliance physicians.

Alternative Delivery System— ADS and Competitive Medical Plans—CMPs

Alternative Delivery Systems or Competitive Medical Plans include almost any organization that combines physician and hospital services that can be purchased on a competitive price basis. These systems compete for members on the basis of specific services, prices, or premiums—conventional or prepaid.

Preferred Provider
Organizations—PPOs

Preferred Provider Organizations have a considerable advantage over HMOs because they can come into being without clinics having to be built and without converting doctors into employees. And with a growing shortage of patients, many doctors will sign on with any plan that offers business. In a PPO, a group insurer agrees to direct its members to specific hospitals and doctors in return for volume discounts. This serves two purposes: The providers (doctors and hospitals) get their needed referrals, and members get lower premiums. What a PPO does is limit the choice of physician in return for reduced prices.

Individual doctors can join more than one PPO, HMO, or IPA in addition to seeing patients who aren't members. Most of the large insurers are forming PPOs to appeal to their largest customers—corporations.

4
The Right to Financial Security

Senior Americans have the right to manage their financial affairs, as well as the right to complete information and full disclosure of possible consequences from those through whom they seek assistance with the management of those affairs.

"Answer questions about money matters in language that can be understood, and if you see a Senior American heading down the wrong road, speak up."
—Art Linkletter

Regardless of the image we're given that allows the Pepsi Generation a corner on the market for fast living, fun, and disdain for the "establishment," there have been some astounding changes among Senior Americans who drink Pepsi, too. Turning sixty-five no longer means the beginning of the end. Today it means we want to continue having fun, looking good, living well, learning, traveling, taking on challenges, and reaching new goals. Luckily, many of us have the money to achieve these things while preserving what we value most— our independence. We're the older half of the Pepsi Generation and don't view advancing age as a time for others to take us under their wings so we can dodder through the last years of our lives without making waves. More of us than ever have planned well and are independently stepping into retirement without undue strain.

That's the good news.

On the other side, there are many Senior Americans wanting the same things who find themselves unprepared to manage in today's complicated financial world and who become easy prey for those deliberately intent on misleading or enticing them into spending money. Still other Senior Americans make *themselves* victims because they won't face up to the economic realities of their current situation, or because they don't know what to do and are anxious to believe anything that sounds good. There are also a sizable number of Senior Americans who ignore the changing times, preferring to cling to beliefs that are no longer valid.

Among the Senior Americans with whom I spoke about financial matters is Jeannette, who is in her early seventies and attempting to weave a path through the maze of money matters that were handled exclusively by her husband. While he was alive they never really thought about retirement. Sure, they put money away for a rainy day, but never believed deep down that the day would arrive. Now, faced with his death and money management in her own hands, where does she turn: to the kids, to the bank, to a financial adviser, to an investment counselor, or does she just let the chips fall where they may and hope for the best?

Then there's Bridget, a new divorcée in her late

fifties who's in her second year of selling real estate and doing well. A stubborn Irish realist, she began to prepare for the inevitable by getting her real estate license when she accepted the fact that her husband was going to force a divorce and she'd have to go it alone. On her own now, she's trying to replace those things that once were part of the marriage package. She's working hard to catch up but doesn't really know what to do. She's discovered that if she works long enough hours she barely has to think about it at all.

I met a man named Joe, who became a widower in his early seventies when his wife died following an extended illness that drained savings and every dime of borrowing capacity against insurance policies. Now he rattles around in a big house filled with memories and isn't sure what he ought to do, so for the most part, he's doing nothing. He did have the carpeting changed in the bedroom where his wife died, repainted the walls a dull beige, and moved in a single bed, converting what once had been their bedroom into something resembling a monk's cell. And in the following spring he plowed the flower gardens under, covering soil needing weeding with lava rock and bushes. He'll never admit it, but he's counting on his serious heart condition intervening before he has to move somewhere else, make any major decisions and—*before the money runs out.*

And then there's Dorothy, who worked in a paper mill all her life. As the youngest of eleven children, she cared for her aged parents until their deaths. Her brothers and sisters felt it was only fair that she inherit the homestead in exchange for the years she'd given up for their parents. After they died, she sold the homestead and paid cash for a tiny house that exactly fit her needs. She continued to work, putting aside a little here and there for her retirement, counting on Social Security and her pension to see her through. As always, she drove around town paying bills in cash, keeping her savings securely hidden in a metal box in the basement root cellar.

Retirement freed time she'd always wanted to concentrate on her garden and the multiple craft projects she enjoyed with her friends. For thirteen years everything went well. Her only nearby relatives were a niece and her husband who looked in on her. Shortly after her niece died from a sudden illness, Dorothy had a severe heart attack. When she was discharged from the hospital, she was faced with recovering, the maze of paperwork involved with Medicare, and severely strained funds. Her niece's husband, Bill, had kept up with her affairs while she was hospitalized and now offered to help her manage her money. He began by insisting that the nearly $8,000 in cash she kept stashed in the root cellar be moved to a bank to earn money until they decided what to do with it. Dorothy wasn't an easy sell. She remembered what her parents went through during the Great Depression. She was barely over the shock of entrusting her money to a bank when Bill insisted she not only could but *would* learn how to write checks and balance a checking account.

She was fortunate. Bill enjoyed the challenge and did such a good job teaching her, faithfully showing up every Wednesday afternoon to help, that her friends began to show up, too. Within a year, Bill was running a virtual investment club— giving lessons on managing checking accounts, handling government paper work, and counseling her friends on their money problems.

Regardless of the common bonds among these five representative Senior Americans, there are also considerable differences. Joe has all the skills he needs; he just doesn't care. Bridget probably will take hold of her finances in the future. Right now she has all she can manage to get through a day at a time without the added agony of looking at a future that depends entirely on what *she* does or doesn't do. Jeannette? She's the perfect example of a live target for whoever offers to carry a burden she has no idea how to handle. It's the relationship among Bill, Dorothy, and her friends that is indicative of the financial know-how that I think is the right of all Senior Americans.

When phrases, acronyms, and assumptions are tossed onto the table without explanation, we literally shut out anyone who isn't fully informed. Several things result. A good number of people remain silent lest they appear ignorant, others continue as they have for years hoping for the best, and still others are victimized by those who recognize their lack of understanding and underlying fears—people who capitalize on a lack of sophistication as they offer to "help."

More than anything, Dorothy's underlying fear was that any foray into the "professional" arena might result in her surrendering the independence she'd fought so hard to preserve. She trusted Bill. He'd never lied to her, had taken the time to look in on her, and factored for her lack of financial skills without insulting her intelligence.

Dorothy isn't alone. How many well-educated, worldly people fake it today where the intricate world of money is concerned? Next time you are with a number of people, do a little homespun surveying to see who can provide an accurate definition of a commonly bandied-about term like CDs. Follow that by asking whether or not they can tell you what licensure is required for those calling themselves financial planners; to define *money market funds;* or tell you what *compound interest* is all about.

I firmly believe that financial institutions like banks and savings and loans have a real responsibility where Senior Americans are concerned—for that matter, where Americans of any age are concerned. Regardless of how large or small the nest egg, what, if any, investments you have, or how much property is involved, it is essential that you know where to go and what to ask those you'll entrust with your money. You have the further right never to be intimidated by language and terms you don't understand or to be patronized by someone with a specialized knowledge you don't share. Backing that statement is *your* right to withdraw *your* money and find an institution that will take the time to help.

On every billboard, in every newspaper, on TV and radio, we hear about the "friendly" banks, savings and loans, financial planning companies, and credit unions that want to do right by us— "trust us," their spokesmen say. The relationship all Senior Americans are entitled to was demonstrated through Bill, Dorothy, and her friends. He took the time to see the holes in information, teach, explain, and guide seventeen women who needed his help.

Don't you wish our bankers would do the same for us?

FINANCIAL CHOICES

Senior American Financial Security

Modern banking's roots extend all the way back to the seventeenth century in The Netherlands and England. What began there spread to the New World when the Bank of North America was incorporated in Philadelphia on May 26, 1781. Since then, we've seen a lot of changes in what began as austere, formidable, pillared sanctuaries. Like hospitals, banks now advertise, offer premium promotions, and make every effort to convince consumers that they care more than their competitors. When they succeed, consumers deposit money, open checking and savings accounts, secure and pay off loans with interest, lock valuables in safe deposit boxes, and use the services of their departments.

Because money is bought and sold, it's a commodity just like poultry or cotton. Consequently, banks are highly competitive. Therefore, it's important to know what distinguishes one from another before choosing where you will entrust your money. And why not? Isn't it fair that your friendly bank should be expected to work as hard for your money as you did to earn it?

It's as important to establish a primary relationship with one person in the bank as it is to choose a primary doctor. He or she is the person you talk to first when you need assistance. Financial choices are no longer confined to buying savings bonds and finding the highest interest on bank accounts— or for the high rollers, the stock market. Today's choices are so extensive it would take several books just to scratch the surface of available alternatives.

The terminology alone is staggering—it's a language that I doubt few people outside those who must use it every day understand.

Financial institutions are fond of proclaiming their "full-service" capabilities. What really defines these words, however, is how *you* are treated and what kind of help *you* receive. My interest is in helping you see that *your* best interest is served. If that's going to happen, you need to establish a mutually trusting relationship with "your banker" as securely as you establish it with "your doctor." It makes no difference where you presently bank or how long you've been there; if you don't already have a banker on your side, you need one. Regardless of how much or how little, it is *your* money and *your* financial security that is at stake. If you keep that thought front and center, you won't hesitate to ask whatever questions need answering and you'll provide complete, accurate information for "your banker" to consider so he or she can best assist you.

A word of advice. Senior Americans tend to be fond of running from one financial institution to another because one offers an eighth of a point more on a CD than a competitor, or a special gift promotion. If you move around every time something is offered, a budding relationship stops and you're back to square one. More important, the real price of the "deal" being offered could cost you the services you need most. It makes more sense to concentrate your financial power—however large or small it may be—in one institution so you can build as much financial clout as possible. A trusted, mutual relationship—once established—can make the difference if and when you need help.

Banks aren't the only financial institutions out there. Savings and loan associations are offering more and more services that overlap those offered by banks. Savings and loan associations are regulated by the Federal Home Loan Bank Board, which protects savers against losses on their deposits up to $100,000 through the Federal Savings and Loan Insurance Corporation (FSLIC). The purpose of the FSLIC is to provide stability to the savings and loan industry while providing safety to small savers by offering insurance for savings accounts. It also is concerned with helping the industry attract funds for economical home financing.

However, a word of warning needs to be sounded.

More than 500 savings and loans nationwide are in very weak condition. It has been reported that one S & L customer in three has a chance of being with a financially troubled institution. Unfortunately, financial statements will not give you the complete picture regarding the soundness of an institution. If you are interested in obtaining a brief and reliable analysis of the condition of an insured savings and loan's—or an insured bank's—financial condition, there is a company that can provide it. The charge for an analysis of the S & L or bank you want to know about is $20. Write:

VERIBANC
P.O. Box 2963
Woburn, Massachusetts 01888

The Federal Home Loan Bank Board also provides a free pamphlet about savings and loan associations entitled *There Ought to Be a Law . . . There Is*. To request a copy, write or telephone:

Consumer Division, Office of Community
Investment
Federal Home Loan Bank Board, 2nd Floor
1700 G St., N.W.
Washington, D.C. 20552

Telephone: 202-377-6209

Since my purpose is to help you establish a primary resource for managing your money, my references are to banks and bankers. However, if you select a savings and loan as your primary financial institution, the same principles apply.

Finding "Your Banker"

Let's assume that you don't have someone you consider "your banker" and want to locate him or her. Before looking inside the bank, you'll want to decide if the bank itself is conveniently located. Although location isn't everything, if "your banker" is nearby, so much the better. If you are in a large city, a bank with a network of branch banks offers considerable convenience and flexibility. You'll also want to consider banking hours and whether or not the institution has drive-in banking and automatic teller machines.

Once you've selected a bank you'd like to consider, telephone and ask if an officer of the bank is assigned to helping Senior Americans. If the answer is "Yes," make an appointment. If the answer is "No," ask for an appointment with an officer of the bank who *can* meet with you. When you keep the appointment, these are the essential questions that need answers:

1. *I'm interested in establishing a working relationship with someone at this bank who can become my personal contact and help me with my affairs. Can you arrange that for me?*

   Legally, banks are not permitted to give investment advice to clients. No problem. You aren't seeking a financial planner or investment counselor. What you are seeking is a person who can guide you through the complexities of banking—someone who becomes familiar with your affairs and can direct you to options you might want to consider, caution you when appropriate, or provide a referral to someone else—like a financial planner or investment counselor. You need someone able to explain things you don't understand and who is willing to answer questions when you have them. Whatever "full services" and benefits are offered, they're meaningless if you don't know how to use them.

NOTE: There is a fine line between knowingly looking the other way when someone is headed down a dangerous road because giving advice is illegal and caring enough to provide warnings that need to be considered. In my opinion, a trusting relationship with "your banker" means he or she will sometimes caution you or ask you to consider other options.

2. *Will this person be my primary contact or is it the bank's policy to have me contact whoever happens to be available?*

If you're told that the bank can't promise that the same person will be available on a continuing basis, find another bank. I feel strongly about this because a trusted relationship involving your finances won't happen if you receive the supermarket approach and end up shifted from person to person. Explaining financial affairs is a somewhat delicate matter. Most people are cautious about those with whom they discuss their affairs and it is a laborious process to go through all the details. You need to lay out your financial condition—income, assets, liabilities, investments, as well as your expectations and needs for financial security in the years ahead. Once that's done, it's time to learn what services the bank offers that can be applied to your particular financial condition and future expectations, as well as any other services you may need that are not offered but can be obtained with a referral.

Banks process a tremendous amount of paper-work, and at times mistakes are made. When a mistake involves you it's upsetting. This is another reason you need a personal contact who can quickly help you straighten out an error. It's easy to get lost in bank bureaucracy.

3. *To what extent will "my banker" oversee my financial affairs and provide assistance and direction; on what basis may I feel free to telephone him/her or schedule an appointment?*

Consider the following example: Suppose you have a Certificate of Deposit (CD) that comes due and needs to be reinvested. Is it the bank's policy to send a form letter telling you it's coming due in the next thirty days and that unless you provide notification it will automatically be reinvested in a similar instrument at the current market rate? Or will you get a phone call and be informed about options and other available choices you might want to consider? You are seeking personalized service that will allow you to realize the greatest benefits you can achieve with your monies. However, it's only fair to point out that no one has the right to expect a relationship that permits daily phone calls. Bankers are busy people and deserve consideration in terms of scheduling appointments and answering or returning telephone calls.

4. *Are the bank's deposits insured by the FDIC— Federal Deposit Insurance Corporation?*

If the bank is not FDIC-insured, find another bank. It is the FDIC that insures your money up to $100,000. And if you want to house more than $100,000 in the bank, that can be done by varying the accounts and their structures. In fact, you can house several hundreds of thousands of dollars and still be FDIC-insured. This is something "your banker" can explain if you are one of the fortunate who needs such advice.

If you'd like additional information about insured deposits, write or telephone the FDIC. Request a free copy of a pamphlet titled *Your*

Insured Deposits. It provides examples of insurance coverage under the FDIC's rules about certain types of accounts commonly held by depositors in insured banks.

Federal Deposit Insurance Corporation
550 17th Street, N.W.
Washington, D.C. 20429

Telephone: 202-389-4221

5. *What special services do you offer for Senior Americans?*

More banks every day are recognizing the importance of Senior American dollars and are offering programs that are educational and informative relating to money management. Some offer special travel programs with significant discounts; others provide free checking accounts. However, it is important that you always weigh the "bonuses" against everything else you need to solidify a strong relationship with "your banker." In my opinion, it is most important to feel that you can call on your banker without being made to feel your questions are stupid or that you are intruding on his or her time.

6. *Do you have a trust department and specialists in estate planning and wills?*

First of all, not all people need trust departments and not all banks have them. If your nest egg is small, you probably don't need this help. And you may or may not need additional expertise to protect possible investments that offer financial growth. If your nest egg is large and the bank doesn't have a trust department, remember the importance of "your banker" and the relationship built on mutual trust. He or she can refer you.

Trust departments may have minimum dollar requirements in order for the department to provide trust services. However, before you decide that $50,000 (should that be the minimum) is out of your reach, consider the home you may own that's paid for and now is valued at $65,000, as well as other assets you have acquired. Although specialists in wills, investments, estate taxes, and other areas generally have their offices in the trust department, that doesn't mean you can't utilize one or more specialists if you need any of their services.

7. *If an emergency were to occur and I had to have a document signed or notarized and I was unable to come to the bank, would the bank send someone to me?*

In my opinion, this is not an unreasonable question or request—and you'll never know the answer unless you ask. If you were ill or unable to get to the bank for a legitimate reason and had to have a document signed or notarized, I think the answer should be "Yes." Expecting a bank to make a "housecall" to cash a check or pick up a deposit hardly qualifies. I am clearly referring to the kind of circumstance that would give you the license to ask a special favor of a friend.

Remember, if you expect the kind of service I've outlined, the bank has a right to expect your loyalty in return. People who jump from bank to bank every time a rate changes or a competitor offers a free toaster can hardly expect personal, caring service from a banker. In the long run, mutual loyalty grows into trust and trust grows into confidence. Once that is established, you are well on the road to building your financial security.

Once you find "your banker," you'll want to discuss basics like whether or not you and your spouse need a joint or single checking account, charges that are attached to certain bank services, minimum-dollar-balance requirements that may exist on certain accounts, bank statements that may not be easily read and understood, overdraft charges, and safety deposit boxes.

I think the overall attitude of the people within the bank toward Senior Americans is really the measuring stick. Politeness, how problems are dealt with, helpfulness, and courtesy mean a good deal. When the overall attitude is good, you have a fair indication that the bank really *is* trying to make its product—money—more serviceable.

Is the Stock Market for You?

Is the stock market a place where your fortune will be made or is it the place where you could be stripped of everything you have? The answer is "Yes" *and* "No." And the explanation for a *yes* or *no* is complicated.

Like medigap insurance policies sold by unscrupulous insurance agents who "twist" their clients from policy to policy to generate high commissions for themselves, unscrupulous stockbrokers can "churn" their clients' accounts to put monies in their own pockets. "Churning" is the practice of buying and selling securities for clients in order to generate commissions for the broker instead of profits for the client.

Before I go any further, let me assure you there are many, many conscientious stockbrokers imbued with integrity and expertise. However, the stock market is no place for an amateur who decides to gamble with a nest egg. It's an arena in which you need a stockbroker with a well-established reputation who fully understands your financial position—a stockbroker who takes the time to make certain you understand what kind of investments you're getting into, as well as the risks involved. And *you* have to be willing to do the homework required in checking references before you sign anything or turn over your money to anyone.

Senior Americans often are approached by stockbrokers saying "Trust me. I'll invest your monies in safe, long-term investments that will make money." Then, for every question posed by an inexperienced, unwitting potential investor, a smooth, warm, reassuring answer follows. After hours of patient give and take, the deal's done and the money is handed over. A "friend" has been found who says he or she understands how important it is to be cautious, that this is the nest egg and you can't afford to lose it. You're handing the money over because you *do* trust and *are* counting on your new friend's extensive knowledge to help fill your coffers.

However, not long ago, Harry Reasoner presented a segment on "60 Minutes" that profiled an eighty-four-year-old widow who turned over $321,262 to a broker at a reputable firm. When the broker was finished with her, she had $820 left. At first he invested her money in mutual funds which usually are long-term, high-quality investments. But he began recommending the funds be bought and sold on a short-term basis. The widow trusted his judgment. She had no idea that the reason he was "churning" her account was to put commissions into his own pockets. She described how the stockbroker was always there to help her with household problems and other tasks, making her feel he was looking out for her because she was alone. She considered him a trusted friend who really cared.

Finally the stockbroker put her funds into index

options—an investment area for only the most sophisticated investors. When someone gets involved in index options, he or she is trying to guess in advance whether average market prices will go up or down. Now, an eighty-four-year-old widow's account was being traded almost every day, resulting in hundreds of transactions in a six-month period. During those six months, she lost $200,000 and the broker earned more than $90,000 in commissions.

The stockbroker later described her as a greedy woman who lusted for big money. His definition of a stockbroker was someone who is there to take the orders and buy and sell for someone who wants to put money at risk. His position was that the only time this posture backfires is when a nice guy like him gets involved with someone people feel sorry for, like a widow.

The widow's only chance to reclaim some of her money was by going to arbitration. She couldn't sue because she didn't know that the standard agreement she signed with the stockbroker had waived her right to sue in federal court—she had put her signature on a document that said any disputes would have to be settled in arbitration. When it was over and all the legal fees and other expenses had been paid, her net loss was in the neighborhood of $200,000.

Horror story? Not really. One of the other people Harry Reasoner interviewed was a securities analyst who testified at the arbitration hearing. He said there was a lot of stock "churning" going on and that it's a growing problem, with the number of claims increasing every year. He said the real problem is that even though brokers *are* advisers to clients, they can't make money without buying and selling clients' stocks.

Here's my advice if you decide to invest in the stock market:

- Thoroughly research a stockbroker's references and those of the firm he or she represents. Ask to see an outline of the standards by which the firm and its brokers operate.
- React immediately—no matter how small the complaint—if a problem occurs. You want to be on record from the onset should something major occur further down the road.
- Understand that legally you cannot sue a stockbroker—arbitration is the only recourse available. However, if you stay on top of your affairs, often problems can be settled quickly and quietly if you take swift and strong action.
- Be aware of the five most common complaints heard about stockbrokers:

    Unsuitability—stockbrokers make inappropriate investments regardless of a customer's financial status.

    Unauthorized trading—stockbrokers operate on their own without their clients' approval.

    Churning—stockbrokers make frequent trades and change investments for personal gain and increased commissions.

    Lack of supervision—stockbrokers operate

freely without strict standards being imposed by brokerage corporations.

Fraud. (See p. 322.)

Do You Need a Financial Planner?

Financial planners are a relatively new phenomenon. Today it's almost an "in" thing to be able to refer to "my financial planner." The truth is that today's complex financial world created a real need for financial planners who can play an important role in or lives—sometimes. That "sometimes" is predicated on having a justifiable need and money you can afford to invest. It's also predicated on finding a financial planner who considers your entire financial picture and personal needs before developing a plan outlining immediate and long-term goals while assuring your ability to meet essential costs like housing, food, health care, and other living expenses.

The world of financial planners is comparatively complicated, and there are advantages and pitfalls you need to understand before turning the management of your finances over to someone else. First of all, while other professionals like doctors, lawyers, architects, and certified public accountants can't practice their professions without having met educational requirements and standards and passed licensing examinations, financial planners can sell their expertise without having to meet any uniform prerequisites or standards. Just about anyone can advertise himself or herself as a "financial planner."

The real question is whether or not you need help or can manage on your own. I think everyone needs some kind of financial plan, regardless of income level, to live successfully within an available income, realize personal goals, maintain a good credit history, spend more effectively, maintain a level of economic confidence, and secure a comfortable retirement. And many people are well able to produce and maintain such a plan without the services of someone else. If you have established a relationship with "your banker," he or she will be a good professional source regarding the advisability of seeking outside financial planning help.

Most financial planners are legitimate. However, be aware that there also are many unscrupulous, self-proclaimed financial planners who cheat their clients out of tens of millions of dollars every year. Anytime your financial future is involved, be cautious.

Before selecting a financial planner you need to be very well informed. To help you do that, I recommend you send for a brochure published by the Better Business Bureau entitled *Tips on Financial Planners*. It contains important information, some of which I've mentioned in this section. You can request a free copy by writing to:

Better Business Bureau
Consumer Information Services
1515 Wilson Blvd.
Arlington, Virginia 22209

Request: Publication No. 24-225 A401286
Tips on Financial Planners

Before entering into any agreements, you need to spend some real time and effort interviewing several financial planners in your area. Schedule appointments to meet with them and ask ahead of time whether or not a fee for consultation is going to be charged. Initial meetings usually are free, but don't leave yourself open to a surprise.

Although a large firm may be appealing because of its diversity of services, an independent financial planner may give you greater personalized attention. The important factors in making your decision relate to the planner's references, competence, experience, and ability to handle your account personally. It makes no sense to choose a financial planner only to find out later that your financial planning has been assigned to a junior associate without comparable experience or background.

A planner should have five or more years experience as a broker, insurance agent, accountant, or lawyer. He or she should also be known by persons you respect within your community who can provide reliable references. I also recommend taking the time to contact your state securities administrator and local Better Business Bureau to make certain the planner is complying with state and federal laws governing broker-dealers and investment advisers. You can also ask for a reliability report.

I recommend you ask for references from at least three clients the financial planner has worked with in the last several years. Then contact these people and find out how satisfied they are, what investment returns have been achieved, and what their future plans are regarding the planner. Don't rely on the recommendations of one or two new clients that you don't know. If a scheme is being promoted, an unscrupulous planner will pay off a couple of people to lure an investor like you.

Find out what professional organizations the financial planner belongs to, as well as any additional trade education he claims to have completed. This information may indicate the extent of the person's dedication to his trade, as well as providing credentials which can easily be verified.

Visit the offices of financial planners you are considering and check them out. Unscrupulous planners like to be able to pick up and leave in a hurry and aren't likely to be located in an established professional setting. Also inquire about the referral base the planner maintains with other professionals such as lawyers, accountants, real estate firms, tax specialists, etc.

Never get involved with a financial planner who

wants you to put your money into anything with a *guaranteed* short-term interest rate that exceeds prevailing market rates. No-risk promises are the number-one tipoff of a possible scheme offered as a tax shelter or new investment vehicle.

If you decide you want financial-planning assistance, first do your homework—it's up to you to protect yourself since no regulations currently exist to protect consumers. There is no question you should hesitate to ask someone you are considering entrusting with your money. Check references and talk to reputable people within your community. If you do all these things, you'll be in good, experienced hands. "Your financial planner," like "your banker," must be someone who comes to know you well and with whom you build a trusted relationship.

Estate Planning, Wills, and Trusts

Everyone needs a will. In fact, a carefully drawn will is the key to effective estate planning that takes into account the needs of your spouse, children, and other heirs. It allows you to pass on the greatest possible benefits to everyone involved. The best time to begin estate planning is ten to fifteen years before you plan to retire. The next best time to begin—if that time is already past and you haven't started—is right now.

An estate consists of whatever investments, property, and personal possessions you have accumulated during your lifetime that have monetary and sentimental value. Estate planning is the process of arranging your financial and legal affairs in a way that will provide as much comfort as possible for you and your spouse while you live—and for your heirs when you die.

A will legally declares a person's intentions after his or her death and can concern itself with the disposition of property, guardianship of children, administration of an estate, or a combination of all three. The penalty that can result—if you don't take the time to plan your estate and write a will—is to make the government one of the major beneficiaries.

Over the years, an estate often increases considerably in value because of inflation and investments. And when the value of profit sharing plans, company insurance, pensions, and other benefits has been calculated and included, it's not surprising for an average Senior American to discover that his or her estate adds up to a sizable amount.

In my opinion, a good attorney specializing in estate planning can be the most important contributor to the development and emergence of a successful estate plan. Although many attorneys can draft and write a will, not all of them have the expertise you need for estate planning. I think it's important that you find someone who does. In one sense, an attorney who helps plan your estate and write your will is like your primary doctor. He or she should be the person with whom you establish a relationship that allows you to discuss candidly your legal affairs and concerns on a continuing basis. He or she should also be a person who can advise your family and administer your affairs after your death.

Unfortunately, it's been estimated that as many as half of all Americans die intestate—without a properly drawn and executed will. However, that's not the whole story. Everyone *does* have a will because if *you* don't bother to write one, the statutes of the state in which you live will—in so many words—write it for you. Without a will, you have no executor (relative, trusted friend, lawyer, or an institution like a bank) to administer your estate. The state will take care of that, too. It will appoint someone who could be a complete stranger to your family. His or her executor's fees will be deducted from your estate, and the executor could be required to post a bond—all of which reduces your estate's value.

The bottom line? If you die without a will, nothing goes to anyone you might have wanted to have receive it. And, depending on the laws of your state, real estate and other possessions may be divided in a way that creates bitter fighting within your family. If your spouse is no longer living, each child will have an equal say in the administration of your estate. There are also a number of tax consequences.

Contrary to often-held belief, wills do not restrict anyone from doing what he or she wishes with property while still alive. A will can be changed at any time as long as it's done in legal form: you can still buy, sell, or give away property in any way you wish. There's no need to itemize possessions before making a will, and there is no public record of your will while you are alive.

If you already have a will and decide to move to a different state, you need to have it reviewed by an attorney in the new state since each state has its own specific requirements for wills. In most states, handwritten—or holographic—wills are not considered valid. And the power to execute a will is subject to several limitations. Age is one factor. So is the mental capability of the person writing the will. He or she must be sufficiently competent to know and understand the nature and act of a will, as well as everything that is being disposed of and its value. Wills must be made voluntarily, the identity of the heirs must be known, and a will cannot require an illegal action on the part of an heir.

A living or inter vivos trust is set up while you are alive and passes to your beneficiaries outside your will after your death. In a living trust, you turn over all, or some, of your assets to a trustee who manages them for your benefit. The trustee can hold, sell, manage, invest, and carry out other activities involving your assets. Whatever dividends or income are earned go to you. A legal and detailed document prepared by your attorney specifies the purposes of your trust, as well as the powers and responsibilities of your trustee. A living trust can also be a directed living trust, which means you have a say in how your investments are managed.

A testamentary trust is very much like a living trust. The difference is that it doesn't become effective until your death. It is the kind of trust that can be particularly useful in providing a well-managed base of assets for children's education, support of elderly parents, or to provide income for a spouse without adding taxable assets to the estate.

If nothing else, making decisions governing your estate will provide considerable peace of mind. Whatever your motivation, I urge you to put your house in order now.

Social Security

A lot has changed since Franklin D. Roosevelt introduced Social Security to "give some measure of protection to the average citizen and to his family against poverty-ridden old age." Although the Social Security Act was passed in 1935, the policy of withholding taxes didn't begin until 1937. Social

Security began by paying an average of $22.60 a month to people who were sixty-five or older who had worked every year since 1935. At that time, they were the only people who could collect benefits.

Social Security is our country's way of providing a continuing income when family earnings are reduced or stop because of retirement, severe disability, or death. Benefits are paid from the Social Security Trust Fund, which is primarily supported by equal contributions from employers and employees.

The philosophy behind Social Security isn't complicated. Employees, employers, and those who are self-employed pay Social Security taxes which go into trust funds to pay benefits for those who are retired, disabled, or survivors. These monies also fund the administrative costs of the program.

In the early 1980s there was considerable concern about large increases in the costs of paying Social Security benefits, as well as the overall financial soundness of the system. This occurred because the original planners had no way of knowing that an aging population, declining birthrate, unexpectedly high inflation, and unprecedented unemployment would combine to produce an unhealthy economy that would also produce an unhealthy system of Social Security.

During 1982 a literal panic ensued. In a three-ring media circus, we found out that Social Security was veering toward bankruptcy. This was followed by the appointment of a presidential commission directed to solve the problem. What resulted was a bailout package for Social Security that included a measure tacked onto the bill converting Medicare to DRGs. (See p.244, What in the World Are DRGs?) In 1983, Congress passed the Social Security Amendments which restored solvency to the Old Age, Survivors' and Disability Insurance program (OASDI). At this point, it appears that the program and its cash benefits are secure into the next century. But, of course, no one—not even the economic experts—can ever really predict what the future holds.

What You Should Know About Social Security

1. *When should you begin collecting information about Social Security?*

   At least six months before retirement so you are ready to apply three months ahead of the time you want benefits to begin. I also recommend that you begin by collecting earnings records two years before retirement. You should also call your local Social Security office and ask how you can obtain an estimate of your projected retirement benefits.

2. *What are the three basic requirements for qualification?*

   You must have enough quarters of coverage,

you must be at least sixty-two years old, and you must meet all retirement criteria.

3. *How many quarters of coverage are required for full retirement at age sixty-two and age sixty-five?*

By definition, "quarters" are four equal, three-month periods of a year beginning with the month of January. You cannot earn more than four "quarter" credits in any year regardless of your salary. For example: In 1988 one quarter of coverage is credited for each $470 earned on a job where Social Security taxes are paid by you and your employer. If you earn $1,880 (4 x $470) in a year, you earn a full year's credit of four "quarters." You'll need thirty-seven quarters of coverage if you turn sixty-two in 1988. Depending on your date of birth, you'll need thirty-four quarters of coverage in order to receive full benefits if you turn sixty-five in 1988.

4. *Should you start collecting Social Security when you are sixty-two or sixty-five years old?*

This is a question only you can answer. You need to consider economic and personal factors that will tell you when the right time is at hand. Here are some of the important issues:

- What will the effect be on your spouse and/or other dependents?
- Can you afford to retire early?

- What effect will retirement have on your pension?
- Why do you want early retirement?
- Have you made plans to replace job satisfaction with new interests, volunteer activities, relocation, or other employment?
- How is your health?

5. *How do you check your official earnings record?*

You'll need to contact your local Social Security office and ask for a copy of Form SSA 7004. Fill it out and mail it in one of the pre-addressed envelopes to the Social Security Data Center that covers your area. Your earnings statement will not seem accurate because the Social Security Administration doesn't keep track of all the money you've earned. It only lists the amount of earnings on which you've paid Social Security taxes and groups together the years 1937–1950, 1951–1978. The years from 1978 to the present are listed separately. If you are concerned about whether you've earned enough quarters of coverage, write "show quarters of coverage" on your completed SSA 7004 form.

Make certain your spouse also obtains information about earned credit and earnings at the same time you do. An insured spouse must apply to receive his or her own benefit. The exception to this rule is a widow who can choose which account to draw from—her own or as a widow of an insured spouse. There are other provisions which affect the spouse's benefit—including minimum age, disability, having a dependent younger than sixteen years of age, and divorce.

6. *How much income can be earned in one year without affecting your "retired" Social Security status?*

*In 1988 you can earn the following without penalty:

If you are under sixty-five years of age—$6,120

If you are over sixty-five years of age—$8,400

If you are older than seventy—no limit

If an established annual earnings limit is exceeded, you will lose $1 in monthly benefits for every $2 of earnings. Beginning in 1990, benefits will be reduced $1 for every $3 earned by people who are sixty-five or older.

If you do return to work full-time or earn more than the Social Security limit for a single year, you must report these earnings. Whether or not benefits cease for a given year or subsequent years that you also work will depend on the amount earned above the limit. However, these additional earnings may give you higher benefits when you stop working again.

---

*These numbers are raised when wage levels increase. During the first year of Social Security, any penalties will be based on monthly earnings.

Social Security will compute new benefits when the additional earnings have been credited to your record. You receive a special credit of about three percent for each year after sixty-five that you didn't draw benefits because you were employed. These credits will begin to increase in 1990, rising from three percent to eight percent in the year 2007. Additional credits can also increase payments for spouses, widows, and widowers.

Social Security is stringent about reclaiming overpayments in benefits. You must report all the wages earned over the limits set by Social Security, including those from jobs where Social Security taxes weren't paid. You must report gross pay, including tips, commissions, and other fees beyond a base salary.

7. *How do you find out what your estimated Social Security benefits will be?*

Call your local Social Security office, give them your Social Security number, and request an estimate. If you are between the ages of sixty and sixty-five, you can obtain an estimate by visiting the Social Security office. They can supply the answer via a computer.

8. *What counts as earnings for Social Security purposes and what doesn't?*

Since Social Security originally was designed to help replace earnings lost because of retirement, the Social Security Administration is only interested in the money you earn as wages from being employed or self-employed.

There are certain kinds of retirement earnings that do not count against your Social Security check:

- Interest on savings.
- Investment income in the form of dividends from individually owned stock.
- Income from pensions, life insurance annuities, other retirement pay or Veterans' Administration benefits.
- Gains from the sale of capital assets.
- Unemployment or worker's compensation.
- Gifts and inheritances.
- Rental income from privately owned real estate.

9. *What protection does Social Security provide for your spouse and dependent children in the event of your death?*

Surprisingly, many people don't realize that Social Security provides the equivalent of very good life insurance coverage for a widow, widower, and dependent children of someone who was employed. Generally, a surviving husband or wife continues to collect full Social Security benefits in the event of the employed's death (if the spouse is of retirement age). The exact amount depends upon the age of the spouse, the age of any children, or the presence of a serious disability within the family.

Monthly payments can be made to the following relatives of a deceased worker:

- Unmarried children under the age of eighteen (nineteen if still in high school).
- A disabled son or daughter eighteen or older; if severely disabled—before the age of twenty-two.
- A widow or widower under the age of sixty if caring for a disabled child or a child beneficiary under the age of sixteen.
- A widow or widower who is fifty or older who becomes disabled no later than seven years after the employed's death, or the date his or her prior benefits terminated.
- Dependents' parents who are sixty-two years of age or older (seldom occurs).
- Certain divorced spouses.

All Social Security survivor benefits contain many detailed provisions. These should be checked at a local Social Security office.

10. *If you disagree with a Social Security decision, how do you obtain a review?*

Begin at the Social Security office by asking to see the claims representative. Make certain you bring any pertinent documents and records with you. Social Security doesn't charge for this service. If, after you've discussed your case with the claims representative, you still believe the decision is unfair or incorrect, you may challenge it by asking that your case be reconsidered. You have a maximum of sixty days from the date you receive a written notice to make your appeal.

There are four steps to follow in an appeals process:

1. Reconsideration
2. Hearing
3. Appeals court
4. Federal court

If you decide to use the appeals process, ask your local claims representative for a booklet explaining the procedure in detail. You should also consult a benefit representative from one of your community senior citizen or retiree organizations, or contact your U.S. congressman or one of your U.S. senators. They have experienced people on their staffs who can advise you regarding Social Security matters.

11. *What changes must be reported to the Social Security Administration?*

It's your responsibility to report promptly changes of income, address, or family status by mail, telephone, or in person at a local Social Security office. In any correspondence with the Social Security Administration, include your claim number (nine digits followed by a letter) and signature.

Here is a list of what must be reported:

- Earnings over the annual limit.
- Work performed outside the United States.
- Change of address.
- A planned trip or change of residence outside of the country that will last 30 days or longer. Social Security will inform you of special reporting instructions about receiving your checks while out of the country.
- Change in marital status: divorce, marriage, or annulment.
- A minor or disabled child who leaves your care.

12. *What relationship is there between your pension plan and Social Security benefits?*

It is very important that you find out whether your pension is in addition to what you will receive from Social Security or whether—and to what extent—it is reduced by Social Security income. Nearly sixty percent of all private pension plans are integrated, which means they are plans in which employers may offset pension benefits by any amount up to eighty-three percent of Social Security benefits.

Social Security Checks

The Social Security Administration can arrange to have your monthly Social Security check directly deposited into a bank, savings and loan association, or credit union of your choice. In order to arrange for direct deposit, go to your bank, S & L, or credit union and fill out Form SF-1199. I strongly recommend doing this to avoid worry about lost checks and the bother of cashing them. Of course, there is an additional worry for people who hand-carry Social Security checks to cash them—robbery.

Social Security checks should arrive by mail on approximately the same day each month—usually the third. If the third falls on Saturday, Sunday, or a legal holiday, checks generally arrive the previous Friday. The check that arrives each month is your benefit for the previous month. For the most part, checks are on time. If they are late, it probably will be caused by a delay in the mail or administrative problems. If your check has not arrived by the sixth of the month, contact any local Social Security office. They can find the cause of the delay and help you get an overdue payment as quickly as possible. If a check is lost or stolen, it will be replaced—but that can take a long time.

When a Senior American is unable to manage monies for any reason, a relative, friend, or guardian should contact the Social Security office and arrange for checks to be mailed to him or her. This person is known as a representative payee.

If a Senior American dies while receiving benefits, a check is not payable for the month during which he or she dies. Payment for that month should be returned. The only exception occurs when a

check is made out jointly to a husband and wife—
in that case, the Social Security office should be
contacted. They will advise you of how to proceed.
And if a Social Security recipient had checks directly deposited, the financial institution should be
notified promptly.

A death benefit of $255 is provided for an eli-
gible husband, wife, or child entitled to benefits
for the month of death. Originally this was created
to cover burial expenses. Since the benefit has not
changed for many years, it is now considered a
payment toward burial expenses. *This is not an
automatic payment—the family must apply for it.*
For information, contact the Social Security office.

Supplemental Security Income—SSI

If Social Security benefits are very low, you may
be entitled to receive a Supplemental Security Income benefit. The law now requires that elderly
people who are potentially eligible for SSI be notified. However, only one notification will be provided.

Supplemental Security Income is administered
by the Social Security Administration and is often
confused with Social Security. It provides benefits
for people who are sixty-five years of age or older,

the blind, and disabled who have little or no cash income, who own little or no property, and who have less than $1,900 ($2,850 for an individual with a spouse) worth of household goods or savings.

The program is financed by general revenues, not payroll taxes. People who receive Supplemental Security Income must pass a "means test" in order to qualify.

If you think you or another member of your family qualifies for SSI, call your local Social Security office and inquire about how to proceed.

Financial Terms
You Should Know

Abstract of title—a complete history of the record of title of a designated parcel of land.

Accrued interest—the interest due on an investment since the last interest payment was made.

Adjusted gross estate—amount upon which federal estate tax is levied after deductions are taken from the gross estate.

Administrator—the individual or institution appointed by the court to administer the estate of a person who died without a will or whose will did not designate an executor or whose designated executor could not or would not serve.

Agent—one who acts for another.

American Stock Exchange (AMEX)—the second largest stock exchange in the U.S., located in the financial district of New York City.

Amortization—loan payment by equal periodic payments calculated to retire the principal at the end of a fixed period and to pay accrued interest on the outstanding balance.

Annuity—a contract between an insurance company and an individual which may be tax-deferred. The company agrees to provide a fixed or variable income for life or for a designated period of time, in exchange for a stipulated amount of money.

Appraisal—an estimate of value. In real estate, an estimate of value of a specific parcel of real estate as of a specific date for a specific purpose.

Arbitrage—a technique employed to take advantage of differences in price. If, for example, XYZ stock can be bought in New York for $10 a share and sold in London at $10.50, an arbitrageur may simultaneously purchase XYZ stock here and sell the same amount in London, making a profit of fifty cents a share, minus expenses. Arbitrage may also involve the purchase of rights to subscribe to a security, or the purchase of a convertible security.

Assessed value—the value of a property for tax purposes. It may or may not be equivalent to the property's market value.

Assets—everything a corporation or individual owns which has monetary value and everything which is due: cash, investments, money due, materials and inventories, which are called *current* assets; buildings and machinery, which are known as *fixed* assets; and patents and goodwill, called *intangible* assets.

At-risk rule—the rule that prohibits an investor from taking a tax deduction for any amount that exceeds the amount of his investment.

Attorney-in-fact—a legal agent appointed to act for another in a power of attorney.

Auditor's report—often called the accountant's opinion, it is the statement of the accounting firm's work and its opinion of the corporation's financial statements.

Averages—various ways of measuring the trend of securities prices, one of the most popular of which is the Dow Jones average of thirty industrial stocks listed on the NYSE.

Balance sheet—a detailed and itemized list of total assets and liabilities on a given date which is used to determine net worth.

Bear market—a declining market. Someone called "bearish" believes the market will decline.

Beneficiary—one for whose benefit a trust is established or to whom a bequest is made in a will.

Bequest—a gift made in a will.

Blue chip—a company known nationally for the quality and wide acceptance of its products or services and for its ability to make money and pay dividends.

Blue sky laws—a popular name for laws various states have enacted to protect the public against securities frauds. The term is believed to have originated when a judge ruled that a particular stock had about the same value as a patch of blue sky.

Bond—an evidence of debt of a corporation or governmental body, on which the issuer usually promises to pay the bondholders a specified amount of interest for a specified length of time and to repay the loan on the expiration date. Bondholders are *creditors*, rather than part-owners or share-owners of the company.

Book value—an accounting term. Book value of a stock is determined from a company's records by adding all assets, then deducting all debts and other liabilities, plus the liquidation price of any preferred issues. The sum arrived at is divided by the number of common shares outstanding and the result is the book value per common share. Book value of the assets of a company or a security may have little relationship to market value.

Broker—an agent who handles the public's orders to buy and sell securities, commodities, or other property. For this service a commission is charged.

Bull market—an advancing market. A person called "bullish" is one who believes the market will rise.

Capacity—soundness of mind required to execute a will.

Capital assets—all property, like securities and real estate, but not including business inventory, business property, accounts or notes receivable, artistic creations of the taxpayer, and certain U.S. government obligations.

Capital gains/capital loss—profit or loss from

the sale or exchange of capital assets. Under current federal income tax laws, a capital gain may be either short-term (six months or less) or long-term (more than six months). The capital gains provisions of the tax law are complicated, and a tax or financial adviser should be consulted about them.

Cash value—the cash reserve element of permanent life insurance, which is created with the excess premium charged above the cost of "pure" protection or term insurance.

Certificate—the actual piece of paper that is evidence of ownership of stock in a corporation.

Certificate of deposit (CD)—a money market instrument issued by banks. The CD is a "time deposit" which earns a specified rate of interest over a given period of time and is generally considered a highly negotiable short-term investment vehicle.

CFP—professional designation meaning Certified Financial Planner.

Charitable deduction—a deduction from gross income or gross estate for contribution to charity.

ChFC—professional designation meaning Chartered Financial Consultant.

Churning—rapid and repeated trading (buying and selling) of securities in order to generate commissions for the broker instead of profits for the client.

Clifford Trust—a type of trust to which income may be diverted to a beneficiary (usually from a parent to a child in a low income bracket) for a period of at least ten years, during which time the income from the trust is taxed to the beneficiary of the trust. Also known as a Short-Term Trust, a Ten-Year Trust, or a Reversionary Trust.

Closing—the conclusion of a transaction. In real estate, closing includes the delivery of a deed, financial adjustments, the signing of notes, and the disbursement of funds necessary to the sale or loan transaction.

Closing costs—costs payable by a buyer and seller for the purchase, sale, or financing of real property. Typically included are appraisal fee, loan origination fee, settlement fee to attorney, title examination fee, title insurance premium, deed preparation and recording fees, and brokerage commission.

CLU—professional designation meaning Chartered or Certified Life Underwriter. Those achieving the designation must meet substantial educational, ethical, and experience requirements.

Codicil—a formal amendment to a will.

Collateral—securities or other property pledged by a borrower to secure repayment of a loan.

Collectibles—assets collected for their aesthetic value as well as their monetary worth.

Commercial paper—promissory notes issued by companies (usually large, solid companies) to meet short-term financing needs.

Commodity—an item of trade or commerce. A commodity can be *tangible*, like gold or wheat, or *intangible*, like stock index futures.

Commodity Futures Trading Commission

(CFTC)—created by Congress in 1974 to regulate exchange trading in futures.

Common stock and preferred stock—securities that represent an ownership interest in a corporation. Common stock is "junior" to preferred stock and bonds—if the company is liquidated, bondholders and preferred stockholders have priority in receiving dividend income and claims on company assets. Preferred stock may not be accompanied by voting rights, while common stock shareholders—by law—have the right to vote at shareholder meetings. Common stock is usually a higher-risk investment than preferred stock, but promises potentially higher gains in the form of dividends and capital appreciation.

Compound interest—interest computed on the sum of an original principal plus the accrued interest, which subsequently creates a larger principal on which more interest can be earned.

Condominium—a form of ownership of real property in which you own individual living units and share ownership of the hallways, grounds, and other common areas with other owners of individual units.

Contingency—a specific event which must occur before a contract is considered binding.

Convertible security—a bond, debenture, or preferred share that may be exchanged by the owner for common stock or another security, usually of the same company, in accordance with the terms of the issue.

Cumulative preferred stock—a stock having a provision that if one or more dividends are omitted, the omitted dividends must be paid before dividends may be paid on the company's common stock.

Debenture—a promissory note backed by the general credit of a company and usually not secured by a mortgage or lien on any specific property. Can also be a corporate obligation which is sold as an investment.

Decedent—a deceased person.

Deed—a written instrument which, when legally delivered and accepted, transfers title to real property from one person to another.

Default—failure to pay principal or interest on a loan when it is due.

Deferral—a means of sheltering income from taxation by deferring the reporting of income during high-tax years until a period of lower taxation (such as retirement).

Defined-benefit plan—a pension plan in which the amount of your retirement benefits is determined in advance but the amount of your contributions to the plan varies, depending on projections of how many employees are to receive benefits and how much the benefits will be.

Defined-contribution plan—a pension plan in which the amount of your retirement benefits is not known but the amount of your contribution to the plan is fixed. Also known as a profit-sharing plan.

Depreciation—charges permitted to be deducted from taxable income to reflect the assets' decline in value as it "wears out."

Direct-deposit system—a system that allows a Social Security check to be mailed directly to your bank or savings and loan institution for deposit to your account.

Discount—the amount by which a preferred stock or bond may sell below its par value.

Discount points—added loan fee charged by a lender. Each point equals 1% of the mortgage amount and is paid to the lender as part of closing costs. Points may be paid by the seller or buyer, except in federal VA loans, where the seller must pay all discount points.

Discretionary trust or account—a trust under which the trustee (such as a financial counselor or broker) has absolute discretion as to how much (if any) income or principal shall be paid over to the beneficiary, or to buy and sell securities or commodities.

Diversification—spreading investment funds among a number of investments (one method of avoiding catastrophic financial losses).

Dividend—a payment by a corporation to be distributed among the shareholders of the corporation. In life insurance terminology, a dividend is a refund of part of the premium paid, reflecting the company's earnings for the year.

Donee—the person who receives a gift; also a person given authority under a power of appointment.

Donor—the person who makes a gift.

Durable power of attorney—a power of attorney which, by state law and in accordance with the terms of the instrument, is not revoked by the incompetence of the grantor of the power.

Earnest money deposit—an amount of money deposited by a buyer under the terms of a contract that is to be forfeited if the buyer defaults but applied to the purchase price if the sale is closed.

Employee Retirement Income Security Act of 1976 (ERISA)—This legislation was designed to strengthen the role of private retirement benefits and personal savings and established such regulations as minimum funding standards. Among other things, it imposed stringent regulations upon plan administrators, trustees, and other "fiduciaries" to prevent mishandling of funds and imprudent investment decisions. It also created a special government agency that insures benefits.

Endowment life insurance—a type of life insurance on which a high premium is paid for a limited term. At the end of the term, the cash value of the policy equals the face amount of the policy. The face amount of the policy is paid to the insured when the policy matures if it has not already been paid out to beneficiaries on the insured's death.

Equity—the excess value of ownership in real property or securities, less claims or liens against them. For example, the current market value of a home less the principal remaining on its mortgage is the equity of that property. Equity also refers to total holdings, including real estate, securities, vested interests in annuities, pensions, etc. The ownership interest of stockholders in a company may also be referred to as equity.

Escrow—*Monthly Escrow:* payment required of a borrower by a lender to cover the anticipated costs for real estate taxes, homeowners' insurance renewals, and mortgage insurance renewals. One-twelfth of the estimated annual costs are included in the borrower's regular monthly payments. *Performance Escrow:* money, securities, instruments, property or evidences of property deposited with a third person, to be delivered on a certain contingency or on the happening of a certain event.

Estate tax—a tax levied against the entire estate of a decedent at death.

Exclusion ratio—the percentage of an annuity that escapes taxation because it represents the portion of the annuity you have purchased with after-tax dollars.

Executor—an individual or institution designated in a will to administer the estate of a person who has died.

Exemption—a tax deduction allowed from gross income for the taxpayer and persons cared for or supported by the taxpayer.

Face value or par value—in the case of a common share, a dollar amount assigned to the share by the company's charter. In the case of preferred stocks, it signifies the dollar value upon which dividends are figured. With bonds, par value is the face amount unless the value is otherwise specified by the issuing company. Face or par value is not an indication of market value.

Fair market value—the price at which property is transferred between a willing buyer and a willing seller, each of whom has a reasonable knowledge of all pertinent facts and neither being under any compulsion to buy or sell.

Federal Deposit Insurance Corporation (FDIC)—The FDIC is an independent agency of the U.S. government, established by Congress in 1933 to insure bank deposits and thereby help maintain sound conditions in our banking system and protect the nation's money supply in case of bank failure. Insurance premiums are not charged to the depositors but are paid to the FDIC by member banks.

Federal Insurance Contributions Act (FICA)—These initials on a worker's paycheck identify the amount paid for Social Security.

Federal Savings and Loan Insurance Corporation (FSLIC)—The FSLIC provides stability to the savings and loan industry by offering insurance for savings accounts, thereby protecting small savers. It is also concerned with helping the industry attract funds for economical home financing.

Fiduciary—one who holds a fiduciary (relating to, or involving, a confidence or trust) position or acts in a fiduciary capacity.

Financial futures—futures contracts based on financial instruments such as U.S. Treasury bonds, CDs and other interest-sensitive issues, currencies and stock market indicators. Commodities traded in futures markets include stock index futures; agricultural products like wheat, soybeans, and pork bellies; metals; and financial instruments.

Fiscal year—a corporation's accounting year. Due to the nature of their particular business, some companies do not use the calendar year for their bookkeeping—for example, a department store may find December 31 too early a date to close its books after the Christmas rush. It may instead close out its accounting on January 31. The store's fiscal year, then, runs from February 1 of a year through January 31 of the next year.

Generation-skipping transfer tax—a tax on the transfer of assets to members of a younger generation which would not otherwise be subject to transfer tax.

Gift tax—a tax on lifetime transfers of assets. (Since 1986 the federal government allows you a lifetime exclusion of $600,000.)

GNMA—an acronym for Government National Mortgage Association, but commonly referred to as "Ginnie Mae." A Ginnie Mae is a type of government-backed securities fund. Other commonly known types include "Fannie Maes" and "Freddie Macs."

Government bonds—obligations of the U.S. government, regarded as the highest-grade securities issues.

Gross estate—the entire estate of a decedent before any deductions are made.

Gross income—the entire income of a taxpayer before any deductions are made.

Holographic will—a will written entirely in the handwriting of the person making the will; not valid in all states.

Individual Retirement Account (IRA)—a private pension plan, the contributions to which are tax-deductible when invested and taxable when withdrawn after age 59½. IRAs permit investment through intermediaries like mutual funds, insurance companies, banks, or directly in stocks and bonds through stockbrokers.

Inflation—occurs when there is an increase in the volume of money and credit in relation to the availability of goods, resulting in the substantial and continuing rise in the general price level.

Inheritance tax—a tax imposed upon the beneficiary of an inheritance, often with the rate increasing as the beneficiary is further from the deceased in relationship.

Interest—payments borrowers pay lenders for the use of their money.

In terrorem clause—a clause in a will which provides that any person who contests the will shall not take any interest under the will.

Inter vivos trust—another name for a living trust.

Intestate—one who dies without a valid will.

Investment bankers—the middlemen between the public and corporations issuing new securities. Often the investment banker will purchase new securities outright, then form a syndicate and sell shares to the public. Investment bankers also distribute large blocks of stocks or bonds from estates.

Irrevocable trust—a trust that cannot be altered or revoked by the person who established it.

Itemized deductions—specific personal expenses permitted to be deducted to reduce gross income.

Keogh Retirement Plan—a pension plan used by self-employed persons, the contributions to which are tax deductible when they are invested and taxable when withdrawn after retirement.

Land contract—a contract primarily designed to protect the seller's interest, in which a purchaser of real estate pays some portion of the purchase price when the contract is signed, and agrees to pay additional sums, at intervals and in amounts specified in the contract. The title remains with the seller until the purchase price or a specified amount of the purchase price is paid.

Leverage—the use of a relatively small amount of capital, which acts like a down payment, to control a larger, more valuable entity. Leverage also describes the effect on a company when the company has bonds, preferred stock, or both outstanding.

Liabilities—all the debts and claims against a person or corporation; the opposite of assets. Liabilities could include accrued taxes payable, bank loans, debentures, accounts payable, wages and salaries payable, and dividends declared payable.

Lien—a legal hold or claim filed by one party

on the property of another as security for a debt or charge.

Life estate—an interest in property that lasts only during the owner's lifetime.

Life insurance—a contract between an individual and an insurance company under which the individual agrees to pay a certain amount of money annually, in return for which the insurance company agrees to pay the individual's beneficiaries a specific sum of money in the event of that person's death during the life of the contract.

Life insurance trust—a trust to which an insured person conveys all the incidents of ownership in a policy of life insurance and which is made the beneficiary of the life insurance policy. On the death of the insured, the proceeds of the policy are not includable in his estate for federal estate tax purposes.

Lifetime exclusion—the amount of assets that may be conveyed during the lifetime of an individual without incurring federal gift tax liability. Since 1986, this amount is $600,000.

Limited-payment life insurance—a variation on whole life insurance in which premiums are not payable during the insured's entire life but for a limited period of time. The premiums paid are higher than comparable premiums for whole life insurance.

Limited partnership investment—business partnerships between a general partner who supplies expertise and ability to operate in a certain industry (such as real estate or oil and gas) and a group of limited partners who invest in capital. The partnership itself pays no taxes, but investors report their partnership profits, losses, and deductions on their own individual tax returns.

Liquidation—the process of converting property or other securities into cash.

Living trust—a trust established by an individual during his or her lifetime. Also known as an inter vivos trust.

Living Will—a signed, dated, and witnessed document which allows you to state, in advance, your wishes regarding the use of life-sustaining procedures when you are dying. It also has a provision for the appointment of someone else to direct your care if you are unable to do so yourself.

Load fund—a mutual fund sold by salespeople who charge a sales charge or "load" to cover commissions and other costs of distribution. The load is usually incurred only on purchase, there being, in most cases, no charge when the shares are sold (redeemed).

Loan-to-value ratio—loan amount divided by the value of the home. Example: $45,000 mortgage on a $50,000 home represents a ninety percent loan-to-value ratio.

Marital tax deduction—a deduction for assets passing from one spouse to another during a lifetime or on the death of one spouse. The effect of this is to remove all the assets that pass from a deceased spouse to the other spouse from his or her estate for tax purposes.

Maturity—the date on which a loan, bond, or debenture comes due and is to be paid off.

Minimum-deposit insurance—the use of loan proceeds from a life insurance policy's cash value to pay for the premiums in whole or in part. Interest must be paid to the insurance company for this "loan," but it is tax deductible.

Money market fund—a mutual fund whose investments are in high-yield money market instruments such as federal securities, CDs, commercial paper, and other short-term securities. Its intent is to make such instruments—normally purchased in large denominations by institutions—available indirectly to individuals. They are available through brokerage firms or mutual funds.

Mortgage—a legal document which pledges real property as security for the repayment of a loan or the performance of a duty.

Municipal bond—a bond issued by a state or a political subdivision, such as a county, city, town, or village. In general, interest paid on municipal bonds is exempt from federal income taxes and state and local income taxes within the state of issue.

Mutual fund—an investment organization that pools the dollars of many people and invests in many different businesses. Mutual funds involve *indirect* investing—investment decisions are made by the mutual fund organization on your behalf—the idea being that the organization can invest the dollars more productively than individuals can for themselves.

National Association of Securities Dealers (NASD)—an association of brokers and dealers in the over-the-counter securities business.

Negotiable—term used to describe a security which can be transferred.

New York Futures Exchange (NYFE)—a subsidiary of the NYSE devoted to the trading of futures products.

New York Stock Exchange (NYSE)—the largest organized securities market in the U.S., founded in 1792. The exchange is a not-for-profit corporation of over 1,300 individual members, governed by a board of directors consisting of both public representatives and exchange members.

No-load mutual fund—a type of mutual fund sold directly from an organization which employs no sales force and for which there is no sales charge. There may be a small charge when shares are redeemed.

Noncupative will—an oral will, valid only for the disposition of personal property under limited circumstances; not valid in all states.

Option—a right to buy or sell a fixed amount of a particular stock at a specified price within a limited period of time. A real estate option is the right to buy or lease property at an agreed-upon price with agreed-upon terms during a limited period of time.

Over-the-counter—a market for securities made up of securities dealers who may or may not be members of a securities exchange. This market deals mainly with stocks of companies without sufficient shares, stockholders, or earnings to warrant listing on an exchange. The over-the-counter market is the principal market for bonds of all types.

Parity—generally, a level of equivalence; more specifically, the point at which a commodity expressed in one currency price is equal to its price in another.

Penny stocks—low-priced issues of stock, often highly speculative, selling at less than $1 per share.

Personalty—personal property.

P.I.T.I.—an acronym for principal, interest, taxes and insurance. P.I.T.I. generally represents a borrower's monthly payment on a loan.

Portfolio—all holdings of an individual or institution; may contain bonds, preferred stocks, common stocks, and other securities.

Pour-over will—a will directing that assets in an estate be added to a trust established by the testator during his lifetime or on the death of one spouse.

Power of appointment—authority conferred by a will or other instrument upon another person, known as the donee, to determine who is to receive property or its income.

Power of attorney—a written instrument by which a person names another person as his agent (known as the attorney-in-fact) for purposes set out in the instrument.

Premiums—money paid for a contract of insurance. "Premium" may also refer to the amount by which a bond or preferred stock may sell above its par value.

Prepayment penalty—a charge imposed on a borrower who pays off the loan or principal early to compensate the lender for interest and other charges that would otherwise be lost.

Prime rate—the lowest interest rate charged by commercial banks to their most credit-worthy and largest corporate customers. Other interest rates, such as personal, automobile, commercial, and financing loans, are often pegged to the prime rate.

Principal—the outstanding balance on a loan at any given time as distinguished from interest charges. "Principal" may also refer to the face amount of a bond or the person for whom a broker executes an order.

Probate—the process of administering a decedent's estate.

Progressive tax—a tax in which the rate increases as the amount subject to taxation increases.

Proxy—written authorization given by a shareholder to someone else to represent him and vote his shares at a shareholders' meeting.

Prudent man rule—an investment standard. In some states, the law requires that a fiduciary, such as a trustee, may invest the fund's money only in a list of securities designated by the state—the so-called legal list. In other states, the trustee may invest in a security if it is one that would be bought by a "prudent man of discretion and intelligence, who is seeking a reasonable income and preservation of capital."

Public offering—the original sale of a company's securities.

Rally—a brisk rise following a decline in the general price level of the market, or in an individual stock.

Ratings—Designations used by investment services to give relative indications of quality. Two of the best known are the bond ratings made by Standard & Poor's and Moody's.

Realtor—a registered trademark term reserved for the sole use of active members of local realtor boards affiliated with the National Association of Realtors.

Revocable living trust—a trust established by an individual during his lifetime that is freely alterable and revocable.

Rollover—the changing of a funding medium of an IRA. For example, moving your IRA investment from a stock mutual fund to a bond mutual fund is a rollover.

Savings and loan—a depository institution whose primary purpose is to promote savings and also homeownership through mortgage lending. Today savings and loans, in many cases, have expanded to provide many of the same services as commercial banks.

Securities—stocks, bonds, and other investments in a common enterprise with the expectation of profit from the effort of others.

Securities and Exchange Commission (SEC)—established by Congress to help protect investors, the SEC administers the Securites Act of 1933, the Securities Exchange Act of 1934, the Securities Act Amendments of 1975, and other acts governing securities investments.

Securities Investor Protection Corporation (SIPC)—a nonprofit membership corporation created by an act of Congress which protects customers of registered securities brokers in the event the SIPC-member firm fails and is liquidated, thereby promoting confidence in U.S. securities markets.

Special power of appointment—a power of appointment which may not be exercised by the donee of the power in favor of himself, his estate, his creditors, or the creditors of his estate.

Speculator—one who is willing to assume a relatively large risk in the hope of gain.

Spendthrift trust—a trust in which the assets cannot be sold, given away, or otherwise transferred by the beneficiary before they are conveyed to the beneficiary.

Split—the division of the outstanding shares of a corporation into a larger number of shares. (A three-for-one split by a company with one million shares outstanding results in three million shares outstanding. Each holder of 100 shares before the three-for-one split would then have 300 shares, although the proportionate equity in the company would remain the same.)

Stock dividend—a dividend paid in securities rather than cash.

Support trust—a trust under which the trustee

is to pay over to the beneficiary only so much income as is necessary for the beneficiary's support.

Survey— a measurement of land prepared by a registered land surveyor, showing the location of the land with reference to known points, its dimensions, and the location and dimensions of any improvements.

T-bills—another name for Treasury bills, which are backed by the government and can be purchased at a discounted price. They are worth the face amount at the time of maturity, which can vary from 91 days to a year. Treasury notes and bonds also are available, with maturity dates of one to seven years and with interest being paid semi-annually.

Tax credit—a dollar-for-dollar subtraction from tax liability. A $100 credit saves $100 in taxes, regardless of tax bracket.

Tax deduction—amounts allowed to be subtracted from gross income or gross estate in order to arrive at taxable income or taxable estate.

Tax-deferred dividends—dividends that are reinvested and not taxable until the stock is sold.

Tax shelters—any means of shielding or sheltering money or assets from taxation by legal methods.

Term insurance—a contract of "pure" life insurance (i.e., life insurance with no investment element). Term life insurance is temporary, and is payable if death occurs within a specified period of time.

Testacy—dying with a valid will.

Testamentary trust—a trust established by an individual in his will.

Testator—a person who makes a will.

Title—the evidence of right a person has to ownership and possession of property.

Totten Trust—a deposit of money in a bank or other savings institution in the name of the depositor, in trust for a beneficiary. The trust is revocable during the depositor's lifetime.

Trust—a legal arrangement under which one person holds and manages property for the benefit of one or more other persons.

Underwriting—the analysis of financial risk and the matching of it to an appropriate rate and term.

Variable annuity—a life insurance policy where the annuity premium is immediately turned into units of a portfolio of stocks. Its objective is to preserve, through stock investment, the purchasing value of the annuity.

Vested—fixed or absolute. A right that is vested is not subject to being withdrawn.

Whole life insurance—permanent life insurance which creates guaranteed cash values payable at a later date to the insured or beneficiary. Whole life insurance is really a combination of life insurance protection and investment. The face amount of the policy and the premium remain fixed even though the insured ages and the risk of death increase. In a "young" whole life policy, the premium is higher than for a comparable term life policy, but the difference in premium is used to build up the cash values.

Will—the document providing for the disposition of a person's estate on death.

Yield—also known as "return"; the dividends or interest paid by a company expressed as a percentage of the current price. For example, a stock with a current market value of $50 paying dividends at the rate of $3.50 has a seven percent return, or yield.

Zero coupon bonds—bonds which pay no interest but are priced at a significant discount from their redemption prices.

5

Freedom from
Fear of Abuse

Senior Americans have the right to freedom from
fear of mental and physical abuse, as well as from
chemical or physical restraint except in medical
emergencies.

*"Those who swindle, mentally and physically abuse,
or deliberately injure Senior Americans must be
stopped."*
                              —Art Linkletter

There is nothing subtle about this right. What is
saddest is that it needs to be put into writing at
all. The truth is, Senior Americans *are* targeted as
"marks," deliberately swindled out of monies, verbally and physically abused in some nursing homes,
and even abused by children and other relatives.
When an eighty-year-old man's suicide note states
that he killed his wife before turning the gun on
himself because both were too terrified to face
another assault and robbery, it's time to say,
"Enough is enough."

As a Senior American who has experienced the
best of what this country has to offer, I have no
stomach for what happens to anyone less fortunate. I'd like to be able to stand aside and say fraud
and abuse really aren't problems, but that just isn't

true. They are. And if one person is harmed, it's too many. We simply cannot excuse or turn aside from problems often portrayed as too big to deal with because they'll continue to grow worse.

We may not be able to convince people to venerate Senior Americans because of their age, but we can come down harshly on those who perpetrate abuse of any kind. Years ago I said that if every family would accept responsibility for just its own members where drug and alcohol abuse were concerned, we'd make a big dent in the problem in a short period of time. Unfortunately, simple solutions are always suspect. Nevertheless, that statement is as true today as it was eighteen years ago. It's also true that if everyone would step forward and speak up who already knows about a Senior American being victimized or abused in any way, we'd make progress in short order.

Our society is far too complex to expect that we can easily legislatively correct the many forms of Senior American abuse. In fact, I'll go one step further. Calling for legislation to correct social and moral problems really represents an excuse of the first order. It's passing the buck. Every year we write more laws when we can't—or won't—deal with problems.

In 1624, John Donne said: "No man is an island, entire of itself; every man is a piece of the continent, a part of the main; if a clod be washed away by the sea, Europe is the less as well as if a promontory were, as well as if a manor of thy friends or of thine own were; any man's death diminishes me, because I am involved in mankind; and therefore never send to know for whom the bell tolls; it tolls for thee."

Isn't it time we all started getting involved?

Senior Americans— Easy "Marks" for Fraud

Among the millions of people who are victims of fraud every year, a large number are Senior Americans because they are perceived as easy targets by confidence men and women, or "cons." In fact, it's estimated that frauds are increasing at the rate of twelve percent each year.

People who live alone, who are ill, in pain, or afraid, or who have a fixed income, making the appeal of quick money attractive, make good targets for fraud. The most sickening aspect of Senior Americans' victimization is that their losses tend to be disproportionately devastating because they have less and their abilities to recover are greatly diminished.

Confidence people most often are kind-looking, middle-aged, conservatively dressed and have carefully cultivated mannerisms that inspire confidence. And the criminal frauds they convince people to buy into amount to *billions* of dollars every year.

There are five common techniques to convince a "mark" or victim to buy whatever fraudulent scheme is being promoted. Every Senior American should be aware of these:

- Scare techniques—The Senior American is warned of something dangerous or an impending peril like a roof about to collapse or other structural damage regarding property. Whatever the supposed problem, it's presented as an immediate danger that must be corrected right away.

- Pressure for down payments—After the "cons" have their "marks" convinced to buy into some scheme, the next step is to obtain a down payment of money. When the "cons" have the money in hand, it's the last time they're seen.

- Rush deals—This approach convinces victims that action must be taken at once: "I can only make this offer today . . . it's so special you have to decide right now!"

- Claims of credibility or special authority—In this instance, the "con" convinces his "mark" that he or she is some kind of an authority or, in some way, specially qualified. The con's pitch centers on establishing himself as highly credible, thereby gaining his victim's trust. If cons sell themselves and their credibility well enough, people buy into their schemes.

- Secrecy—Many times the "con" will try to convince his "mark" that this deal is so good that it has to be kept quiet because there just isn't room for everyone—"this deal is limited to an exclusive few." At other times, the "con" sets out to convince the "mark" that the plan he presents is highly confidential. For example, he's a bank examiner and needs help trapping a dishonest bank employee. Obviously, if this is to be accomplished, the "mark" must keep the plan a secret.

Ten Common Frauds

According to the U.S. Senate Special Committee on Aging, the ten most harmful frauds are quackery and medical related frauds, home repair and improvement frauds, "bunco" schemes, insurance frauds, social frauds, land and housing frauds, business and investment frauds, nursing home frauds, automobile frauds, and funeral frauds.

This is how they work:

Medical Frauds—Senior Americans are deliberate targets and easy victims for those promising cures or relief from pain. It would take pages and pages just to discuss the number of frauds that involve arthritis. Because *hope* sells, people will continue to become victims. Before buying anything related to your medical health that promises a relief, cure, or anything else, call your primary doctor, pharmacist, or Better Business Bureau.

Home Improvement/Repair Frauds—These frauds offer to replace or repair roofs, furnaces, driveways, chimneys, etc. A phony repairman or someone posing as a city official could knock on your door saying he's been referred by a neighbor or is employed by the gas company or some other company. This person will offer to make a free inspection of your home which of course will result in the discovery of a major problem that has to be fixed immediately. This will be followed by an offer of a quick, efficient repair at bargain prices. You'll be asked for a down payment or partial payment then and there. Chances are good you'll never see the person again. If someone *does* return, the quality of workmanship will be inferior, the balance of the money will be collected, and then the person will disappear. Either way, your money will be gone.

Home improvement rackets are too numerous to list. These basic rules can help you avoid being taken in:

- Don't sign anything or verbally consent to anything without finding out who the people or companies are. You can check references by calling your local Better Business Bureau or the Chamber of Commerce. You can also make a phone call to your local Police Department to ask if any reports of home repair frauds have been called in.

- Insist on references and then check them carefully. Many con men and women are prepared to provide references—in fact, they may offer them before you ask—because they know that most people will never bother to check them. They know that victims tend to believe that people with references are trustworthy. Remember, if someone is trying to con you out of money, the references provided will be as phony as the scheme.

- Make sure all of the salesman's promises are written into the agreement. People operating honestly and with integrity have no reason not to cover everything in writing and carefully review it with you before you sign it.
- Get competitive bids from contractors you know or whose reputations can be verified before you begin any form of home repair or improvement. Nothing is so urgent that you have to hand money over the same day or sign some form of agreement at your front door—no matter how much you want to believe the understanding, nice person working diligently to convince you.
- Never sign a completion certificate before the work has been completed to your satisfaction.

Bunco Schemes—"Bunco" is a term used for frauds that swindle and are based on gaining your confidence so you'll turn over money. Although hundreds of different bunco schemes have been identified, some of the most common include the Bank Examiner Racket, the Money Pitch, the Pigeon Drop, and C.O.D. Packages, plus schemes aimed at selling medigap insurance, land and housing, automobiles, and business investments.

Here's how they work:

The Bank Examiner Racket—Someone telephones claiming to be a bank examiner saying that he or she needs your help to trap a dishonest bank employee. The racket centers on getting you to withdraw money from your account—which of course you'll be told will be returned to you immediately after the employee is caught. Once the money is withdrawn and turned over, the con man disappears with your money. Even though people say, "I'd never fall for that," professional con artists are so convincing that people are entrapped every day. If you ever get such a call, telephone the police at once.

The Money Pitch—This fraud is intended to get you to sign an installment contract to buy something—even though you'll be told it really won't cost you anything because you'll get your money back when you refer the salesman to friends and neighbors who also buy. Instead of getting your money back, you could end up paying installments each month, possibly for a long period of time.

The Pigeon Drop—When you least suspect it, a kind, honest-looking man or woman in a public place might show you a package full of money telling you he or she just found it and is willing to divide it with you if you'll show some good faith by "putting up some money of your own." Believe it or not, this fraud continues to make millions of dollars for confidence people. If anyone ever approaches you with such an "offer," walk away and go to the nearest phone and call the police.

C.O.D. Packages—If someone dressed like a deliveryman arrives at your door with a package telling you that your neighbor isn't at home and that you can save him or her the trouble of going to the post office if you'll accept it and pay for it, refuse and close the door. Unless a neighbor has made arrangements with you to accept a C.O.D. delivery and given you the money in advance, you'll end up stuck with a package of unordered and unwanted junk. Also take the time to inform your local post office.

Medigap Insurance Frauds—These frauds are targeted at Senior Americans because of Medicare's "gaps" in coverage—they're presented as insurance policies that plug what's missing in Medicare insurance. It's estimated that twenty million of these policies have been sold at the cost of some $4 billion.

Social Frauds—These frauds target a person's natural compassion and charity. Their objective is to get Senior Americans to contribute to some worthy cause that often involves bogus charities or religious groups. You could be contacted by mail or by someone telephoning to ask for your "help." If you have any question about a solicitation you receive in the mail, call your local post office.

Housing and Land Frauds—More and more of these frauds involve vacation homes, time-sharing properties, and retirement homes. Buyers discover that what they've purchased may be missing utility connections, that more time was sold than is available, that the property they expect to look like the picture in the brochure is located in a swamp, desert, or miles from the nearest town. *Never* invest in any property without the most intense scrutiny and detailed investigation of everything involved. Anyone operating on the up and up has no reason to object—in fact will welcome your questions and provide whatever information you request.

Business and Investment Frauds—These kinds of frauds deliberately target the elderly on fixed incomes. They offer opportunities to "make money" quickly and easily. Whatever is presented, it always looks irresistible and requires an investment of money in exchange for a promise of large returns. Some involve "business opportunities" where, in exchange for your money, you might get a worm farm, sew-at-home, or envelope stuffing and addressing business. The Committee on Aging heard about a Cleveland promoter selling jewelry franchises to 540 investors who responded to newspaper ads. The con man collected $3.5 million and each victim received $100 worth of costume jewelry.

Other schemes make you work just to be "lucky" enough to qualify for whatever "opportunity" is being offered. Victims are asked to take some kind of qualifying test for which a modest fee must be paid. In one sew-at-home scheme, 200,000 people paid a registration fee to take a sewing test to see if they were qualified for employment. Not surprisingly, no one qualified.

Nursing Home Frauds—This kind of fraud covers everything, including overcharges for specific services, paying for things that are already included in the daily rates, paying for things never received, being charged an "admission fee" to get on a Medicaid facility list, and many others. (See "Nursing Homes," p. 140).

Automobile Frauds—For the most part, automobile salesmen and repairmen stop just short of committing outright fraud. Their form of "conning" involves increasing profit margins by raising the price of a new car so a "big trade-in" can be offered on the car being traded, misrepresenting a car's performance or history, or substituting a car that has fewer options.

Funeral Frauds—take advantage of the emotion surrounding a loved one's death. Some of the abuses include implying that embalming is required before burial when, in most states, there is no such requirement unless the body is to be transported by a common carrier; others require cash advances (that have been inflated) for standard items like flowers and obituary notices, and excessive markups on things like burial vaults. If you haven't got the emotional energy to review an itemized bill carefully, have someone else carefully cross-check it for you.

You Can Stop Fraud
Before It Happens

Except for a very few "lucky" people, most victims of fraud never get their money back. There aren't enough government agencies or law-enforcement personnel to stop those who deliberately set out to defraud those they see as vulnerable. Confidence schemes and frauds are perpetrated by amoral, unscrupulous people who care nothing for someone's age, vulnerability, or the consequences that result from what they do.

Most fraud can be prevented. Common sense is your best weapon against being lured into a fraudulent scheme. Handing over money to someone who appears at your door or telephones you asking for it, or allowing someone to come inside to inspect your property, or signing something you really don't understand just doesn't make sense.

A real blow to con men and women could be rendered if everyone would just decide to take the time to check on what someone is saying, offering, promising, or trying to sell. Remember, it is the need and hope for fast, quick money, a cure for a medical problem, or some "high-return deal" that confidence men and women feed on. Like it or not, people who con others enjoy the thrills associated with what it takes to pull it off. They thrive on their own cleverness in tricking, luring, and scaring victims into turning over money. Because many operate just barely within the confines of the law, they often get away with their schemes. If you get taken in, the chances are that whatever you've spent is lost forever.

A two-minute telephone call to the Better Business Bureau, the Chamber of Commerce, the Police Department, the Sheriff's Department, your pharmacist, your banker, your doctor—depending on what someone is trying to sell—could make the difference in stopping someone from making you— or someone else—his or her next victim.

6

The Right to a Healthy Lifestyle

Senior Americans have the right to the information and assistance needed to ensure a continuing healthy lifestyle.

"We're willing to learn and appreciate any assistance offered that will help us stay active and healthy."
— Art Linkletter

Although men in the United States live to be an average of seventy-two years of age and women seventy-eight, there are remote areas of the world where pockets of people are reported to live 100 years and longer. This kind of longevity is attributed to lots of reasons, including diet, but it's difficult to prove that relationship because people who maintain overall good health habits tend to do the same where nutrition and diet are concerned. Believe me, if I knew the secret to living more than a hundred years, I'd bottle and sell it.

Even though our overall environment and genetic makeup are beyond our control, choosing what we eat and how much we exercise are major contributing factors to our health, well-being, and longevity. In this section I'm presenting you with some important information about nutrition, as well as recommending the best exercise program available for Senior Americans—walking.

Lifelong habits are hard to break—especially lifelong food habits. One of my Senior American friends has German ancestry on both sides of his family. He grew up accustomed to rich foods saturated in butter and grandmothers who—when he was a child—felt insulted if he didn't clean his plate twice during Sunday dinners. Not only were the desserts rich; whipping cream was a standard topping. He still loves meat, potatoes, gravy, creamed vegetables, strudels, and rich chocolate desserts. When he recalls how he threatened his mother as a small boy when he didn't get his way, he laughs out loud. He told us he'd say, "All right then, I will go to Grandma's and she will fix me rice." The rice he loved was covered with warm cream and sugar, and sprinkled with cinnamon.

Just think about a holiday dinner like Thanksgiving. This traditional meal was—and is—served from a "groaning board" loaded to capacity. We call it a real success if we end up stuffed so full that discomfort borders on pain.

One person's Thanksgiving dinner might include yams in butter and brown sugar, while another's has green beans and corn as vegetables. In an Italian household a frequent side dish is homemade ravioli. Some turkeys are stuffed with rich oyster dressings, others have apple and raisin dressings, or rice and sausage laced with nuts and seasoned bread cubes.

Think about all the changes in our lifetime regarding the cultivation and storage of food. Years ago, summer months were spent raising vegetables and harvesting fruits to be canned or preserved for the winter. A root cellar was used to keep potatoes, onions, carrots, and apples fresh long into the winter months. Many of us remember helping our mothers can tomatoes, pickles, peaches, applesauce, carrots, beans, peas—everything the family ate during the winter. What a good feeling it was to go into the basement to see the shiny jars lined up and ready.

Senior Americans remember putting a card in the window to let the iceman know how many pounds of fresh ice were needed for the "ice box" inside. Freezing as a common method of food preservation didn't really begin until about forty-five years ago. Refrigerated railroad cars, trucks, and the airlines brought us to where we are today—a nation of people who can have anything we want to eat all year round.

Years ago, county fairs rewarded the best cooks with blue ribbons and celebrations centered on events tied together with rich foods. One woman I talked to laughed as she remembered her mother's tirade when packaged cake mixes were first introduced. What was at issue, she said, more than the fact that angel food cake came from a box, was the "laziness" of any woman unwilling to separate and beat a dozen egg whites and "do it right."

Two large, deep drawers in our kitchens once were lined with sheet metal to hold the quantities of flour and sugar needed for baking that was done at least weekly in every household. One man with whom I spoke remembered, with tears of delight, racing home to eat the "heels" of freshly baked bread drenched in butter. He said one of the happiest memories of his life was associated with the bellyaches caused by overeating what his mother baked.

New England gave us the boiled dinner of corned beef and cabbage; we credit the South with deep-fried chicken and honey-glazed ham; the Midwest is known for its solid, rich, rib-sticking food. Regardless of where we're from, all our tastes are based on those things we associate with our childhoods: warmth, love, caring, social status, special people, and special events.

So, here I am writing and thinking about freshly baked, butter-drenched bread, homemade fudge, caramel apples, meats, potatoes and gravies, ravioli, sugar-coated yams, and Southern fried chicken. Since I've gone this far, I might just as well mention a new dessert I recently encountered called "Death by Chocolate." For me, making food choices is an opportunity for personal triumph. As much as I love food, I've learned that my choices in food are as much in my control as are other choices that affect my life and health. I've also learned that good nutrition involves a lot more than choosing foods and a good diet. It means understanding the science of how our bodies use the food we eat.

Our bodies change as we grow older and so does our ability to absorb, transport, store, and excrete nutrients found in food. Senior Americans often develop an impaired ability to utilize nutrients, and they also tend to choose inadequate diets which doubly compromise their health. Foods are made up of nutrients essential to good health. They must be absorbed and transported to be converted or broken down and used in the bodily processes essential to our lives.

Good nutrition at this later stage of our lives is just as important as it was when we were growing up. As inadequate nutrition slows growth in children, it can accelerate deterioration in Senior Americans. On the other hand, *overnutrition*—too much fat and calories—can contribute to obesity and killer diseases like heart disease, cancer, diabetes, and hypertension. There is growing evidence that we really are what we eat.

Even though we're all inclined to follow lifelong eating habits, reducing fat and cholesterol—even after sixty years of a regular diet of eggs, fatty meats, and butter—can make us healthier, especially if the changes made don't affect a diet's overall quality. It's also true that when Senior Americans lose interest in preparing foods, just a few weeks of compromised nutrition may result in lowered resistance to infection, nutritional deficiencies, or loss of lean muscle.

Because Senior Americans have a lowered reserve of body nutrients and a diminished capacity to bounce back from bouts of illness or stress, it's even more important to be consistent in maintaining sound eating habits. Like it or not, a number of things happen in later years. There are physical changes in the way our organs function which affect the way our bodies use foods, alter our senses, lessen the number of taste buds, and slow the flow of saliva, causing a reduction in sensitivity to sweet, salty, bitter, and sour tastes. If dentures don't fit properly, chewing is compromised. Many nutritional problems are related to disease and, unfortunately, susceptibility to disease increases with age. Not surprisingly, drugs often are included in a Senior American's overall management of health—drugs that sometimes affect appetite and the way the body uses nutrients found in foods.

Where choosing food is concerned, growing old is most definitely *not* for sissies. Choosing to eat well is essential to feeling well and staying healthy. This is no time to throw up your hands in surrender to habits maintained throughout your life. If I can make changes in *my* diet (like occasionally saying "No thank you" to a piece of creamy cheesecake and instead choosing fresh fruit), so can you. Simply stated, proper dietary habits and sound nutrition can keep nutrition up and poor health at bay. Choosing to eat well is up to you. And if you make that choice, you need to know how nutrition recommendations should be tailored to meet the special needs of Senior Americans.

NUTRITION CHOICES

Many Senior Americans eat poorly because they don't enjoy eating alone and food doesn't seem that important. Others find that preparing food requires too much effort and it's easier to eat whatever is handy rather than take the time to cook a nutritious meal. When it comes to nutrition, Senior Americans are no different than any other Americans—they don't know enough.

Without a doubt, I love good food, but I confess I never knew much about nutrition. Luckily, I have a friend who is an expert in this field. So I asked if she would develop and write this special chapter to meet the informational needs of Senior Americans.

Jamie Pope is the director of nutrition for Vanderbilt University's Weight Management Program. She has her master of science degree in nutrition and is a Registered Dietitian. She credits many of her personal food habits and career choices to her grandparents, Gilley and Ruth Stephens, who run a 100-acre farm in middle Tennessee. Her grandmother is seventy-eight and her grandfather is seventy-nine. Their active lifestyle and lifelong diet-conscious attitudes confirm, in Jamie's view, the direct link of proper nutrition and exercise with continuing good health, vigor, and a positive outlook on life.

What follows is a thorough approach to how to eat well. I think you'll find it direct and informative. What's most important is that all the information included has been tailored to meet the specific needs of Senior Americans. We can tell you what to do and why to do it, but choosing to listen and perhaps making some changes in the way you eat is up to you.

Nutritional Requirements for Senior Americans

The Food and Nutrition Board of the National Research Council released the first edition of its recommended daily allowances—RDAs—for nutrients in food in 1941. Since then, it's been updated as new developments and research in the field of nutrition have occurred. The recommended levels for the various nutrients are intended to maintain health and prevent nutritional deficiency diseases in just about all healthy people. The RDAs are not intended as a guarantee for good health, but they are the basis for planning and evaluating adequate diets.

The most recently published RDAs (1980) divide adult population into two age groups—twenty-three to fifty, and fifty-one years of age and older. There has been concern, however, that these classifications are too broad, and that the needs of Senior Americans have not been addressed adequately. Senior Americans show greater complexity in their health and in their corresponding nutritional requirements than younger adults. An individual's physical condition at fifty-five is very different from what it is at eighty-five. In spite of that fact, until recently there has been very little research done concerning the nutritional needs of older Americans. In fact, most data used for people older than fifty-one has been taken from studies involving younger people. Nevertheless, there *is* light on the horizon. Research is gaining momentum as centers like the one at Tufts University in Boston are established to deal primarily with nutrition research related to Senior Americans. Also, a nutrition analysis, diet improvement software package for the Apple Computer and the IBM-PC, called the Dine System, is available from DineSystems, Inc., of Buffalo, New York. Dine was developed, in part, with the help of the Department of Health and Human Services. A study has been completed, funded by the National Institute on Aging, to identify nutritional guidelines for Senior Americans. I've used this computer program, and it's useful and revealing where one's eating habits and nutritional need are concerned.

Although current RDAs provide a sound base for determining the nutritional needs of people over fifty-five, it is important to understand that

RDAs, as well as other recommendations in this chapter, are generalized. Your physician and a dietitian can offer individual advice and guidance about tailoring dietary recommendations to fit your needs. This help may be especially important for Senior Americans because of an increased tendency to have one or more diseases or disorders that require a special diet. The American Dietetic Association estimates that as many as half of all Senior Americans have nutritional problems requiring professional assistance.

What foods you select, how you prepare them, and how and when you eat them determine the nutrients you'll consume—the more varied the food selection, the more likely you'll be to get the daily nutrients you need. National nutrition surveys tell us that a large percentage of Senior Americans are getting less than two-thirds of the RDAs needed for many essential nutrients. When this fact is combined with an impaired ability to use the nutrients in food because of physical changes associated with aging, the problem becomes even greater.

Senior Americans tend to have a difficult time meeting nutritional requirements for a number of reasons: limited budgets, a lack of interest or inconvenience in preparing food from "scratch," feelings that depress appetite, and difficulty shopping for food. Any or all of these reasons make prepackaged products attractive even though they may lack nutrients, may be overly refined, high in salt, and expensive. Missing teeth or poor-fitting dentures can further complicate the situation and result in limiting food choices to soft, low-nutrition items. Finally, many older Americans are encouraged by their doctors to modify their diets in certain ways—cut calories, cut fat, cut cholesterol, cut salt, and so on. These modifications may appear overwhelming, particularly if lifetime favorites must be eliminated.

The first step toward improving diet and health is learning what may be compromising your nutrition. A brief review of the major nutrients in food, as well as special considerations for Senior Americans, follows.

Calories

Calories are a measure of the energy value in food. Everyone needs a certain number of them each day to fuel the body to perform basic functions like breathing, blood circulation, body temperature regulation, and digestion. Any physical work done above this level like walking, housecleaning, or gardening requires additional calories. Foods provide calories in differing amounts. The type of foods selected, the quantity consumed, and how often we eat determine the number of calories we take in daily. Our body's needs and our activities determine the number of calories we use up or burn. If we take in too few calories to meet our daily needs, we lose weight. Our bodies turn to their calorie reserves in the form of body fat to supply additional energy when needed. If we eat more calories than are needed or burned, the result is weight gain when excess calories are stored as fat. Eventually, daily accumulation of fat from too many calories results in obesity.

As we grow older, the proportion of body fat to lean tissue changes. Lean tissue, namely muscle and bone, gradually decreases with age. Even if at the age of seventy-five you weigh the same as you did in high school, you actually have more fat.

It takes more calories to fuel muscle than to fuel fat, which accounts in part for the decrease in calories we need as we grow older. Since most people become less active, calorie utilization is further decreased, which also lowers calorie requirements.

RDA recommendations for people between fifty-one and seventy-five years of age is ten percent lower than calorie requirements for younger adults. After the age of seventy-five, calorie needs decrease another ten to fifteen percent. However, this drop in necessary calories doesn't change the need for essential vitamins and minerals. Consequently, it becomes necessary to pack more nutrition into *fewer* calories. This can be quite a challenge, leaving less room for foods that provide lots of calories with little nutrition like sweets, candy, fats, and alcohol. Unfortunately, many Senior Americans actually consume more of these foods than their younger counterparts, making it even more difficult to achieve a balance in calories and good nutrition.

Calories are of particular concern for those trying to manage their weight. Obesity is prevalent in older adults and contributes to the development of heart disease, high blood pressure, diabetes, and other diseases. It also puts stress on bones and joints. If you've been told you have a condition associated with being overweight, you'd be well advised to consult your physician or a dietitian about safe and effective weight loss. If you're only *slightly* above your ideal body weight (ten to fifteen percent) and don't have a condition related to excess weight, evidence suggests that a little excess weight in otherwise healthy Senior Americans *may* actually be protective. Your body may need to pull from those fat reserves in the future for unforeseen illnesses, surgeries, or infections. Ideally, weight should be "managed" with regular physical activity and a sensible diet, preventing extra pounds from building up to the point that secondary diseases become a risk.

Many Senior Americans are interested in weight management and are attempting to control calorie intake. If you fit into this category, dietary fat is the place to start. An ounce of fat has more than twice as many calories as an ounce of any other food. Replace fat with more nutritious, lower-calorie foods like vegetables, grains, and fruits. Prepare foods with little, if any, added fats. Try low-fat cooking methods like baking, broiling, steaming, or boiling. Season with spices and herbs rather than reaching for a pat of butter. Try some of the low-fat products on the market like reduced-fat salad dressings or spreads. With an open mind and a little creativity, you *can* reduce fat without losing flavor or food quality.

It's important not to overlook the other side of the energy equation that includes exercise and physical activity. Remaining active helps maintain muscle mass and muscle tone, boosts spirits, aids in weight control, and may even extend years of life. Walking, cycling, tennis, golf, or swimming are activities enjoyed by millions of healthy Senior Americans. A brisk, thirty-minute daily walk invigorates body, mind, and soul. Before making any significant increases in physical activity, consult your doctor.

Protein

Our bodies need protein to build and repair cells and tissues. Regardless of age, our protein requirements don't decline, even though our ability to grow and repair cells and tissues slows down. In fact, Senior Americans may need more protein than younger adults because of a decreased ability to digest and absorb protein from foods. Protein requirements for people older than seventy years of age can be as much as fifty percent higher than for their younger counterparts. It's important to remember, however, that the diet of Americans— in all age groups—frequently exceeds the RDA for protein, and therefore an increase in protein intake is usually not warranted.

Even though protein is found in almost all foods, our bodies must have "complete" protein to make or repair tissue. Complete protein is found in animal foods like meat, poultry, fish, eggs, and dairy products. And beans, peas, and nuts make complete proteins when combined with grains. A complete protein should be included at each meal. The "Grocery List" at the end of this chapter gives specific advice about getting the most protein for your food dollar.

Carbohydrates

About forty percent of our total calories come from carbohydrates. Nutritionists recommend that we eat more complex carbohydrates in place of fatty foods to boost the total carbohydrate in our diets to at least fifty percent of our total calorie intake. Carbohydrates are classified as "simple" or "complex." Simple carbohydrates are sugars, honey, sweets, sugary desserts, and candy. They're high in calories but provide very little in the way of nutrition and are often called "empty" calorie foods. Trying to achieve the best nutrition within a reasonable calorie level doesn't permit frequent use of these foods. Simple carbohydrates require little breakdown by the body and enter the bloodstream fairly rapidly. They are restricted in diabetic diets and should be used with discretion by all Senior Americans because the body's ability to manage blood sugar is frequently impaired in later years. Complex carbohydrates, on the other hand, provide an excellent source of nutrients without lots of calories. Complex carbohydrates like vegetables, grains, breads, and legumes should have a prominent place in everybody's diet.

Fats

Fats are used primarily to flavor and prepare foods. But flavor, in this case, is accompanied by lots of calories. One teaspoon of a fat like butter contains about forty-five calories—the same number of calories found in one cup of broccoli, three crackers, or a small apple. Pure and simple? We eat too much fat in this country, and the high incidence of obesity proves it. Cutting back on fat automatically reduces calories, usually without compromising nutrition. And if we replace fat with complex carbohydrates, we get a nutrient bonus.

Although fat does provide essential fatty acids in the absorption of certain vitamins, the amount of fat needed for these functions is minimal.

There are different types of fat present in foods. Although the calorie values are the same, they differ in chemical structure. Some fats are considered "saturated" while others are "unsaturated." The significance of a fat being saturated or unsaturated lies in the effect it has upon our blood cholesterol levels. Saturated fats raise blood cholesterol and elevated levels of cholesterol in the blood increase the risk of heart attack. Unsaturated fats—usually referred to as monounsaturated or polyunsaturated—don't raise cholesterol levels in the blood. Replacing saturated fats with unsaturated fats in the diet can help control blood cholesterol levels.

Saturated fats tend to be hard at room temperature and usually are animal in origin. Butter, lard, marbling in meat, and the fat found in cream and whole milk are examples of fats that are primarily saturated. Saturated fats also predominate in certain vegetable fats like hydrogenated margarines, shortenings, palm oil, coconut oil, and cocoa butter. Substitute unsaturated fats like corn oil, safflower oil, sunflower oil, soybean oil, or olive oil in cooking and recipes. Use margarines made from these oils in place of butter. It is important to remember that the number of calories in saturated and unsaturated fats are the same—so don't overdo it.

The bonus we get when we reduce the amount of fat and saturated fat in our diets is a simultaneous reduction in dietary cholesterol. Cholesterol is not only present in our bloodstream and in other parts of our bodies; it also is found in foods of animal origin. Eggs, fatty meats, and high-fat dairy products all contain cholesterol. Prudent use of these foods helps control the amount of cholesterol we get through our diets which, in turn, aids in achieving or maintaining a good blood cholesterol level. Ask your physician about your blood cholesterol level.

Considerable debate has centered on whether reducing saturated fat and cholesterol in the diets of older Americans is warranted. Here again, it's important to recognize the need for individualization. Senior Americans who have eaten high-fat, high-cholesterol diets most of their lives are at higher risk for a first or *second* heart attack, and any reduction in blood cholesterol that can be achieved with diet reduces that risk. Lowering elevated blood cholesterol levels is particularly beneficial for people who have other risk factors present for heart attack, like high blood pressure, diabetes, a family history of heart attack, or obesity. It's never too late to take preventive action.

Vitamins

Vitamins are classified as *water-soluble* or *fat-soluble*. Water-soluble vitamins (the B vitamins and C) *can't* be stored in our bodies and must be supplied every day through the food we eat. Fat-soluble vitamins (A, D, E, and K) *can* be stored in the body and then utilized when our diets do not provide a sufficient supply. In general, Senior Americans' reserves of most nutrients—including fat-soluble vitamins—are much lower than in younger adults, making it even more important for older individuals to obtain needed nutrients through a varied and well-balanced diet every day.

Vitamin intake can be affected by the status of our health, the presence of disease, and the foods we choose to eat. Maintaining an adequate diet can also be hampered by physical, social, financial, and emotional barriers. Research indicates that many Senior Americans don't consume enough B vitamins, Vitamin A, Vitamin D, thiamine, and riboflavin. Although Senior Americans' vitamin needs aren't necessarily greater than those of younger adults, the impact of an inadequate intake upon health and susceptibility to disease can be greater. If a wide variety of foods are eaten in adequate amounts, they can provide sufficient vitamins to maintain health.

Vitamin supplementation usually isn't necessary when a sound, sensible diet is followed. Interestingly, the use of vitamin and mineral supplements is quite common in later life. The decision to take vitamin and mineral supplements, especially when they exceed the RDA, should be discussed with your doctor. "Megadose" supplements, which exceed the RDA, can actually be dangerous.

Minerals

Foods contain certain minerals in trace amounts that are essential to life. However, when examined in national nutrition surveys, the food choices and diets of many elderly Americans were found to be low in several important minerals—particularly iron, calcium, and zinc. It's interesting to note that a number of maladies associated with aging can actually be attributed to a lack of these minerals. Consequently, the question arises: Are all the disorders of Senior Americans a consequence of growing older or could they be due to dietary or lifestyle practices?

A low intake of calcium is strongly associated with the development of a bone condition called osteoporosis, especially in postmenopausal women. Calcium requirements for women after menopause are higher than for younger women because of hormonal changes and an acceleration of bone loss. Dietary practices and amount of exercise influences the strength and integrity of the bones throughout life—including the later years. When you consider that the majority of older women get less than half of the calcium they need each day, it's no wonder fragile and broken bones are so common. Milk is the richest source of calcium and its consumption goes down as people get older. Unless Senior American women are careful to include at least three good calcium sources a day, calcium supplements may be necessary. Check with your doctor or a registered dietitian about whether or not you need supplementary calcium and which supplement to use.

Calcium is not only essential for healthy bones and teeth; it's also required for muscle contraction and blood clotting. Evidence is also present to support calcium's role in controlling blood pressure. An increased incidence of high blood pressure has been associated with low levels of calcium in the blood.

Iron is an essential mineral involved in the formation of red blood cells that carry oxygen to all parts of the body. A woman's requirements for iron are almost double that of a man's until she reaches menopause, at which time the RDA for iron becomes the same for both sexes. This is due to the cessation of menstruation. Studies show that Senior Americans' intake of iron is less than two-thirds of the recommended level. This inadequate intake is further compounded by a decreased ability to retain iron once it is absorbed. The status of iron in our systems is measured through a blood count of hematocrit. Because a low hematocrit, or "iron-poor blood," can be caused by a variety of factors aside from a diet low in iron, a careful evaluation is needed before any treatment is started. Iron-poor blood, or iron-deficiency anemia, can result in listlessness, fatigue, and a general lack of get-up-and-go. Some people relate these symptoms to aging when they may be due to low iron levels in the blood. Lean meats, organ meats, fortified cereals and breads, and certain dried fruits like apricots and raisins are good sources of iron. Although iron supplementation may be beneficial to some people, it should only be started with your doctor's direction.

Fluids

Fluids keep the body hydrated and assist with proper digestion of foods. Without fluids, namely water, we couldn't survive much longer than a few days. The intake of fluids frequently declines as people grow older. This decline may be caused by taste changes affecting the flavor and appeal of beverages, or the misconception that limiting fluid intake will control the number of trips one has to make to the bathroom. Even mild dehydration can result in fatigue and other physical complaints that can lead to serious problems if not resolved. Although the exact fluid requirements for Senior

Americans is unknown, drinking six to eight glasses (forty-eight to sixty-four ounces) of fluids every day—preferably water—is a good rule to follow.

Fiber

Fiber is not necessarily recognized as a nutrient, but its importance in our diet has been well established. It's vital to proper intestinal function and passes through the body undigested, which adds bulk and holds water. The result is an improved movement of waste through the intestine. Low-fiber diets are associated with chronic irregularity, certain forms of cancer, diverticulosis, and intestinal disease.

Constipation is a common complaint among the elderly and is often caused, or aggravated, by a diet low in fiber. Insufficient fluid intake, inactivity, and loss of muscle tone also can be contributing factors. Boosting fiber in the diet with whole grains, bran cereals, fruits, and vegetables, plus moderate activity and plenty of fluids, can help alleviate irregularity and constipation. If you feel you need an over-the-counter remedy to help, use stool softeners rather than laxatives. If constipation becomes a chronic problem, consult your doctor.

Special Concerns of Senior Americans

Modified Diets

The presence of certain conditions or diseases often warrants a restriction or manipulation of various dietary components in order to control or treat the associated disorder. People with heart disease may have been instructed by their doctors to control cholesterol, fat, and salt. Diabetics are restricted in the use of concentrated sweets and fats.

Special or modified diets generally are nutritionally adequate, especially when planned by a Registered Dietitian or qualified health professional. When people try to restrict their own diets, they sometimes go overboard and may eliminate important foods, compromising their overall nutrition. Medical supervision is very important in the monitoring of a prescribed diet to assure its appropriateness and effectiveness.

Following any special diet is difficult—especially when it means a major change in lifelong food habits. An even greater challenge arises when more than one restriction is involved. Advice or suggestions from well-meaning friends and relatives can further complicate the situation. Unless people have a real understanding of the reasons for special diets and whatever modifications are involved, it's not likely they'll be correctly followed or maintained. A restriction of favorite foods or interference with someone's food patterns can result in not following the prescribed diet at all, compromising the diet's quality and quantity, or a flat-out refusal to take the time needed to purchase and prepare special foods.

When a modified diet is prescribed by your doctor, it makes sense to seek professional nutrition guidance. It's essential for good health, as well as treatment or prevention of a related disease condition, to maintain adequate nutrition while incorporating any changes. When planned creatively and approached with an open mind, a modified diet can be just as tasty and varied as a "normal" diet. The services of a Registered Dietitian can be very helpful in tailoring your doctor's recommendations to your eating habits and individual needs.

This chapter's purpose isn't to discuss all modified diets. However, because of the high percentage of older Americans with diet-related conditions, it's worthwhile to discuss briefly the modifications most commonly prescribed.

Calorie Modification

Calories are controlled in diets of those people who need to reduce or control body weight because of diabetes, hypertension, or heart disease. Restricting calorie intake results in weight loss. Senior Americans must "diet" with caution because reducing calorie intake results in a reduction of vitamins and minerals as well as a reduction in weight. If weight loss is recommended, calorie restriction should be moderate so that weight loss is very gradual. When done this way, the body's store of important nutrients isn't depleted. Weight loss and dieting should be undertaken only with the supervision of your doctor. A Registered Dietitian can help plan a calorie-controlled diet for safe and effective weight management.

Cholesterol Modification

Cholesterol is a fatlike substance essential for many of the human body's chemical process. Our bodies make sufficient amounts of cholesterol to meet our needs. We get additional cholesterol from animal foods like eggs, meats, and high-fat dairy products consumed in our diets.

When high levels of cholesterol are present in the blood, it's been found to increase the chances of having a heart attack or stroke. Unfortunately, Americans' blood cholesterol levels are among the highest in the world, due primarily to high cholesterol and saturated fat content in our country's diet.

Reducing the intake of saturated fat and cholesterol helps lower blood cholesterol and reduces the risk of heart attack. People with elevated blood cholesterol levels or with heart disease generally are instructed to follow low-cholesterol diets. Although considerable debate has taken place governing the effectiveness of low-cholesterol diets for

Senior Americans, recent evidence indicates that a moderate restriction of cholesterol and saturated fats can lower blood cholesterol levels and slow the progression of heart disease.

Saturated fats like butter, lard, meat fat, or hydrogenated vegetable fats contribute to high blood cholesterol levels and they are restricted on low-cholesterol diets. Substitution of polyunsaturated fats like corn oil, safflower oil, or vegetable oil margarines is generally recommended.

Sodium/Salt Modification

Sodium is a mineral needed to balance fluids in the body. We get sodium primarily through table salt—and plenty of it! Americans have been estimated to consume ten to thirty times the amount of salt needed every day.

People with high blood pressure or medical histories of fluid retention—particularly fluid retention around the heart (congestive heart failure)—most often are placed on low-sodium diets. Salt doesn't cause high blood pressure, but it can make high blood pressure worse or cause sodium-sensitive people to increase their chances of high blood pressure. It's also important to know that medications prescribed for blood-pressure control are more effective with moderate sodium restriction.

Diet and Drugs

Senior Americans tend to take prescription and over-the-counter medications for everything from minor aches to serious diseases. In comparison to the overall population, Senior Americans consume a disproportionate quantity of drugs—considerably more than the young and middle-aged. They're also more likely to take more than one medication at a time and usually for longer periods of time. The higher rate of drug use is primarily related to an increased incidence of disease and age-related conditions that are treated with medication. However, an additional factor appears to be the inclination shared by Senior Americans to use medications to remedy everyday maladies or derive benefits promoted through the media.

Excessive use or misuse of drugs is a real problem among Senior Americans. People sometimes have several prescriptions from different doctors—some of which may be unnecessary or harmful when used in combination. And the notion that if low dosages don't relieve symptoms higher dosages will can lead to overdose. Other drug misuse can be caused by a preoccupaion with minor symptoms or bodily functions like bowel movements and use of laxatives. "Doubling up" on dosages when medications are forgotten or failing to follow a prescribed drug regimen can have serious consequences. So can taking another household member's medications—even if symptoms are the same. Medications and their prescribed use are completely individual. Misuse of drugs can also result through a misinterpretation or misunderstanding of advice given by health professionals, as well as through inappropriate recommendations given by nonprofessionals and the media.

Foods and eating patterns can be directly influenced by the action and use of certain drugs. For example, beverages that contain caffeine slow the absorption of some medications. Meal content—and timing in relation to drug dosages—influence how quickly drugs reach the bloodstream. It's very important to find out from your doctor what, if any, impact your diet can have on medication you may be taking.

Just as food can influence a drug's effectiveness, drugs affect the way our bodies utilize and store the nutrients in food. When you consider that a Senior American's health status and nutrient reserves already may be compromised, the nutritional impact of multiple drug usage can be serious. Some drugs deplete the body's store of certain nutrients, which can be significant if the person's usual diet isn't nutritionally sound. Senior Americans are especially at risk where a drug-induced nutrient depletion may be concerned. This can happen not only because of extensive drug use, but also as a result of aging, a low-quality diet, or the presence of disease. The problem can be further compounded because of the negative effect some drugs have on appetite and the taste of food.

Important Reminders*

- Take medication only when necessary and as prescribed.
- Don't keep medications too long; they may lose their effectiveness if kept longer than a year.
- Don't take medications prescribed for someone else—even if the symptoms are similar.
- Never double up on medication if you miss a dose.
- Check the label each time you take a medication to be sure it is the correct bottle.
- Don't drink alcohol when taking medication.
- Keep medicine bottles tightly capped in a dark, cool spot away from children's reach (the medicine cabinet in the bathroom is too warm and moist).
- Drink plenty of water when taking any medication.
- Find out if it is best to take your medication with or without food.
- Inquire about interactions or complications of combining one drug with another or with certain foods.
- Tell your physician about any over-the-counter medications or nutrition supplements you may be taking.

*Also review "Common Drug Sense," p. 219.

- Do not use antacids or laxatives on a regular basis.
- Be aware that some over-the-counter drugs contain salt, sugar, and/or caffeine.

Nutrition Supplements

"Health" foods and nutrition supplements have created a billion-dollar-a-year industry in the United States. Among the prime targets for these businesses are Senior Americans. This industry suggests that its products can improve your health, prevent disease, and extend your life, and often exploits the findings of scientific studies to promote them. The sensational claims that are made often stop just short of violating the Food and Drug Administration (FDA) regulations. It's no wonder many Senior Americans are enthusiastic. When certain foods or supplements promise vitality, improved well-being, relief from health complaints, and longer life, there's reason to get excited. The truth is that the vast majority of these claims and promises are false or partial truths that have been lifted from scientific research or created to meet advertising needs. And these products tend to be expensive. The real loss is when Senior Americans use money to buy these products and end up diverting funds that could be used to buy healthful and nutritious foods.

It's been estimated that more than sixty percent of Senior Americans take one or more nutrition supplements. Heading the list are vitamin and mineral preparations used every day and frequently in large dosages. For the most part, supplementation just isn't necessary when a person's usual diet is well-balanced, with a wide variety of foods eaten in appropriate amounts. All the vitamins and minerals we need each day can be supplied through foods. These are the reasons for which supplementation *is* indicated:

- Your body's reserves of certain nutrients drop because of illness, prolonged stress, or poor nutrition.
- Your usual calorie intake is less than 1,500 calories daily.
- Your diet doesn't include a variety of foods, or you are following multiple diet restrictions.
- You are taking a medication(s) that depletes your body of one or more nutrients and have been so informed by your doctor or a Registered Dietitian.

When supplements are needed they should provide approximately 100 percent of the RDA. Avoid "megadosages" of vitamins and minerals that contain several times the RDA. Large dosages are not necessary or beneficial for most people. In fact, they can actually be harmful when used over an extended period of time. Although most excess nutrients are lost in urine, some are stored in the body. Vitamins A, D, E, and K are fat-soluble vitamins that can accumulate to toxic levels when taken in megadosage amounts over a period of time. Excess B vitamins and C are excreted—*along with the money you paid for them*. Relatively inexpensive vitamin-mineral supplements can be purchased that provide 100 percent of the RDA at any pharmacy or food outlet. Your doctor, dietitian, or pharmacist can advise you regarding supplements and brand-name products to purchase.

Nutrition Programs

The growing number of Senior Americans who have nutrition and health needs has prompted development of various private, state, and federal programs intended for persons over sixty years old. The programs are directed at those who have difficulty purchasing foods and eating an adequate diet because of limited income, those who have a limited ability to shop or prepare foods, and those who are limited by mobility or motivation in meal preparation.

Although low-income and minority groups represent target populations, eligibility isn't based upon economic status. The Nutrition Program for Older Americans (NPOA) was instituted by Congress in

1972 through the Title VII Amendment to the Older Americans Act of 1965. This bill mandated the establishment of community-managed locations where food can be obtained. Community-based meals are now provided free of charge (voluntary contributions accepted) under a revised amendment, Title III, through congregate locations at churches, senior citizen centers, and other institutions. Title III programs strive to provide approximately one-third of the recommended dietary allowance (RDA) at least five days a week for Senior Americans who are in need. In many communities, hot "main meals" can be delivered to the homes of shut-in elderly.

Title III has also been expanded to provide "boxed" meals that can be delivered with a hot lunch for a shut-in's supper. And a special nutrition formula is being used experimentally that can be mixed with water for a milk-based, nutrient-rich drink that can be used when regular home-delivered meals aren't possible. In some areas, shut-in Senior Americans also can make use of shopping aides to do their shopping at local markets. (Also see "Assisted Independence," p. 119.)

Many Senior American food programs provide more than nutritious food. They may include education and counseling, referral services, a means of transportation for those who need it, economic benefits, and an opportunity to socialize. The long-term goals are to improve the physical, nutritional, and social well-being of Senior Americans in need of help.

Living Alone—Eating Right

Many Senior Americans are faced with the challenges of shopping and cooking for one or two persons—often on a limited budget. Here are some tips that can help:

- Buy fresh fruit and vegetables in small quantities. If you can only make it to the grocery store once a week, buy underripe produce to use at the end of the week. Promptly refrigerate what you purchase to help prevent spoilage. (See the Grocery List, p. 368, for specifics.)
- Whenever possible, buy individual-serving packages. These may be more expensive, but there is less likelihood of waste and spoilage. Individual servings also help avoid the monotony of having the same foods a number of times in succession—and they take less space.
- If you have enough freezer space, you can buy certain items in larger quantities. Buy several varieties of frozen vegetables in the large bags and use them as you need them. Securely reseal bags and return them immediately to the freezer. Family-size meats and poultry also can save money and be broken up and frozen in individual packages for later use.
- Date any leftovers (a piece of masking tape will do) to help you remember to use them within the next few days or to throw them out.

- Double or triple recipes you cook, and freeze extra servings for reheating later. These are generally more nutritious, economic—and tasty—than commercially packaged dinners.
- Pay special attention to the color, texture, and flavor of food. Choose a wide variety of foods and season them creatively.
- Freeze foods in clear plastic bags or wrap so you can easily tell what they are and to prevent "freezer burn." If you wrap foods in aluminum foil or freezer paper, be sure to label and date the packages.
- Organize your kitchen for convenience and safety. Keep items you use frequently within easy reach.
- Serve meals in a pleasant environment. When eating alone, use an attractive place setting and enjoy your meal free of other distractions (television, newspaper, etc.).
- Organize a group of friends to take turns with potluck meals or arrange outings to restaurants or cafeterias. Surround yourself with those you enjoy.
- Purchase (or suggest it for a gift) one of the many cookbooks designed for one or two persons. They can be an invaluable kitchen resource.

Good nutrition is essential for good health—just as good health is the basis for good nutrition. Even the very best nutrition cannot guarantee super health and freedom from disease. And, as far as we know, nutrition cannot reverse the aging process. But sound nutrition throughout life can improve the *quality* of life. Eating well and making positive health choices can help us enjoy more disease-free years, help us recover more quickly from illness or surgery, and help us keep infections at bay. As we grow older, proper food choice continues to be a primary avenue to attaining and maintaining health.

Grocery List

Alcohol is high in calories, it has no nutritional value, and it's a drug that affects our bodies like any other drug. When used in moderation by healthy, active individuals, it may not be hazardous. However, habitual use and excessive quantities can result in multiple physical and emotional problems—including addiction.

Alcohol should never replace nutritious foods in the diet. Regular use of alcohol can deplete the body of certain nutrients and increase the need for others. This can be serious for Senior Americans whose body nutrient reserves are already reduced and who—without alcohol—already need increased nutrients. Senior Americans, more than younger adults, have to make every calorie count just to assure nutritional quality—which leaves little room for alcohol calories.

Alcohol influences the effectiveness of many drugs, making its consumption of particular concern for Senior Americans because of the increased number of prescribed or self-administered medications ingested.

A very serious and addictive disease, alcoholism is prevalent among Senior Americans. Its use may be the result of a lifelong habit or represent an "escape" from loneliness, boredom, or depression. Whatever the cause, alcoholism kills and is particularly debilitating as age increases. There are many professional treatment programs available.

Assuming you are in good health and enjoy an occasional drink, alcohol should be used only in moderation and, of course, no one should ever drink and drive.

Beans and legumes are one of the best protein, vitamin, and mineral buys for the money. Beans, peas, and lentils make a complete source of protein when combined with whole grains, wheat, nuts, seeds, or dairy products. They make a great high-protein main dish for meals, like the Spanish favorite, red beans and rice.

Dried beans come in a variety of colors, sizes, and flavors. Store them in their packages until opened. Then transfer the beans that aren't used to a covered container. Dried beans will last up to six months in an airtight container. After cooking, they'll last about one week in the refrigerator.

Prepare beans by washing them in cold water first. Most varieties of beans, except lentils and split peas, should be soaked in water overnight, or boiled for two to three minutes and then soaked for at least two hours. After soaking, bring the beans to a boil in the same water they were soaked in, leaving enough room in the pan for the beans to expand. If they begin to stick, add more water. Reduce the heat to low and simmer until tender (about two hours). Don't add salt until after cooking. Check your favorite cookbook for bean recipes.

Canned beans are nearly twice as expensive to serve as dried beans and they are generally high in sodium. If convenience is important, buy canned beans that aren't cooked or seasoned with fat or fatty meats.

Breads are most healthful when made from unbleached and whole wheat flours. White bread isn't *bad;* it just doesn't contain as much fiber or wholesome nutrition as whole grain varieties. Specialty breads like rye or pumpernickel can lend variety to the diet.

Although breads usually stay freshest out of the refrigerator, that isn't true in warm weather, when refrigeration can prevent molding. Always keep breads securely sealed in a plastic bag to retain the moisture. Keep a loaf of your favorite bread in the freezer in case you can't get to the supermarket. It freezes well and will last up to six months if stored in an airtight package.

Butter is high in saturated fats and contains about forty-five calories in each teaspoon serving. If you want to control saturated fat and cholesterol, replace it with margarine. Remember: The calories are the same—so go easy. Try cutting whatever you use in added fats in half. Many recipes work just as well with half the fat. If you do enjoy butter, keep it refrigerated.

Cheese is a very popular food and provides many of the same nutrients as those found in milk, although you generally have to eat more calories of cheese to match the nutrients. Cheese is available at a reasonable cost and the protein it contains is high in quality.

Cheese comes in many varieties, lending versatility for use in recipes and for quick meals and snacks. Remember, however, that cheese contains about 100 calories an ounce and those ounces can add up quickly for people watching their waistlines. Cheese is made from cream, whole milk, or part-skim milk. The part-skim varieties contain less fat, saturated fat, and cholesterol. Also available on the market are reduced-fat cheeses.

Keep several varieties of cheese on hand. Melted cheese on toast with tomato slices, along with fruit, can make a quick and nutritious lunch. Keep cheese refrigerated and be sure to check expiration dates. A little mold can be cut off if the cheese is not older than its date of expiration. Sealing cheese in an airtight plastic bag or container will prevent it from drying out.

Because cheese is usually considered a salty food, people on sodium-restricted diets may have to limit its use to an ounce or two, a few times a week. Processed or pasteurized varieties of cheese are especially high in salt.

Contrary to popular belief, cheese does *not* cause constipation. Constipation may result from insufficient fiber and fluids in the diet, but not from eating cheese.

Cream is loaded with fat and cholesterol. It can easily be replaced in beverages or recipes with low-fat milk or canned, evaporated skim milk. Beware of commercial cream replacements in the form of nondairy creamers. Some of these products contain saturated fats (palm and coconut oil) and should not be used on a regular basis.

Eggs are excellent sources of high-quality protein. You can use them in so many ways that it's easy to make them part of your diet several times a week. Because the yolk contains a high quantity of cholesterol, it's a good idea not to use more than three whole eggs a week. The white of an egg is cholesterol free. Try using one whole egg combined with two egg whites as a replacement for two eggs in recipes or omelets. When preparing eggs use minimal fat. Try poaching, boiling, or scrambling in a nonstick skillet.

Keep eggs refrigerated to retain freshness. They'll last about ten days from the date posted on the carton.

Fish consumption is at an all-time high in this country. The media and the scientific community tell us fish is a heart-healthy, low-fat, high-protein food. They're right; it *is*. Choose *fresh* fish in all varieties. White fish like haddock and cod are lean and very low in fat and cholesterol compared to meat—or even poultry. Cold-water varieties like herring, mackerel, or salmon are higher in fat; however, the fat is primarily unsaturated and appears to protect against heart disease. Health authorities recommend two to three fish meals a week.

Fish should be purchased as fresh as you are able to obtain it. Keep it refrigerated and use it within a day or two of purchase. If you don't use it right away, freeze it in moisture-proof paper. It will keep one to two months without much flavor loss.

Don't overcook fish or it will become dry and tough. To control fat, fry only on occasion—otherwise bake, broil, poach, or steam fish. Herbs, spices, and lemon juice easily—and deliciously—replace butter and salt.

Frozen or canned fish also are popular items and can easily be kept on hand. These items generally have added salt and may have batter coatings. Buy canned fish like tuna packed in water rather than oil if you are trying to control fat and calories. If your trips to the supermarket are limited, frozen or canned fish can provide convenient, high-protein main dishes.

Fruits are nature's "sweets." Available in a wide array of flavors, colors, shapes, sizes, and textures, they make the perfect dessert or snack. Carbohydrate is the major nutrient in all fruits. The variety of fruit selected and its ripeness determine vitamin and fiber content.

Because of consumer demand, most fruits now are available year round. However, it's best to choose fresh fruit in season for peak flavor and juiciness. This is also the time when prices are generally lowest and fruits are of the highest quality. Don't buy more fresh fruit than you need—it perishes quickly. Although refrigeration will help fruit last longer, it should be ripened at room temperature first. Wait to wash fruit until just before it is eaten.

If you like to keep canned or frozen fruit on hand, try the varieties with no sugar added or those packed in their own juices.

Cutting fruit into small, bite-sized pieces can make it easier to chew. Try combining several varieties of fruits for a delicious salad or dessert. And it's best to leave the skins on fruits like apples and pears because of the fiber they provide.

Dried fruits are convenient to keep on hand for snacking or to add to cereals, salads, cookie or bread batters, cottage cheese, and yogurt. Many dried fruits like raisins, prunes, and apricots are good sources of iron.

Grains are the core of the diet of three-fourths of the world's population, yet in the United States most people center their diets on meats. Grains are complex carbohydrates in the form of wheat, rice, and corn. Purchase "whole" grains whenever possible because they haven't been refined and will be higher in fiber and other nutrients. For example, use brown rice instead of white rice and whole wheat flour instead of white flour. Try mixing wheat and white flour in baked goods.

Brown rice is an inexpensive source of many B vitamins and minerals. It can be bought in quantity because it will last at least six months if sealed airtight. Flavor it with herbs and spices, or use it in a vegetable casserole for variety.

Margarine is about eighty percent fat and has the same calories as butter; however, it contains a different kind of fat. Margarines are generally made from vegetable fats or oils, while butter is made from animal fat. Margarines are more unsaturated than butter and can be substituted for butter, lard, or shortening in any recipe. When used in place of butter, margarines made from vegetable oils like corn or safflower can aid in the control of blood cholesterol levels. Avoid using hydrogenated margarines because they are chemically saturated. Although margarine is unsaturated, it's still high in fat and calories—use it sparingly.

Meats—specifically red meats—are good sources of high-quality protein, vitamins, minerals, and especially iron. Although red meats are higher in saturated fat than poultry or fish, they should not be excluded from your diet. Prudent use of red meats is recommended for Senior Americans, who frequently don't get enough iron and certain B vitamins in their diets. Choose lean, well-trimmed, fresh meats with the. U.S.D.A. grade of Choice, Good, or Standard. The more expensive Prime cuts are heavily marbled. Not only do they cost more, they provide more fat and less protein for your food dollar.

Unless you've been otherwise advised by your doctor, feel free to include lean cuts of red meat three to four times a week. Keep portion sizes between three and five ounces and prepare meat without added fat by baking or broiling.

Fresh meat spoils quickly, so keep it refrigerated or freeze it if you aren't going to use it within a few days. Properly frozen, meat will keep about three months in a conventional freezer and longer in a deep freeze. Do not refreeze meat once it has been thawed. Thaw meat in the refrigerator and *never* soak it in water to thaw—water is an ideal breeding ground for bacteria. And you don't necessarily have to thaw meat before cooking. It will take a little longer to prepare, but a fresher flavor will be retained.

Processed meats can have as many as half their calories in fat. When you read the list of ingredients, you'll find fillers, chemicals, corn syrup, flavorings, and nitrates (suspected in causing cancer). Processed meats like frankfurters, bologna, sausage, bacon, and cold cuts contain significant amounts of saturated fat and cholesterol. Using sliced, lean roast beef or turkey breast for sandwich fillers is a much better alternative. You also get more protein for your money even though they won't keep as long in your refrigerator. Freeze individual slices and use them as needed.

Milk isn't just for kids. Rich in calcium and protein, milk provides many essential nutrients throughout our lives. Ideally, older adults should have at least two servings each day of milk and other dairy products. Skim or low-fat milk products are your best choice—all whole milk provides is extra fat and cholesterol, no extra nutrition. If you are an avid whole milk fan, try adding two or three tablespoons of nonfat dry milk to skim or low-fat milk. It will "bulk up" the flavor and boost nutrients without adding fat. Women should be certain to include at least two or three servings of milk or milk products every day in order to achieve their calcium needs. Look for the new calcium-fortified milks now available in the supermarket.

Some people find they have a reduced capacity to tolerate milk and may experience cramping, diarrhea, or bloating after drinking it. Check with your doctor if these symptoms occur, but don't just eliminate milk without replacing the nutrients you lose with other foods or a supplement. And if an intolerance is related to the inability to digest sugar in milk lactose, there are special products available that can help your body break down the lactose, which will help alleviate the intolerance.

Nuts and seeds are a rich source of energy, protein, iron, and other vitamins and minerals. Combining nuts and seeds with dried beans, grains, or milk products forms a complete, high-quality protein. Remember that nuts and seeds *do* contain a significant amount of fat and calories—go easy on the quantity if you're watching your weight.

Store nuts in covered jars or containers to protect them from heat, air, and moisture. This will help keep them fresh and crunchy for as long as six months.

Pasta is rich in complex carbohydrates and is a low-fat way to round out a meal. Because it contains very little protein, pasta should not be used as a substitute for protein foods, but as a side dish with tasty, low-fat sauces. Top whole wheat pasta with meatballs made from lean ground beef that you bake on a cookie sheet instead of frying.

Poultry is a low-fat, inexpensive source of high-quality protein. Turkey and chicken head the list in popular choices. Buy U.S.D.A. Grade A varieties in quantities that satisfy your preference and needs. It's a good idea to sometimes bake a whole bird and freeze parts, or slices, for use at later meals. For one or two people, buy meaty parts like breasts in small packages. Removing the skin before cooking will help reduce saturated fat content. Although it is commonly believed that removing the skin will cause chicken to be dry, that won't happen if you cook with moderate heat and use liquids like fruit juices, wine, or a touch of fat in preparation.

Chicken and turkey are extremely versatile choices for a creative chef. You can keep cooked poultry on hand for sandwiches, salads, or soups. Baking, broiling, boiling, or stir-frying in a minimal amount of oil are recommended preparation methods.

Fresh poultry will keep in your refrigerator for approximately two days before cooking. If you need to store it longer, be sure to freeze it in moisture-proof paper. Frozen properly, it will keep for two to three months.

Sauces can add flavor and variety to meals. Packaged and canned sauces usually contain less wholesome ingredients and more salt than homemade sauces. However, canned spaghetti sauces can be convenient and are good to have on hand for quick, easy dishes. Choose brands without added meat or sugar. When making cream sauces, use evaporated skim milk or low-fat milk thickened with nonfat dry milk in place of cream—you'll save fat and calories without losing out on flavor.

Seasonings or flavor enhancers in the form of herbs, spices, and extracts turn ordinary foods into delicious dishes that appeal to our senses of smell and taste. Experimenting with a variety of fresh or dried herbs can be helpful when you are cutting back on salt in your diet. Look for seasoning and spice suggestions in your favorite cookbooks.

Soups vary in their nutritional value according to the ingredients they contain. Commercially canned or dehydrated soups tend to be high in sodium, but occasionally can be part of a convenient, healthy meal. People on sodium-restricted diets may need to choose reduced sodium varieties. Homemade soups offer the opportunity to choose fresh ingredients and seasonings. Make them with the stock from chicken or a roast and skim the fat. Add fresh vegetables, pasta, rice, or lean meats. Use low-fat or skim milk in place of cream or whole milk for cream soups to reduce fat content. Soups made with milk or meat provide protein and, when combined with bread or crackers, fruit, and maybe a little cheese, make a great meal.

Sweets include cakes, cookies, pies, pastries, and so on. Human beings have an instinctive attraction to these high-fat, high-sugar delicacies. And occasional sweets—in moderate amounts—probably aren't harmful to healthy, active Senior Americans. Problems arise when sweets replace more nutritious foods in our diets because they compromise diet quality. Sweets can also lead to weight gain when eaten in addition to a regular diet because of the extra calories.

Calorie needs for Senior Americans are lower than for younger people, but vitamin and mineral needs *don't* change. They may, in fact, be higher. This leaves little room for high-calorie, low-nutrition foods like sweets. Don't make sugary sweets a mainstay in your diet—try fresh or dried fruit for a sweet snack or dessert.

When you do choose to include something sweet, choose items that are not loaded with fat. Ice milk, sherbets, gelatin, frozen fruit bars, or Popsicles are good choices. If you like baked goods, try angel food cake, animal crackers, ginger snaps, fig bars, or shortcake—and for toppings try low-fat yogurt, ice milk, or assorted fresh fruits.

If you make desserts from scratch, try making a few modifications or substitutions in the ingredients to control fat, cholesterol, and calories. For example, try evaporated skim milk in place of creams; vegetable oil margarines for butter or shortening; low-fat, plain yogurt for sour cream; or two egg whites for a whole egg. Cut back on fat and sugar in recipes by at least twenty-five percent—your taste buds will never know the difference.

Vegetables provide a very rich source of vitamins and minerals in delicious, relatively low-calorie varieties. Because there isn't a single vegetable endowed with all the essential nutrients, it's important to include a broad selection in your diet.

Many people have negative feelings about vegetables possibly because they think something so nutritionally good can't possibly taste good, too. With proper preparation and seasoning, vegetables can be a meal's highlight in both sensory appeal *and* nutritional value.

Whenever possible buy fresh vegetables for the best nutrition and flavor. When cooking vegetables, steam them until just tender or bake them in their own skins. Boiling vegetables, especially for any length of time, may destroy some of the nutrients. If you do boil, use only enough water to prevent burning—never add baking soda because it depletes the B vitamins. If you pan-fry or sauté, use a minimal amount of fat over medium-high heat; add water or broth if extra liquid is needed.

Frozen vegetables can be more convenient, especially if cooking for one or two people and when making trips to the supermarket are difficult. A wide selection can be kept on hand for quick and easy preparation. Buy plain, frozen vegetables. Sauces and other toppings increase calories, salt, and fat content. Add the seasonings or a dab of butter or margarine yourself.

Although they may be less nutritious than their fresh or frozen counterparts, canned vegetables are quick to prepare and easily stored. If you do use canned vegetables and are concerned about your sodium intake, rinse them briefly under running water in a strainer before cooking—this will remove some of the salt. Look for popular brands with *no salt added,* as indicated on the labels. The special "low-sodium" varieties are not significantly lower in salt or sodium, but usually are more expensive. If you are on a sodium-restricted diet, using special low-sodium products may be warranted. If not, buy fresh or frozen vegetables. For the record, celery is *not* high in sodium.

Yogurt is not a "wonder" food, but it can provide calcium, vitamins, and protein. It's made from the interaction of special bacterial cultures and milk. Its smooth consistency makes it a good choice for people who have difficulty chewing. Look for low-fat varieties. Yogurt is available plain, or flavored with extracts, fruits, and sugar. Try the plain, low-fat varieties and mix them with your favorite fresh fruits and just a touch of sugar or honey. You can even stir in a tablespoon or two of bran to boost the fiber content.

Plain yogurt makes a great substitute for sweet or sour cream in recipes. You can also blend it with mayonnaise to reduce calories and fat in salad dressings.

Table 1—Major Vitamins and Minerals: Sources and Functions

NUTRIENT	FOOD SOURCES	SOME FUNCTIONS
Vitamin A	Liver, broccoli, turnips, carrots, pumpkin, sweet potatoes, winter squash, apricots, butter, fortified margarine, fortified dairy products.	Helps maintain eyesight, especially in dim light; aids growth of healthy skin, bones, and teeth; helps resist infection.
Thiamine Vitamin B-1	Pork, liver, lean meats, whole grains, dried beans and peas, nuts.	Helps the body obtain energy from food; aids in keeping healthy; promotes good appetite and digestion.
Riboflavin Vitamin B-2	Dairy products, liver, green leafy vegetables, fortified grain products.	Helps the body use nutrients for energy and tissue repair; important for vision and healthy skin.
Niacin	Lean meats, poultry, fish, dark green leafy vegetables, fortified grain products, peanuts.	Required for healthy nervous system and skin; helps in the use of fats for energy.

NUTRIENT	FOOD SOURCES	SOME FUNCTIONS
Folic Acid	Liver, dried beans and peas, leafy green vegetables.	Important for the use of protein by the body; helps to form red blood cells.
Pyridoxine Vitamin B-6	Lean meats, poultry, fish, shellfish, green vegetables, whole grains, wheat germ, beans and peas.	Helps the body use protein and fats; essential for normal growth.
Vitamin B-12	Lean meats, poultry, fish, dairy products.	Necessary for producing red blood cells and for building new proteins in the body.
Vitamin C	Citrus fruits, strawberries, cantaloupe, tomatoes, potatoes, broccoli, sweet and hot peppers, green leafy vegetables.	Aids in building the materials that hold cells and tissues together; helps in healing wounds and fighting infection; needed for healthy teeth, gums, and blood vessels.
Vitamin D	Fortified dairy products, egg yolk, fish oils; also produced by direct sunlight on skin.	Helps the body use calcium and phosphorus to build strong bones and teeth.

Vitamin E	Vegetable oils, green leafy vegetables, nuts, dry beans and peas, nuts.	Functions are not clearly understood, but is thought to help form red blood cells and muscle tissue; protects Vitamins A and D.
Vitamin K	Green leafy vegetables, cauliflower, egg yolk, liver, soybean oil.	Promotes normal clotting of blood.
Calcium	Dairy products, green leafy vegetables, broccoli, canned mackerel and salmon (with bones), tofu, figs.	Builds and maintains healthy bones and teeth; aids in blood clotting; important in wound healing and fighting infection.
Copper	Green leafy vegetables, seafood, whole grains, dried fruits.	Needed for formation of blood.
Fluoride	Fluoridated water.	Protects against tooth decay and strengthens bones.
Iodine	Iodized salt, saltwater fish and shellfish.	Needed for formation of hormones made by the thyroid gland.
Iron	Lean meats, organ meats, egg yolk, enriched whole grains, dried beans, raisins	Necessary for production of red blood cells and the transport of oxygen in the

NUTRIENT	FOOD SOURCES	SOME FUNCTIONS
	and other dried fruits, dark green leafy vegetables.	body; prevents iron-poor blood (anemia).
Magnesium	Whole grain cereals, soybeans, nuts.	A must for strong bones and teeth; helps with muscle contraction; necessary for transmitting nerve impulses.
Phosphorus	Dairy products, nuts, whole grains, dried beans and peas.	Works with calcium to keep bones and teeth healthy; involved with proper use of fat in the body; needed by the "energy" enzymes.
Potassium	Lean meats, dried apricots, avocados, bananas, dried beans and peas, potatoes, most other fruits.	Keeps nerves and muscles healthy; helps to maintain fluid balance.
Sodium	Table salt, processed foods, luncheon meats, pickled foods, most cheeses, salted snack foods.	Preserves water balance in the body.
Zinc	Green leafy vegetables, shellfish, organ meats.	Used for building proteins in the body.

Table 2—Dietary Guidelines for Senior Americans

The Basic Four Food Groups represent a practical way to achieve or approximate the RDA (recommended daily allowance) for the nutrients in food. Listed below are the groups of foods and recommended number of servings for Senior Americans. These recommendations are very generalized and indicate the minimum number of servings Senior Americans should try for each day.

FOOD GROUP	FOODS INCLUDED	RECOMMENDED MINIMUM NUMBER OF SERVINGS
Milk and Milk Products	Milk, yogurt, cheese, cottage cheese, ice cream, ice milk, pudding.	2—postmenopausal women should aim for 3.
Meats and Meat Substitutes	Lean meats, poultry, fish, eggs, beans, legumes, peas, tofu.	1–2 three-ounce servings.

FOOD GROUP	FOODS INCLUDED	RECOMMENDED MINIMUM NUMBER OF SERVINGS
Fruits and Vegetables	All fruits and vegetables (preferably fresh). Average serving about ½ cup.	2 servings of fruit (one that is rich in Vitamin C); 2 servings of vegetables (one of which is a leafy green).
Breads and Cereals	Breads, cereals, crackers, macaroni, pasta, grains, rice. Average serving is one slice of bread or ½ cup cereal or grain product.	4—preferably whole grains.
Other	Fats, oils, sweets, alcohol.	*

*There is no recommendation for this group. Foods included here are essentially "empty calorie" foods that offer relatively high calories with minimal or no nutritional value. These foods should only be included after the recommended number of servings from the other groups are met and if the individual's calorie needs allow for these additional "empty" calories.

SAMPLE MENUS

The following menus provide 1,500 to 1,800 calories. They are planned according to the "Basic Four" food-group plan (see Table 2). These menus are controlled in cholesterol and saturated fat. Concentrated sweets and high-fat foods are not included. The menus were designed to provide rich sources of dietary fiber. Use your imagination and your favorite cookbooks to expand upon these basic menus, using the foods and portion sizes as a guide. Feel free to interchange the lunches and dinners if your main meal is midday. Enjoy!

DAY 1

Breakfast
1 cup low-fat milk
½ cup unsweetened orange juice
Cheese toast: 1 oz. cheese,
1 slice whole grain bread
1 cup high-fiber dry cereal
Coffee or tea

Lunch
Tuna-Macaroni Toss:
½ cup water-packed tuna
½ cup sliced carrots and celery (raw)
1 cup cooked macaroni, chilled
1 tbsp. mayonnaise
5 whole grain crackers

(Or substitute a tuna-salad sandwich
with fruit for this meal)

Snack
Apple, sliced and spread
with 1 tbsp. peanut butter
1 cup low-fat milk

Dinner
3 oz. lean hamburger, broiled
1 multigrain hamburger roll
Lettuce and sliced tomatoes
Mustard and/or ketchup
Fresh fruit salad—about 1 cup

DAY 2

Breakfast
1 cup low-fat milk
½ grapefruit
1 egg, poached, boiled or scrambled
without added fat
2 slices whole grain toast
1 tsp. margarine
Coffee or tea

Lunch
Tomato or vegetable soup
Cheese toast
Fresh fruit

Snack
5 vanilla wafers or 2 graham crackers
1 banana

Dinner
5 oz. broiled fish with
lemon juice and parsley
1 cup steamed broccoli
½ cup steamed carrots
(try seasoning with ginger)
1 cup brown or wild rice
2 tsp. margarine
½ cup apple crisp or baked apple

DAY 3

Breakfast
1 cup low-fat milk
1 cup whole grain hot cereal
2 tbsp. raisins
1 slice whole grain toast
1 tsp. margarine
Coffee or tea

Lunch
½ cup low-fat cottage cheese
½ cup pineapple or fresh fruit
Bran muffin

Snack
5 whole grain crackers
1 tbsp. peanut butter

Dinner
4 ounces turkey loaf (try ground turkey
to make your favorite meatloaf recipe)
1 cup green beans
Medium baked potato with 2 tsp. margarine
1 cup tossed salad with 1 tbsp. regular or
reduced-calorie dressing
½ cup sliced peaches, fresh or
in their own juice
½ cup ice milk

DAY 4

Breakfast
1 cup low-fat milk
1 oz. lean ham or Canadian bacon (fat trimmed)
¼ melon or seasonal fruit
English muffin
2 tsp. margarine, 2 tsp. preserves
Coffee or tea

Lunch
3 oz. leftover turkey loaf sandwich
with 2 slices whole grain bread
Lettuce and sliced tomatoes
Grapes

Snack
8 oz. low-fat plain or vanilla yogurt
Stir in 2–3 tbsp. bran cereal
Sliced banana

Dinner
4 oz. baked chicken
1 cup cauliflower
½ cup green peas
2"-square cornbread or dinner roll
1 tsp. margarine
1"-slice angel food cake or shortcake
1 cup fresh berries as topping

DAY 5

Breakfast
1 cup low-fat milk
1 cup high-fiber or fortified cereal
1 banana, sliced on cereal
1 slice whole grain toast
with 1 tbsp. peanut butter
Coffee or tea

Lunch
Chef's salad:
Lettuce, tomato, cucumber, etc.
2 oz. lean ham or turkey strips
1 oz. cheese, cut into strips
¼ cup croutons
1 tbsp. regular salad dressing or
2 tbsp. reduced-calorie dressing

Snack
½ bagel or English muffin
¼ cup low-fat cottage cheese
Spread cottage cheese on bagel or
muffin half;
sprinkle lightly with cinnamon sugar and
broil until bubbly.

Dinner
Baked pork chop (3–4 oz., cooked)
½ cup applesauce (unsweetened)
½ cup corn or one ear corn-on-the-cob

½ cup Brussels sprouts or other green,
leafy vegetable
1 slice whole grain bread
with 1 tsp. margarine

DAY 6

Breakfast

French Toast—for 2 servings or
4 slices, use:
2 whole eggs, 2 egg whites,
and 3 tbsp. low-fat milk
1 cup sliced fresh fruit
2 tbsp. syrup (or try fruit as a topping)
Coffee or tea

Lunch

Soup of choice
5 whole wheat crackers
1 oz. cheese
½ cup grapes or other fresh fruit

Snack

One-half peanut butter sandwich
1 cup low-fat milk

Dinner

Spaghetti with meat sauce (use extra-lean
ground beef in tomato sauce)
1 cup spaghetti noodles
2 tbsp. Parmesean cheese
Tossed salad
1 tbsp. regular or reduced-calorie salad dressing
½ cup sherbet with fresh fruit topping

DAY 7

Breakfast

1 cup low-fat milk
½ grapefruit
1 cup high-fiber or fortified cereal
1 slice whole grain toast with 1 tsp. margarine
Coffee or tea

Lunch

Mini-Pizzas: spread 2 English muffin halves with
leftover tomato-meat sauce
Top with 1 oz. cheese (try mozzarella).
Bake at 400° until cheese melts
Small apple

Snack

Assorted raw vegetables
6 oz. yogurt dip (flavor plain,
low-fat yogurt with herbs, spices, or powdered
salad dressing mix)

Dinner

4 oz. baked chicken
Baked potato with 2 tsp. margarine
1 cup greens—collards, spinach,
kale, or mustard greens
½ cup steamed carrots
1 slice whole grain bread or roll
½ cup pudding—if homemade,
use low-fat milk

WALK FOR YOUR LIFE

Last year my friend Dr. John Pleas wrote a book entitled *Walking*. John teaches psychology at Middle Tennessee State University in Murfreesboro, Tennessee, and he practices what he preaches. He sold his car in the mid-1970s when the gas crisis was at its peak, and for the next five years he walked everywhere he went. As an expert on the subject, he pulls no punches. John flatly states that *all* Senior Americans who *can* should walk for their lives—regularly.

As we have become a more automated and technologically advanced society, Senior Americans, along with everyone else, have become less active. In fact, a review of available evidence concerning frequency of exercise suggests that a significant number of Senior Americans have bodies that are deteriorating—or "rusting out" just because they're not being "used." John puts it this way: "If you don't use it, you lose it." Isn't it interesting, however, that most Americans, faced with having to choose between a new automobile and one "rusting out" or "wearing out," wouldn't even consider the "rusting" alternative.

I enjoy walking as often as I can and have been doing it for years. However, I never thought about its real impact on my health; the fact that it makes me feel good has been reason enough. As John and I discussed this chapter, I learned why walking makes me feel so good and why it's the recommended physical activity for Senior Americans. In fact, at a recent conference sponsored by the National Institute of Health entitled "Exercise in Aging—Its Role in Prevention of Physical Decline," researchers concluded that walking is the *most* effective form of exercise and the only one that can be *safely* followed throughout an entire lifetime. And it's growing in popularity. In 1976 there were 36 million active walkers and, in 1986, that number had grown to 55 million people.

There are three reasons why I hope you'll choose to *walk for your life:*

- You want an exercise program that will stimulate you to think about ways to move your body more.
- You want to engage in physical activity that will reduce physical complaints and lessen the chances of injuries.
- You want to develop a lifelong, noncompetitive, personalized walking program.

According to Dr. Pleas, there are two basic elements that underlie most physical activity programs: starting gradually and learning to enjoy what you do. The first element—starting gradually—is extremely important for Senior Americans. Those who start fast may finish last—or not at all. "Fast starts" are, in part, based on the natural tendency to want to achieve instant success. Yet this kind of a beginning is often the reason why people drop out of exercise programs. How many people—including yourself—have you known who decide to take up an activity, rush out to purchase the necessary equipment, pay membership dues, overexert, or injure themselves, and then, as quickly as they began, abruptly stop? I'd love to know how many closets and attics throughout America are filled with golf clubs, tennis rackets, bowling balls, jogging suits, and other sports equipment collecting dust.

If your lifestyle is sedentary and you make up your mind to change it gradually, you'll succeed. Your body will adjust as a new, active person emerges, and you won't overexert or injure yourself. The goal is to make a lasting change—no matter how small it may be—that will continue throughout your life.

Enjoyment is a critical and basic element in any exercise program. College coaches understand and agree that the enjoyment of a particular sport is critical to an athlete's top performance. Professional athletes have also recognized the importance of enjoyment of a sport. In retirement speeches, their messages are usually the same: "I'm tired of training and practicing. . . . I don't enjoy the game anymore . . . it just isn't fun." Even though many professional athletes receive large annual salaries for participating in a sport in a given year, money is rarely enough reason. The game has to be enjoyable for them to perform day after day, season after season. This same principle can be applied to walking. If it isn't fun, it will soon become boring and you'll lose interest in it; you won't give it your best; you'll gradually begin to find excuses to avoid it and eventually you'll stop entirely. The message is simple: Set a modest walking goal, take it a step at a time, enjoy it, and you'll succeed.

Walking Shoes and Clothes

Walkers have a distinct advantage over joggers, tennis buffs, golfers, and other sports enthusiasts where clothes are concerned. There's no need to go out and buy a special wardrobe. With the exception of shoes, you're likely to find all the clothing you need to become a full-fledged member of the silent walking majority right in your own closet.

For the most part, any shoe that is comfortable and feels good can be used for walking. Consider the amount of walking you are doing right now and, if your own shoes fit this description, continue wearing them. Here are a few recommendations made by Dr. Pleas concerning the characteristics of a good walking shoe.

- It should fit as snugly as a glove at the heel and instep and should conform to the natural outline of your foot. The longest toe should be ½–1″

from the front of the shoe, and you should be able to lift, wiggle, and spread your toes without difficulty.

- Heel support is very important because the heel strikes the walking surface millions of times in your lifetime. The heel should be broad enough to provide enough support to absorb the impact of the weight of your body. The heel of a walking shoe should be elevated ½–¾″ higher than the shoe sole to relieve strain on the back of the leg.

- Most walking shoes are constructed with soft absorbent padding that conforms to the arch of the foot. However, this *isn't* an arch support. If you have a history of fallen arches or if you are prone to injuries in this area of your foot, see a podiatrist and have a special arch support constructed that can be transferred from shoe to shoe.

- A good walking shoe will also be pliable, will bend easily at the top third of the shoe, will be durable, and will be able to handle the terrain where you plan to walk. The shoe should also be able to "breathe" and allow proper aeration and ventilation.

Walking clothes should be comfortable and practical. During the spring and summer months, light-colored clothes reflect the sun and are cooler. Loosely fitting clothes allow adequate ventilation. In the fall and winter months, dress in layers according to the temperature. A long- or short-sleeved cotton shirt or blouse, a pair of cotton trousers, and a light windbreaker or sweater are enough for most areas of the country during the autumn months. Heavy jackets and coats cause you to perspire after a few blocks of walking—especially if you are walking at a brisk pace. Thermal underwear, leotards, or an extra pair of pantyhose are recommended in cooler climates. However, undergarments should not fit so tightly that they interfere with the natural flow of walking.

A good pair of walking shoes is basic to ensuring comfort and reducing the possibilities of injury, and one general rule covers walking clothes: Less is best.

When and Where to Walk

The early hours are best for walking all year long for several reasons. Walking becomes a high priority when it is one of the first items on each day's agenda. When that happens, days are then scheduled to *include* walking rather than *fitting it in* if and when time permits. Morning hours allow for a minimal number of distractions, which helps you to concentrate on specific aspects of your body or the environment. For example: One morning you can concentrate on elevating your heart rate to achieve the best possible fitness benefits; on another morning you can enjoy the birds, trees, houses, buildings, and other points of interest where you walk. Walking into daylight, as you see the sun rise every morning, and being an active partner in the production of a new day can be, as you will discover, an exhilarating experience. A morning walk should remain at the top of your list of things to do every day. When it's incorporated into a daily routine, it will become an integral and inseparable part of a new lifestyle.

Resolving the issue of where to walk is straightforward since there are only two choices: indoors or outdoors. If you select an indoor walking place, just about any interesting indoor area that is spacious enough for continuous walking and won't bore you is adequate. It may well be that an appropriate indoor walking site is located nearby. Make a careful assessment of your neighborhood; look for a building where you can walk continuously.

Throughout America, shopping malls have become very popular and are especially appealing to Senior American walkers. In Nashville, Tennessee, for example, three shopping malls allow cardiac patients, Senior Americans, and others to walk in the mall each day before it opens to the public. Some merchants even provide attendance books in their stores for walkers to enter the number of miles walked each day. Check out the malls in the area where you live—the odds are three to one that you'll find happy people walking there seven days a week.

Another good place for indoor walking is a large hospital or a university medical center. Have you ever tried to find a particular clinic in a hospital, turned left instead of right, and ended up having to walk a quarter of a mile to reach your original destination? Think how much better you might have felt if you'd taken that "wrong" turn intentionally. The next time you visit a friend or a family member in the hospital, stop by the information desk, pick up a map, and go for a walk around the hospital first. The stimulation of a walk before you enter a sick friend's room could make the difference between a pleasant, cheerful, visit and a depressing one. After your visit, take another brief walk before you leave and focus on the positive things that occurred during your stay.

Safety Precautions

Because walking is an ideal activity doesn't mean that there aren't areas in which difficulty can be encountered. New walkers share the same common concerns. What happens when a person who is afraid of dogs encounters a ferocious one? How does he or she distinguish a friendly bark from a dangerous one? What about encountering a suspicious stranger or a would-be robber? Although these concerns are valid, they shouldn't be used as excuses to avoid or stop walking. There are some things you need to learn and use that help prevent a problem. Dr. Pleas points out in his

book, *Walking,* the following things you need to
learn to help prevent problems.

Dogs

DO	DON'T
Ignore the dog.	Show that you are afraid.
Continue walking briskly and with confidence.	Run from the dog.
Walk with a friend or in a group.	Intimidate the dog.
Stop and tell the dog to go home in a firm voice should he pursue you.	Pet the dog.
Check the leash law and call the owner and/or appropriate officials.	Give up walking.

As you begin to walk a particular route, neighborhood dogs will get to know you and will bark
less. In time, they'll ignore you. More than anything else, dogs react to "strangers" walking in
their neighborhoods, which is entirely normal. After
a few days of walking the same route, you won't
be a stranger and they'll begin ignoring you.

Suspicious Strangers

DO	DON'T
Leave your purse, money, and valuables at home, or lock them in the trunk of your car.	Carry a purse.
Walk on main thoroughfares, indoors, or other public areas.	Walk alone in isolated or deserted areas.
Occasionally vary the time that you walk.	Wear provocative clothing.
Vary your walking route.	Stop and talk to strangers.
Carry an umbrella or walking stick.	Overreact.
Walk briskly and with confidence.	Give up walking.

Tips to Increase Daily Walking

As important as any objective in a walking program is increasing the movement of your body.

That objective comes closer to being achieved each time you find new ways to walk. You can incorporate more walking into a daily schedule by:

- Not spending extra time and gas looking for a parking space that's close to an entrance when you go shopping. Park your car as far away as possible and walk to the store.
- Walking to the neighborhood store instead of sending someone else.
- Answering the telephone in the house that is farthest from where you are.
- Taking the garbage out after each meal.
- Going window shopping without your purse or wallet.
- Doing some comparative grocery shopping first. Walk up and down the aisles, then return to the entrance of the store and *start* shopping.
- Not taking all the mail out of the mailbox at one time. Take out one piece, then another an hour later, and so on.
- Walking to the next stop instead of standing and waiting for the bus to arrive.
- Getting off the bus several blocks from your destination.
- Taking the stairs instead of an escalator or elevator whenever you can.
- Getting off the elevator two or three floors below your apartment and walking up several flights of stairs.

Physical and Psychological Benefits

When walking has been established as a regular part of each day, it becomes pleasurable and the following physical and psychological benefits will occur naturally and continue. You'll notice that the ordinary demands of daily life require less effort as your endurance and energy levels increase. Brisk walking will increase the efficiency of your heart and lungs. A quickened walking pace will elevate your heart rate, and when your heart rate is elevated and sustained at a certain level, the muscles of the heart become stronger and the supply of oxygen throughout your body increases. Other physical benefits that may occur as a result of brisk walking are toned muscles, decreased blood pressure, a lower *resting* heart rate, increased reserves of energy, an improved resiliency in case of an injury, a decreased possibility of degenerative disease, and increased artery elasticity—to name but a few.

The long-term physical goals are to strengthen your heart muscles and increase your physical stamina to a point where you can climb several flights of stairs, carrying on a normal conversation, without exhaustion or having to grip the handrail in order to climb.

The benefits outlined above are by no means the

only ones that you can expect to receive from walking. You'll also discover the additional pleasure of just plain feeling good after a walk. There's an old physics principle that says a body at rest tends to stay at rest until some force acts upon it. This is another way of saying that inactivity breeds inactivity. You *can* overcome a sedentary lifestyle and become physically active with a walking program. And if you stick with it, you'll become physically and psychologically addicted to the point where walking will encourage more walking.

It's up to you to decide whether you think as much of your body as you do of your car, and whether or not you'll let it "rust out" or "wear out." I hope you'll choose to start *walking for your life* today. It could be one of the best choices you'll ever make.

7

The Right to Unrestricted Travel and Leisure

Senior Americans have the right to choose how and with whom they spend leisure time, as well as the right to expect considerate assistance when they travel.

"We aren't seeking editorial opinions on our choices of friends and activities, just give us a willing and friendly helping hand when we need it."
—Art Linkletter

Whenever Lois and I travel together, with our children, our grandchildren, or a combination of both, we have wonderful times. We scuba dive, backpack in the mountains, surf, and in the winter carry our skis and head for snow country.

We've had the opportunity to see the United States and the rest of the world in a way few people ever experience it. We've walked on the Great Wall of China, cruised down the Nile in Egypt, seen sunrises in Australia, walked in the streets of New Delhi, and talked with people in East Germany, Hungary, Russia, and Rumania—people who will never know the kind of freedom we take for granted.

We've been everywhere. During a recent cruise

that took us from Glacier Bay to the Panama Canal I had a chance to get a firsthand look at Senior Americans who did everything *but* sit around knitting and not moving. They were up at the crack of dawn and didn't quit until late at night. They kept up such a pace that I finally stopped going to the evening parties because of the women who stood in line waiting to dance with me. I told Lois that I finally knew what it must have felt like to have been a dance hall floozy who dropped from exhaustion every night.

In spite of being savvy travelers, we've also had our share of harried experiences long distances from home. One that stands out happened a few years ago after we'd left Australia for our next destination—a remote island near Tahiti with no phones and no outside contact except for one plane a day that brought people and messages in and out. We had just arrived and were looking forward to a week of peace and quiet. Little did we know that half a world away Lois's mother, Peg—in her early nineties and one of my favorite people—had been admitted to a San Diego hospital in a coma. Our first information came from someone else on the island with a radio who received a message and brought it over to us—*after* the only plane of the day had already come and gone. There we were—frantic about Peg and unable to leave until the next day.

All Lois could think about was that she would never see her mother alive again and we were stuck on an island, two days from San Diego if everything went perfectly flying home. I kept reminding Lois that Peg had too much spunk not to wait for her and that we'd make it. As I kept reassuring her, I was none too confident myself.

We finally made some unbelievable connections and managed to land in San Diego two days later and rushed to the hospital. When we walked into Peg's room, Lois's father, sister, and brother-in-law were at her bedside as Peg lay motionless in a coma. Lois had tears streaming down her face as she leaned over and kissed her mother as we were told it "didn't look good." Then I bent down and quietly—but authoritatively—spoke these words into her ear: "Now listen, Peg, I didn't travel all the way from Tahiti for you to lie here with your eyes closed while I talk to you. Wake up, open your eyes, and speak to me—right now!"

With that Peg turned her head, opened her eyes, looked me straight in the face, and said, "Well . . . hello, Art."

Later her doctor asked me, "Tell me, how *did* you travel here, Art? Did you bother with a plane or just walk on water?"

As much as anything, I enjoy traveling throughout America. I have been deeply moved while speaking at the base of Mt. Rushmore in listening shadows of four great men. I've eaten dinner overlooking San Francisco Bay, remembering tugboats escorting World War II ships and submarines into the safe harbor—ships carrying weary men who fought in the Pacific defending our freedom. When I see the span of desert and mountains from a plane, I wonder what it must have been like for those who crossed in covered wagons believing in an uncharted future. I have been welcomed in fifty states by people who have shared part of their lives with someone a long way from home. Because of my work in the fight against drug abuse, I have also been in those parts of our country that represent the worst of what some Americans must endure . . . areas loaded with pathos, misery, pain, and degradation.

We are quite a mix of people. Some of us seem to set the world on fire and some don't. A fortunate and comparative few earn recognition while thousands of equally deserving others don't. Others spend their lives in this country labeled "underprivileged." However, from my perspective—having seen the world from so many viewpoints—I'm here to tell you that no one living in freedom ever is completely "underprivileged." We may achieve, be recognized, and rewarded differently, but we share the same freedoms, rights, and choices accorded all Americans, not the least of which is the freedom to travel however and wherever we choose. And on that subject, have I got good news for you.

Travel for Senior Americans has never been better. The travel industry has caught on to the fact that Senior Americans are traveling and that many of us have the means to use airlines, take cruises, rent or buy RVs, or set out on cross-country trips by train or bus. The scramble is on to get our attention by offering packages that are within our means and as varied as the people in this country.

The best part? Time is on our side. We can do our homework in advance, choose our seasons, move at a leisurely pace, and take advantage of the "deals" that really *are* out there.

If you don't already know one, get to know a travel agent. I have worked with travel agents all my life and can attest to their skills. A travel agent's services, for the most part, cost you nothing. They are paid through commissions from the airlines, hotels, cruise lines, and so forth. Of course they're interested in earning commissions by booking your reservations but they also know the pitfalls, can arrange special transportation and assistance if you need it, and, if something goes wrong, help straighten it out. They can alert you if you're headed in a direction they've learned from other experiences isn't such a good idea. If you'll take the time to tell a travel agent what your interests are, don't be surprised if you discover some opportunities you had no idea existed.

Planning is the key. In addition to travel agents, read books, talk to your friends who travel, put some work into it. You can travel by air, by bus, on a ship, in an RV, by train, or in a car. The choices are limited only by your imagination and resources. There are theme tours where you can pursue your interests, including everything from polka dancing to gourmet food. You can take tours that follow in the footsteps of someone famous or spend two weeks cruising down the Nile, stopping at the Pyramids and every other point of interest. You can take a vacation on a farm or ranch and even get involved in the daily chores. You can trade houses with someone else in another part of the country, or take what is often called a "cruise to nowhere," just relaxing and enjoying each day as it comes in a climate you enjoy or a part of the world you've always wanted to see.

If time is no problem, you might want to consider traveling on a freighter. A lot of travelers will tell you these ships can be as comfortable as a luxury liner. They are less crowded and less expensive because schedules must change to accommodate the demands of what is being shipped. The numbers of people on board tend to be small. A freighter can be quite an adventure.

Luxury cruises can range in duration from a few days to two or three weeks. And don't be put off by what at first looks "too expensive." Remember that a cruise includes all your living expenses and often includes the airline fare to and from your point of departure. There are cruises that are based on themes, such as your favorite music, golf courses you always wanted to play, the study of a favorite subject, or improving your bridge game. If you have a special interest, the chances are good a tour is available.

Traveling in recreational vehicles (RVs) has become very popular because of the independence and flexibility they allow. Although a lot of people own them, because they are expensive purchases I think it makes sense to rent one first to find out if this is a mode of travel you really want. The joy of an RV is that you set your own pace, make your own meals, and sleep in the "house" you literally carry with you. This kind of travel provides the opportunity to see this country in a way you may never have seen it before and at a pace you want to keep.

Travel Like a Pro

No one will dispute that I come as close as anyone to being a professional traveler. I have no idea how many air miles I've flown, but there have been years where it's been more than 300,000 air miles in a twelve-month period. Taking a trip isn't a question of making a reservation or two, packing the night before you leave, taking the dog to the kennel, and saying, "Good-bye." Over the years, I've learned that there are some do's and some don't's that can make travel a lot less complicated, safer, and pleasant. The do's first:

Do:

• Travel in the off season. It's a lot less expensive and there is considerably less "hassle."
• Sign up for frequent-flyer programs. With few exceptions, these programs are free of charge. You can often accumulate bonus miles just for signing up, as well as through car rentals and for using certain hotels.

- Read books, talk to friends, write to tourist offices in cities and countries you are interested in visiting. Most foreign countries have tourist offices in New York City. Call telephone information to get the numbers.
- Read the fine print in any tour, cruise, charter, or air fare package you are considering before you sign anything or spend any money.
- Get in touch with your travel agent as far ahead as possible. Special "deals" and "fares" generally get booked quickly, and most of them need to be booked well ahead of the day you plan to travel. Let your travel agent know the approximate dates you'd like to leave and your areas of interest, and let him or her do the looking for you. You might be pleasantly surprised at what turns up.
- Look into less expensive guest houses, "bed and breakfast" accommodations, tourist homes, and budget motels. Most foreign countries have tourist bureaus that often are located in airports or railway stations to help you find lodging you can afford.
- Investigate "shared accommodations" if you are single. The travel industry bases most costs on double occupancy, and the "single supplement" can add a lot of cost on a tour or cruise.
- Consider traveling in an organized group if you aren't an experienced traveler. It's a more secure, worry-free way to get started.
- Travel light. After you've crammed the last piece into your luggage, start over and take half out.

Remember that there will be times that you have to handle your own bags and you may want to do some shopping during the trip.

- Purchase some "tip-packs" of foreign coins before you leave the country. They can be used for your immediate needs when you reach your destination.
- Use toll-free 800 telephone numbers when making hotel reservations in the United States. These numbers can be obtained through telephone information.
- Use public transportation. It's a better way to see the area and it's less expensive.
- Consider obtaining a major credit card if you don't already have one, since it may be extremely difficult to rent a car without one—even if you intend to pay cash. A major credit card will also be helpful in obtaining guaranteed hotel reservations.
- Check travel discounts available through organizations you may already belong to, such as AARP, alumni associations, the military, etc.
- Carry medications, current medical information, copies of your prescriptions, an extra pair of glasses, and your eyeglasses prescription with you. If you need them, they don't do much good in locked or lost luggage.*
- Purchase membership in International S.O.S.

*For information about obtaining an American Security Card™ like the one I carry, see p. 440. It has an area for you to list your prescriptions, eyeglasses prescription, your current medical information, and the S.O.S. number.

Assistance, Inc., if you are traveling outside the United States, and obtain an International Association for Medical Assistance to Travelers (IAMAT) pocket-sized world directory of IAMAT centers. (For more information, see p. 428.)

- Review your health insurance to find out if you have coverage out of the country. If not, consider purchasing coverage for your trip.
- Have your travel agent make arrangements for a cart or wheelchair in airports, special diet meals if they are needed, and nonsmoking rooms in hotels.

Don't:

- Carry any more cash than necessary or use credit cards more than is absolutely necessary. Credit cards can place you in an exchange-rate risk because rates are figured the day your bill is processed, not the day the card was used.
- Wear or carry valuable jewelry.
- Hesitate to ask for help in airports or for directions to where you are going.
- Be fooled by discounts that appear too good to be true. Some discounts are designed to give you reduced rates only on "top of the line" rooms, services, and products. If this is the case, you'll probably save money purchasing lower-level services. Your travel agent is the best person to evaluate discounts.

A Special Word of Warning

Recently travel/vacation "scams" have once again surfaced like a rash across the nation. In many cases, a person receives notification of having been selected to receive a terrific vacation that includes free airfare and accommodations. Often, in order to receive the free trip, you will be required to purchase a product or service, and/or attend a sales presentation. You may have to deposit a $50, $100, or more "processing and handling" fee up front. And in most cases, there will be undesirable conditions or limitations stated in the fine print.

Sometimes, people are contacted by phone with a completely phony offer that sounds too good to pass up. The only purpose of this type of contact is to obtain your name, address, and credit card number. Of course, there is no free trip or vacation package at all. But you'll find a sizable charge recorded on your next credit statement.

There are numerous variations on the basic schemes. Again, the thing to remember is that if an offer sounds unbelievable, it usually *is* unbelievable. I recommend that you never respond to a "free offer" until you've done some careful checking. And never give out personal information—especially a credit card number—over the phone. Ask the caller to send written information for your review, or just hang up.

Four sources of help and information regarding

the reliability of such offers include: your travel
agent, the Better Business Bureau, your county
occupational license office, and the Secretary of
State's office in the state in which the offer originated.

Elderhostel

Elderhostel is a program combining education
with travel, culture, and recreation specifically for
Senior Americans sixty years old and older. Just
leafing through a catalogue of available programs
can cause enough excitement to make you want to
begin packing on the spot. The word "hostel" traditionally implies simple accommodations at a
modest cost and that's exactly what Senior Americans can expect from Elderhostel—along with excitement, challenge, and adventure.

Introduced in 1975 on five university campuses
in New Hampshire, Elderhostel has since grown
to include more than 1,700 educational programs
offered in more than 800 locations around the world.
Its founder, Marty Knowlton, spent years observing the youth hostels of Europe and folk schools
in Scandinavia. He was impressed by the way in
which the availability of a network of modest accommodations encouraged an adventuresome hos-
teling spirit in European young people. He also
witnessed the positive impact residential settings

had on adult education programs offered by local high schools.

Elderhostel courses are as varied as your imagination—Roman History, Shakespeare's Othello, Healthy Living Through Love and Laughter, The Great Depression, Genetic Engineering, Japanese Art, Propaganda: The Power of Words, Marine Biology, How to Make Your Own Sausage, Photography, The Wines of Portugal, Political Processes in Israel, Baroque Art, The Gardens of Northern England—the list goes on and on and on. You might begin at the Feather River College in Northern California by taking a course called Mountain People Are Living History. The following year, how about a three-week program in Australia, where you'll study the history, government, culture, and architecture of the country at major universities? Part of the course includes a field trip to a sheep ranch to learn firsthand about wool production.

Participating Senior Americans must be willing to adapt to simple, no-frills dormitory rooms—where they are most often housed—dining in school cafeterias, and sharing communal bathrooms. It's not the kind of activity everyone wants, but for people who don't mind making a few lifestyle adjustments and who want to learn and experience new adventures, Elderhostel provides endless opportunities for study, travel, and companionship.

In the United States and Canada, programs generally last one week and cost between $215 and $240. This fee covers all costs of the program except transportation and some outside excursions or evening entertainment. For people who can't afford the cost of Elderhostel, limited assistance within the U.S. and Canada is available through "hostelships." (For more information about hostelships, write to the address listed below.) Each program offers three courses and is scheduled to permit attendance at all three. Participants must attend at least one course. Although the primary focus is on high-quality education, a variety of social, cultural, and recreational activities is also offered to complement each program. Instructors are faculty members of the host institution. There are no exams, no grades, no required homework; to qualify, all you need is enthusiasm. No previous knowledge of subject matter is needed and there are no requirements for formal education at any level.

A wide variety of international programs is also available. These usually last about three weeks; the cost varies from $1,400 to $3,500. Fees cover round-trip air fare, all travel within the country while visiting, full room and board, all course-related excursions, admissions fees, and limited insurance coverage. It's not unusual to attend classes at three different campuses in a country you're visiting, and in some locations programs include a one-week stay with a local family.

I think Elderhostel presents a unique opportunity for Senior Americans of all ages and backgrounds to remain intellectually active, expand horizons, develop new interests, and meet interesting, new people. The program operates on the belief that retirement does not represent an end to significant activity or new experiences but a new beginning filled with challenge and adventure.

For more information and a program catalogue contact:

Elderhostel
80 Boylston Street, Suite 400
Boston, MA 02116
617-426-8056

Senior Americans and the Airlines

The airlines place a high value on Senior Americans because of the high number of them traveling each year. It's been estimated that more than 5 million Senior Americans traveled by air last year and that number is going up. Many of the programs I've listed (see p. 432) have come about in the last year and each is a little different. Some require joining a club and paying a small annual fee; others charge no fee at all. Some airlines sell coupon booklets with four to eight one-way tickets and others sell a year's pass that can be used as often as once a week.

Most discounts apply to any available air fare,

including thirty-day advance purchase tickets which already are discounted. The age when Senior Americans become eligible varies depending on the kind of discount and the airline. Sign-up procedures vary where proving one's age is concerned. Depending on the airline, you may need a driver's license, birth certificate, passport, or affidavit attesting to age.

Airline programs involving club membership are a little more complicated because they include tie-in discounts with certain hotel chains, car rental agencies, and cruise lines. A few even send out quarterly newsletters to keep members informed about special bargains.

The highlights of these programs from the major airlines that were available at the time this book was published, like airline fares, are likely to change fairly often. I suggest that you contact a travel agent to make certain information is current as of the date you make the inquiry.

Before joining any Senior program, find out about any special restrictions that may curtail days of the week you can travel, discounts that are suspended during peak travel periods like Christmas, and so forth. And if one airline doesn't offer a discount for the day you want to fly, have your travel agent check to see if a competitor does.

Before You Leave the Country . . .

Do three things: Find out whether you have medical insurance that will cover health care in a foreign country; contact the International Association for Medical Assistance to Travelers—IAMAT—and request a copy of their pocket-sized world directory of IAMAT centers; and enroll as a member of International S.O.S. Assistance, Inc.

The horror stories that can be told about people getting ill in a foreign country are legend. Hardly anyone who has ever spent much time outside the United States is without such a story. *Remember, Medicare doesn't cover health care provided outside the United States*. And foreign medical services more often than not will require payment on the spot—a real problem if the costs are high. Knowing that you have the security of medical and financial resources where you visit can be mighty reassuring—just in case. Arrangements should be made as soon as you complete your travel plans.

Health Insurance

The following reputable firms offer a variety of services on a per-day basis for travel in just about every country in the world. Services include payment for doctor and hospital bills, provision for a nurse or traveling companion, and assistance in locating or replacing lost documents. You can write to the addresses listed below or call toll-free:

World Access Inc.
2115 Ward Court N.W., Suite 200
Washington, D.C. 20037
1-800-482-0016

Healthcare Abroad
1511 K Street
Washington, D.C. 20005
1-800-336-3310

Medical Assistance

International Association for Medical Assistance to Travelers—IAMAT—is an extensive network of English-speaking physicians located in more than 120 countries and 450 cities around the world, including Canada (the United States is not included). Participating doctors' fees are set at $20 for an office call, $30 for a call to hotel or home, and $40 for night calls, Sundays, and local holidays. You will be provided with a pocket-sized world directory of IAMAT centers. If trouble arises, you can telephone a twenty-four-hour answering service at the nearest center. Although membership is free, donations are gratefully received. I urge you to make a donation to this superb service that has helped so many people.

International Association for Medical
Assistance to Travelers
IAMAT
417 Center Street
Lewiston, N.Y. 14092
1-716-754-4883

International S.O.S. Assistance, Inc., has thirty-two centers located throughout the world that can be telephoned twenty-four hours a day. Membership is $15 a week and $2 for each additional day; $45 a month or $195 a year.

In the event of a member's serious injury or illness outside his or her country of residence, S.O.S will take charge of the medical supervision and arrange evacuation to the nearest facility capable of providing care. After stabilization, S.O.S. will provide repatriation to medical facilities nearest the patient's home.

Other client services include telephone access to a worldwide multilingual network of medical centers; return of unattended member children to their place of residence with qualified attendants when necessary; transportation for a person to join a member who is traveling alone and hospitalized seven days or more; emergency hospital deposits; access to both interpreters and legal assistance; repatriation of mortal remains in the event of death.

> International S.O.S. Assistance, Inc.
> 1 Neshaminy Interplex
> Trevose, PA 19047
> Outside PA, toll-free 1-800-523-8930
> PA 1-215-244-1500

Disabled Travelers

The Physically Disabled Traveler's Guide was published in 1987 to help the thirteen percent of all travelers who need canes, braces, wheelchairs, or walkers. It's estimated that if thirteen percent of the disabled travel, another two or three times as many disabled persons don't because they don't know which airlines, airports, trains, and hotel chains have the special facilities they need. The book was written by Rod W. Durgin and Norene Lindsay and provides facts, on cruises, package tours, and travel agents who specialize in arrangements for the disabled. The book sells for $9.95 plus $2 postage. For more information write:

> Resource Directories
> 3103 Executive Parkway
> Suite 212
> Toledo, Ohio 43606

Finally, I want to extend a special "thank you" to the Westin Hotels on behalf of people traveling because they have cancer and need treatment. They provide free hotel rooms for cancer patients (and their families) who are receiving—or are en route to or from—scheduled treatments. Reservations must be made in advance. For information and details on how you may apply, call your local office of the American Cancer Society.

If you are planning on traveling abroad and are unsure about safety, call the U.S. State Department Citizens Emergency Center at 1-202-647-5225. They will tell you what countries should be avoided and provide any other information you may need.

A new hotline has been established by the U.S. Department of Transportation (DOT): 1-202-755-2220. If you should have trouble with the airlines, try working it out with the airline first. However, if you get no satisfaction use the hotline number to find out if the Department of Transportation can help you.

After all this, I have only one thing left to say. Have a good trip . . . and don't forget to write.

Special Travel Opportunities for Senior Americans*

AIRLINE	SENIOR PROGRAM FEATURES	ELIGIBILITY	FEES
American	"*Senior SAAvers Club*" offers a 10% discount on all flights, 15–50% discounts at participating hotels, selected cruises, and American Airlines European tours. The 10% discount also applies to flights within the U.S. (including Alaska and Hawaii), the Virgin Islands, Puerto Rico, Canada, Mexico, Switzerland, and Germany. New Senior SAAvers members receive 3,000 bonus miles for joining and are automatically enrolled in the Advantage Program, which entitles members to an *additional* 3,000 bonus miles. Members who travel within 60 days of enrollment receive another 2,000 bonus miles. For information call 800-433-7300.	Age 65	$25/yr. single member fee, $75/yr. (additional) fee for companion
Braniff	15% discount on any fare within the U.S. or Mexico for qualifying member, as well as for	Age 65	No fee

	one companion of any age. Both tickets must be purchased at the same time. The senior traveler must simply present proof of age at the time of purchase in order to qualify. For information call 800-BRANIFF.		
Continental	"Golden Travelers Club" offers a 10% discount on all flights in mainland U.S. (not Hawaii) and Mexico. New members also receive a certificate good for 4 days' car rental from Thrifty Rental for $65; another certificate for the purchase of a round-trip ticket anywhere in the U.S. for $130; room, meal, and gift shop discounts (from 10 to 50%) at Marriott hotels. For information, call a Continental ticket office or reservation operator, or call 800-525-0280.	Age 65	$25/lifetime member fee, $75 (additional) lifetime companion fee
Delta	The *Senior Citizen Coupon Booklet* offers two programs for Seniors. One contains 4 one-way tickets for $348 ($87 each or $174 round-trip). The other contains 8 one-way coupons for $592	Age 62	No fee.

AIRLINE	SENIOR PROGRAM FEATURES	ELIGIBILITY	FEES
	($74 each or $148 round-trip). The coupons may be used during a one-year period beginning at the time of purchase. Travel is limited to Tuesdays, Wednesdays, Thursdays, and Saturdays. Reservations must be made within 6 days of the start of the trip. Destinations include anywhere in the U.S. (including Alaska and Hawaii) and Puerto Rico. For information call a Delta ticket office or reservation operator, or call 800-221-1212.		
Eastern	Eastern offers 3 different programs: (1) The "Get-Up-and-Go" year's pass designed for frequent travelers costs $1,299 per person and is available to Seniors age 62 and over. The pass is good for up to one trip per week within the U.S., Canada, or Puerto Rico. For an additional charge, you can purchase options for	Age 62 or Age 65	(1) Get-Up-and Go pass: $1,299 per person (2) Coupons: $348 for 4 one-way tickets, or $592 for 8 one-way tickets

discounts to the Caribbean, the Bahamas, and Latin America. (2) *Coupons* sold are similar to Delta's—4 one-way tickets for $348 or 8 one-way tickets for $592. Eligibility is age 62 for this program. (3) The *Senior Citizen's Discount Card* is for people age 65 and over and provides a 10% discount on all fares within the U.S., Puerto Rico, or the Bahamas. There is an annual fee of $25 for the senior member and $75 for a companion's discount card. Call 800-EASTERN for more information.

(3) Senior Discount Card: $25/yr. single member fee, $75/yr. (additional) companion fee

Northwest   Northwest has joined forces with Holiday Inn and Sears Roebuck and Co. with the *Travel Venture Club/Mature Outlook* program. Members between the ages of 55 and 64, along with their spouses, are entitled to 5% off on Northwest air fares. Members age 65 or older and their spouses receive a 10% discount on air fares—including Ultimate Super Saver fares. Participating Holiday Inns offer members and   Varies   No fee

AIRLINE	SENIOR PROGRAM FEATURES	ELIGIBILITY	FEES
	spouses 20% off room rates and 10% off restaurant meals. Discounts are also available on Hertz and National car rentals through this program. Some restrictions may apply. Call a Northwest ticket office or reservation operator for more information, or call 800-272-9273.		
Pan Am	Offers special Senior fares on the shuttle to New York's LaGuardia Airport, and on select off-season overseas flights. For example, Seniors traveling from New York to Warsaw can fly round-trip for about $699, or round-trip from New York to Amsterdam or Brussels for about $338. Since air fares are approximate and subject to change, call any Pan Am office for current information, or call 800-221-1111.	Age restrictions vary from 60 to 65	No fee
Piedmont	*"Senior Class Travel Club"* offers members a 10% discount on all flights, plus awarding dou-	Age 65	$25/one-time member fee,

	ble mileage toward its Frequent Flyer Bonus Program. Members also are entitled to various discounts at participating Radisson and Stouffer hotels as well as on Hertz rental cars. Piedmont publishes a quarterly newsletter for members. Call 800-251-5720 for information.		$75/one-time companion membership fee.
TWA	TWA currently offers 2 programs: (1) The *Senior Travel Card* entitles members to a 10% discount on all U.S. flights as well as to the Bahamas, Puerto Rico, and some flights to Europe and Israel. The card also provides discounts on Marriott hotel rooms, meals and gift shop purchases (from 10 to 50%), and Hertz rental cars. A newsletter is published for members. (2) *VSP (Very Special People) Senior Passes* cost $1,399 (1987) and provide a year's travel to all U.S. destinations and Puerto Rico. Options for international travel may also be purchased. A companion VSP ticket can be purchased for the same price. Pass owners	(1) Age 62 for Senior Travel Card, (2) Age 65 for VSP Pass	(1) $25/one-time fee for member, $75/one-time fee for traveling companion (2) $1,399 for VSP member pass, same price for companion pass

AIRLINE	SENIOR PROGRAM FEATURES	ELIGIBILITY	FEES
	must make reservations 7 days in advance but not more than 45 days in advance. Some other restrictions apply, and certain holiday periods are blocked out. For information call 800-221-2000.		
United	"Silver Wings Plus Travel Club" offers members a 10% discount on flights to all 50 states. Discounts are also available on flights to Canada, Mexico, the Bahamas, Singapore, Thailand, Korea, and the Philippines. Also, members may obtain a 10% discount on flights to over 20 Western European countries via Lufthansa airlines. In addition, discounts of up to 50% are offered at all Westin hotels in the continental U.S., up to 25% at participating Ramada Inns, and up to 10% on Hertz rental cars. Special tour packages for Silver Wings	Age 60 for most benefits, Age 65 for full benefits	$25/yr. or $50/lifetime member fee $75/yr. or $150/lifetime fee for any companion traveler

members are available as well. For more information call a United ticket counter or reservation operator, or call 800-628-2868.

| U.S. Air | Age 65 | No fee |

"Senior Saver Program" offers members with proper identification a 10% discount on all flights. Members are not required to carry a special card, and a companion also receives the 10% discount. For information call a USAir ticket office or reservation operator, or call 800-428-4322.

*Prices are subject to change; be sure to check with the airlines.

AMERICAN SECURITY CARD℠

Throughout this book I've referred to the American Security Card℠ and recommended that you consider purchasing one for yourself. You might be interested to know how the card came about. It's a direct result of talking with Senior Americans, listening to their problems, and hearing the needs they outlined. We all agreed that if it could be found, *one* card was needed that consolidated all the essential information we identified.

I did a lot of looking and located cards that contain individually important information like medical and drug history. But, to the best of my knowledge, until the American Security Card℠ there hadn't been such a comprehensive card.

The American Security Card℠ is laminated and contains a piece of microfilm about half an inch square. The microfilm carries your medical and drug history; primary physician; primary hospital; physician specialist choices and their phone numbers; Medicare claim numbers and policy numbers for medigap insurance policies; other insurance policy numbers like those for an automobile, home, or personal possessions; eyeglasses prescription; pertinent telephone numbers for various help organizations; telephone numbers for your regional ombudsman and the state and local Departments of Health and Social Services; drug and allergy information; special medication information; personal legal information; Living Will information; bank information; names and telephone numbers of people who may be needed in an emergency; special authorizations; and so on.

All you have to do is fill in the form that's mailed to you. Then it is reduced to microfilm, and your card is individually made. It comes in its own imprinted case with a paper-thin magnifier that allows the microfilm to be read easily by you or anyone else.

Two fluorescent red stickers also are provided so that the card can be attached to your driver's license and your car windshield to alert emergency personnel that you carry an American Security Card™.

You can obtain an American Security Card™ for $19.95 by writing or telephoning:

American Security Card™
Med-Card Systems, Inc.
3165 Cahaba Heights Plaza
Birmingham, Alabama 35243
Telephone: 1-800-962-CARD

Index

FOR THE BEST IN PAPERBACKS, LOOK FOR THE

In every corner of the world, on every subject under the sun, Penguin represents quality and variety—the very best in publishing today.

For complete information about books available from Penguin—including Pelicans, Puffins, Peregrines, and Penguin Classics—and how to order them, write to us at the appropriate address below. Please note that for copyright reasons the selection of books varies from country to country.

In the United Kingdom: For a complete list of books available from Penguin in the U.K., please write to *Dept E.P., Penguin Books Ltd, Harmondsworth, Middlesex, UB7 0DA.*

In the United States: For a complete list of books available from Penguin in the U.S., please write to *Dept BA, Penguin*, Box 999, Bergenfield, New Jersey 07621-0999.

In Canada: For a complete list of books available from Penguin in Canada, please write to *Penguin Books Canada Ltd, 2801 John Street, Markham, Ontario L3R 1B4.*

In Australia: For a complete list of books available from Penguin in Australia, please write to the *Marketing Department, Penguin Books Australia Ltd, P.O. Box 257, Ringwood, Victoria 3134.*

In New Zealand: For a complete list of books available from Penguin in New Zealand, please write to the *Marketing Department, Penguin Books (NZ) Ltd, Private Bag, Takapuna, Auckland 9.*

In India: For a complete list of books available from Penguin, please write to *Penguin Overseas Ltd, 706 Eros Apartments, 56 Nehru Place, New Delhi, 110019.*

In Holland: For a complete list of books available from Penguin in Holland, please write to *Penguin Books Nederland B.V., Postbus 195, NL–1380AD Weesp, Netherlands.*

In Germany: For a complete list of books available from Penguin, please write to *Penguin Books Ltd, Friedrichstrasse 10–12, D–6000 Frankfurt Main 1, Federal Republic of Germany.*

In Spain: For a complete list of books available from Penguin in Spain, please write to *Longman Penguin España, Calle San Nicolas 15, E–28013 Madrid, Spain.*

In Japan: For a complete list of books available from Penguin in Japan, please write to *Longman Penguin Japan Co Ltd, Yamaguchi Building, 2-12-9 Kanda Jimbocho, Chiyuoda-Ku, Tokyo 101, Japan.*